D0918552

**Historical Dictionaries of Ancient Civilizations
and Historical Eras**
Series editor: Jon Woronoff

1. *Ancient Egypt,* Morris L. Bierbrier, 1999.
2. *Ancient Mesoamerica,* Joel W. Palka, 2000.
3. *Pre-Colonial Africa,* Robert O. Collins, 2001.
4. *Byzantium,* John H. Rosser, 2001.
5. *Medieval Russia,* Lawrence N. Langer, 2001.
6. *Napoleonic Era,* George F. Nafziger, 2001.
7. *Ottoman Empire,* Selcuk Aksin Somel, 2003.
8. *Mongol World Empire,* Paul D. Buell, 2003.
9. *Mesopotamia,* Gwendolyn Leick, 2003.

Historical Dictionary of Mesopotamia

Gwendolyn Leick

Historical Dictionaries of Ancient
Civilizations and Historical Eras, No. 9

The Scarecrow Press, Inc.
Lanham, Maryland, and Oxford
2003

SCARECROW PRESS, INC.

Published in the United States of America
by Scarecrow Press, Inc.
A Member of the Rowman & Littlefield Publishing Group
4501 Forbes Boulevard, Suite 200, Lanham, MD 20706
www.scarecrowpress.com

PO Box 317
Oxford
OX2 9RU, UK

British Library Cataloguing in Publication Information Available

Library of Congress Cataloging-in-Publication Data

Leick, Gwendolyn, 1951-
   Historical dictionary of Mesopotamia / Gwendolyn Leick.
      p. cm. — (Historical dictionaries of ancient civilizations and
historical eras ; no. 9)
   Includes bibliographical references.
   ISBN 0-8108-4649-7
   1. Iraq–History–To 634–Dictionaries. I. Title. II. Series.
DS70.82.L45 2003
935'.003–dc21   2003000835

$\otimes$™ The paper used in this publication meets the minimum requirements of
American National Standard for Information Sciences—Permanence of
Paper for Printed Library Materials, ANSI/NISO Z39.48-1992.
Manufactured in the United States of America.

Contents

Editor's Foreword *Jon Woronoff*   vii

Conventions   ix

Map of Mesopotamia   x

Chronology   xiii

Introduction   xv

THE DICTIONARY   1

Appendix I. Mesopotamian Rulers   139

Appendix II. Museums   149

Select Bibliography   155

About the Author   187

Editor's Foreword

Mesopotamia was one of the oldest and broadest cradles of civilization. Unlike Egypt, which was a relatively unified state, it was the site of many different city-states, kingdoms, and empires, frequently at odds with one another, and replacing one another as the locus of power—Akkad, Ur, Babylon, the Kassites, Isin, Assyria—and then tending into the more "modern" Achaemenid, Seleucid, Parthian, and Sassanian Dynasties. The transfer of power resulted from a superior capacity in warfare, not so different from our times, and the rise of great leaders such as Sargon of Akkad, Hammurabi, Nebuchadrezzar, Darius, and Alexander the Great. All the while, the Mesopotamians also are known to have been practicing the arts of peace; developing agriculture, metalworking, and trade; devising forms of writing; constructing monumental buildings; organizing an administration and bureaucracy; worshipping various gods; laying down laws; and determining who was higher and who was lower in society. Not so different from our times. That is why Mesopotamia remains so intriguing, showing where we came from and part of how we got where we are, and maybe even giving us some insight into where we're heading.

The message would obviously be much clearer if, like Egypt, there had been a relatively unified state rather than many statelets that tended to wipe away earlier traces left by predecessors, and if the sands of time—and the desert—had not covered over so many of their remains. Thus, what we have been able to uncover, and do know with a reasonable degree of certainty, is particularly precious. So it is nice to have much of it presented in a handy form by the *Historical Dictionary of Mesopotamia*.

The dictionary section helps us sort out the many city-states, kingdoms, and empires; the famous and less well-known rulers (some far from glorious); the arts of war and the arts of peace; the signs of a maturing civilization and high culture; plus aspects of everyday life, including food and drink, clothing and jewelry, housing and cities, social relations and the formation of families, marriage, and even divorce. The whole time frame is too complicated for a straightforward chronology, but the periods are located in the chronology and the rulers in Appendix I. The bibliography is very helpful in suggesting in some detail where further readings can be found.

Writing this book, with its myriad periods and aspects, was no easy task. But it was certainly easier for someone, Gwendolyn Leick, who has already written several books on the ancient Near East, its architecture, literature, and mythology, as well as a "who's who" and an introduction to the Babylonians. Dr. Leick has spent nearly three decades studying, lecturing on, and writing about Mesopotamia. She has also taught at the universities of Glamorgan, Cardiff, Reading, and in London City, and is a fellow of the Royal Anthropological Institute. This long and varied experience is the basis for the latest volume in the steadily growing series of Historical Dictionaries of Ancient Civilizations and Historical Eras.

Jon Woronoff
Series Editor

Conventions

The pronunciation of ancient names is a modern reconstruction and a convention rather than an accurate phonetic rendering. Although cuneiform writing indicated vowels (unlike ancient Egyptian), it is not clear how they were spoken at any given period. Consonants were sometimes written in several different ways, hard or soft, which indicates that there were phonetic variations (e.g., *Hammurapi* as well as *Hammurabi*). Sumerian may have had nasal sounds, but this is not clearly indicated in writing.

Conventionally, the vowels of Sumerian and Akkadian words are pronounced as in German, partly as a result of the pioneering work of German scholars in cuneiform lexicography and grammar. The letter *a* is therefore as in *far, e* as in *very, i* as in *is, o* as in *core*, and *u* as in *full*. Diphthongs are not in evidence, and two successive vowels, as in *Eanna*, should be pronounced separately, as in *theater*. Akkadian, as a Semitic language, had a number of guttural sounds, such as the 'ayin, the qof, and the throaty *h*, and several sibilants (sade, sin, and shin), as well as dental *t* (tet). These are not indicated as such in this volume, except for *š* in Akkadian words, which is rendered as *sh* in transcribed names. The accent is generally on the penultimate syllable.

The names, order, and dates of ancient rulers are not fixed, due to gaps in the transmission, damages on the surface of tablets, and insufficient data for some periods. Dates in the dictionary follow the "middle chronology."

The use of boldface type serves as a cross-reference to other entries in the text.

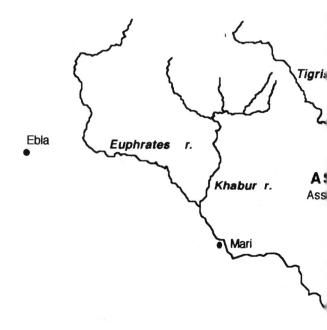

Lake Urmia

Zab r.

Lesser Zab r.

Diyala r.

Karkeh r.

Ešnunna

Cutha

Kiš

Tigris r.

Babylon

Susa

AKKAD

ELAM

Nippur

Isin

Umma

Adab

Girsu

Badtibira

Lagaš

Uruk

Larsa

Karun r.

SUMER

Ur

Eridu

Chronology

PREHISTORIC PERIODS

Middle paleolithic	c. 78.000–28.000 B.C.
Upper paleolithic	c. 28.000–10.000
Neolithic	c. 10.000–6000
Chalcolithic	c. 6000–3000
Hassuna	c. 5500–5000
Halaf / Ubaid	c. 5000–4000
Uruk	c. 4000–3200
Jemdet-Nasr	c. 3200–3000

HISTORICAL PERIODS

Southern Mesopotamia:

Early Dynastic I	c. 3000–2750
Early Dynastic II	c. 2750–2600
Early Dynastic III	c. 2600–2350
Dynasty of Akkad	c. 2350–2150
Third Dynasty of Ur	c. 2150–2000

Old Babylonian period	c. 2000–1600
Isin-Larsa Dynasties	c. 2000–1800
First Dynasty of Babylon	c. 1800–1600
Kassite Dynasty	c. 1600–1155
Second Dynasty of Isin	c. 1155–1027
Second Dynasty of Sealand	c. 1026–1006
Dynasty of E	979–732
Assyrian domination	732–626
Neo-Babylonian Dynasty	626–539
Northern Mesopotamia:	
Old Assyrian period	1900–1400
Middle Assyrian period	1400–1050
Neo-Assyrian period Empire	934–610
Achaemenid Empire	539–331
Seleucid Dynasty	311–126
Parthian period	126–227 A.D.
Sassanian period	224–642 A.D.
Islamic period	Since 642

Introduction

The Greek name *Mesopotamia* means "land between the rivers." The Romans used this term for an area that they controlled only briefly (between 115 and 117 A.D.)—the land between the rivers Euphrates and Tigris, from the south Anatolian Mountains ranges to the Persian Gulf. In modern usage the geographical definition is the same, but the historical context is wider and reaches much further back than the period of the Romans. It comprises the civilizations of Sumer and Akkad (third millennium B.C.) as well as the later Babylonian and Assyrian empires of the second and first millennium. Although the "history" of Mesopotamia in the strict sense of the term only begins with the inscriptions of Sumerian rulers around the 27th century B.C., the foundations for Mesopotamian civilization, especially the beginnings of irrigation and the emergence of large permanent settlements, were laid much earlier, in the fifth and fourth millennium. Archaeological research is the main source for these prehistoric periods, but it also plays a very important part in the process of understanding and interpreting later periods, complementing the written evidence.

The key element in the development of Mesopotamian cultures was the gradual adaptation to the ecological conditions of the region. The original homeland for Stone Age man was the Levantine coast. The first experiments in cultivating cereals and domesticating animals had occurred in this more naturally fertile region, which received a higher amount of annual rainfall. In the Neolithic period (c. 10,000–6,000 B.C.), other areas in the lee of mountain ridges, in Syria and Anatolia, became inhabited, and the first densely occupied settlements with permanent architecture appeared as a gradual shift took place from hunting and gathering as the main form of subsistence to more specialized forms of life, either agriculture or nomadic pastoralism. Northern Mesopotamia (between the south Anatolian Mountain ridge and the latitude of present-day Baghdad) was situated in the geographical zone in which rainfall agriculture was possible. The earliest Mesopotamian settlements, dating back to the sixth millennium, were found here. Excavations at sites such as

Tell Brak, Tell Arpachiya, Tepe Gawra, and Nineveh have yielded plentiful polychrome painted pottery and sometimes substantial buildings.

In contrast, the alluvial plains of the south lie in one the driest and hottest regions of the world, neighboring the great deserts of Syria and northern Arabia. The oldest archaeological sites there date from the fifth millennium and were concentrated in the marshy areas of the south. Their material remains appears simpler in comparison to the finds of the north. However, in the late fifth and throughout the fourth millennia, this began to change as the southern alluvium began to be more densely inhabited. Making use of previous experience with extensive agriculture, people began to intensify the exploitation of the fertile river valleys. This demanded much greater investment in terms of labor and expertise than in the more temperate climates but offered the potential of achieving substantial surplus yields that could feed large populations. In the following historical periods, such knowledge was perfected to allow for intensive cultivation of subsistence crops, especially barley, later also date palm, using sophisticated systems of irrigation, crop rotation, and collective labor deployment on large parcels of land.

During the height of the Uruk period (c. 3400–3200 B.C.), called after the old city of Uruk, southern Mesopotamia had close economic links to northern and eastern neighboring regions. Sites in southern Anatolia, northwest Syria, and eastern Iran show the same material culture, architecture, and account devices as in Uruk. This city appears to have been the center of administration for this complex system of trade and exchange, the largest and earliest urban settlement, with its impressively monumental public buildings and evidence of early bureaucracy (discussed later). Though it is still a matter of debate to what extent Uruk exercised political control over the vast area in which Uruk-style buildings and artifacts have been found, it is clear that the regularized contact with an urban center made an impact on the peripheral regions and that the administrative expertise gained during this period was invaluable for the subsequent development of Mesopotamian economy.

The Uruk "world system" fell apart toward the end of the fourth millennium, and southern Mesopotamia became relatively more isolated. During the Early Dynastic period (c. 3000–2350 B.C.), many new urban centers developed. The most efficient exploitation of the cultivated land was achieved through institutional control over coordinated seasonal tasks, storage, and distribution of food and seed. The city-state emerged as the most suitable socioeconomic unit in response to these demands, with its productive and administrative centers, the temples and palaces. Such city-states were composed of a more or less coherent territory of fields, canals, and villages. The walled city accommodated the majority of the population as well as public buildings and sanctuaries that embodied the "identity" of the community as residences of the city gods. City dwellers rather than rural people provided the bulk of the labor force to sustain the agricultural basis of the Mesopotamian economy. They were also recruited to maintain the irrigation works and public buildings. Most of the general workforce labored for subsistence rations in one of the large institutional or, later, also private households. Of great importance for the efficient management of such complex land-holding organizations were written records. The achievements of the Uruk literacy became superseded by a system that allowed phonetic values to be represented in writing. The scribal skills were taught in a largely homogenized system, making use of syllabaries, sign lists, and lexical lists. By the mid–third millennium, cuneiform writing, still primarily pictographic, was used for several languages with very different linguistic structures (e.g., Sumerian, the Semitic Akkadian and Eblaite, as well as Elamite).

The success of Mesopotamian agriculture was its ability to produce enough surplus not only to feed the laboring masses but to free a large sector of the population from subsistence efforts. There was enough grain to support full-time craftsmen, bureaucrats and administrators, cult performers, and other professionals. The early lists of professions from the Early Dynastic period enumerate a great variety of occupations. Prolonged intensive exploitation of the available resources, however, could lead to conflict over rights to land and water. The historical records of the Early Dynastic period document violent clashes between neighboring cities. Mesopotamia was also seen as a breadbasket by peoples inhabiting less fertile lands. Raids on villages and fields were a constant threat in border regions, and population pressures from such peripheral areas with limited carrying capacity for expansion, such as the desert in the west and the mountains of the east, could result in sometimes massive waves of immigration. Mesopotamia is marked by the ability to absorb new populations, but the process was by no means smooth and unproblematic because it demanded considerable social adjustment to settled and urban life. Although the literate sources always stress cultural continuity, the different values of immigrant peoples did contribute to changes in the political structure and social norms. Mesopotamian culture was always heterogeneous. In the third millennium, Akkadian and Sumerian were two of the languages that were expressed in writing side by side. In later periods, too, ethnic and linguistic differences within the population continued to exist and some ruling dynasties were of foreign origin. The fact that there were always a number of urban centers, with their own institutional bases and traditions, mitigated the overwhelming influence of mass immigration and centralizing politics.

Although cities were the most typical and arguably the most efficient sociopolitical units in Mesopotamia, competition between them could lead to violent conflicts that at times spread to engulf the whole region. To counterbalance such threats to overall stability, cities could unite to form alliances; there is some evidence that this was attempted during the Early Dynastic period. A more lasting solution was the formation of a unified state governed by a king whose authority was recognized voluntarily or imposed forcefully by and on all cities. As long as kings respected the prerogatives of the more powerful religious institutions and provided an efficient and coherent military policy toward neighboring countries and raiding tribes at the borders, they could count on the collaboration of the urban citizenry. The palace was responsible for the maintenance of infrastructure (especially canals) and of public buildings (e.g., city walls) and the repair of sanctuaries. The king could order conscripted labor for the army and civilian projects. He could invest revenue from military campaigns (slaves, tribute in kind, as well as silver and gold) for such purposes as well as for the endowment of temples. At some periods land, especially in peripheral regions, could be awarded to trusted individuals in perpetuity.

The first unified state was that founded by Sargon of Akkad around 2350 B.C. His inscriptions stress, on the one hand, that he secured access to far-flung trading sources (e.g., the timber-bearing mountains of the Amanus or the silver mines of Anatolia) and that he honored the great gods of "Sumer and Akkad." His successors had to suppress internal rebellions and campaign to secure control over their foreign conquests. They also interfered in land ownership and redistributed large tracts of agricultural land to private persons. The Akkad Dynasty was the first experiment with centralization, after its demise the country reverted to the particularism of independent city-states. Too stringent demands in the form of taxation and conscription and insufficient investment in public works, as well as lack of respect toward the old centers of religion, usually provoked rebellions and insurrection. Determined rulers with a well-motivated army could repress such challenges to their power for a while but not forever. Internal unrest often invited foreign aggression, either from neighboring states or from tribal groups looking for new territories. Many a Mesopotamian dynasty was brought to an end in such circumstances. The strong reaction against repressive states often led to a more or less prolonged interval between the end of one regime and the implementation of another.

Toward the end of the third millennium the Third Dynasty of Ur reunited the country once more and initiated centralization on an unprecedented scale: All cities were forced to adopt a standard system of time reckoning, weights, and measures; all senior appointments were made by the king; and all local institutions were subject to central control and taxation. This was sustained by a well-trained army of bureaucrats who supervised all areas of production. In subsequent periods, the control of the state was relatively weaker, and Old Babylonian kings relied on personal charisma and the use of force to command allegiance.

The Kassite Dynasty (1600–1155 B.C.) ruled Babylonia for some 500 years and seems to have managed to curb the political independence of the old cities by encouraging smaller economic units, such as small towns and villages, in the countryside. However, how successful this policy was is hard to determine because of the lack of written sources for much of this period. The last 200 years of Kassite rule were also overshadowed by massive immigration from the east, ecological problems, and foreign invasions. Such natural and man-made upheavals of the countryside had devastating effects on the population. Famines and epidemics decimated the densely inhabited urban quarters and caused cities to be more or less abandoned, sometimes forever.

Throughout Mesopotamian history, there were cycles of prosperity and economic and political stability, interrupted by ecological depravation and social unrest. The myths of the flood as a punishment for human "noise"—a result of overpopulation—articulates that the ancient world was well aware of how precarious the balance between growth and sustainability was, despite the unprecedented carrying capacity of the alluvial landscape.

Northern Mesopotamia, whose geographical conditions were more like those of its western and northern neighbors than the southern alluvial plains, also had different political and cultural patterns than the south. Small-holding farmers, as well as large landowners, together with seminomadic pastoralists were in charge of the agricultural exploitation, as opposed to urban centers. Tribal organization under the leadership of a patriarchal sheikh was the common pattern. Cities were primarily trading centers rather than agricultural producers. Charismatic kingship played an important role in the political development. The north also experienced the influx of different ethnicities. Of great importance were the Hurrians, for instance, who brought their own religious customs to northern Mesopotamia, as well as an expertise with horses and metalworking. The kings of Akkad and the Third Dynasty of Ur claimed hegemony over the north and built temples and public buildings in cities such as Nineveh and Assur. The Ur administration introduced literacy and sparked a local development of writing.

The early Assyrian period, from the early second millennium, is mainly known from texts found in the trading centers of Cappadocia (in modern

Turkey) since the residential levels of Assur have not been excavated. As-syrian traders brought tin and textiles to Anatolia and brought back silver. The first important ruler of the north was the Amorite leader Shamshi-Adad I who operated from a base in the Habur Valley and obtained control over the Assyrian cities. He became a powerful king whose influence reached deep into Babylonia, but he did not leave a lasting legacy.

The Hurrians, governed by an Indo-European elite, established their own state—Mitanni—in the mid–second millennium that was engaged in in-tense rivalry with the Hittites of Anatolia. In the 14th century, Assyria be-gan to grow into a strong and expansionist state under such kings as Ashur-uballit I and Adad-nirari I. They began to intervene in the affairs of Babylonia, and this started a long period of tenuous relations between the two countries in which Assyria emerged the stronger. Both countries suf-fered a decline from the 12th to the 10th centuries B.C., experiencing mas-sive immigration of tribal groups from the west and ecological disasters. Assyria recovered more quickly than the south, and a number of energetic warrior kings established the basis of what was to become the most power-ful state in the whole of the Middle East.

The Neo-Assyrian empire was built on a highly efficient, well-equipped, and professional army, a well-trained civil service, and the principle of co-opting subjugated local rulers as allies. The symbolic center of the state was the capital city, which housed the royal residence, the administrative center, the arsenal, and the sanctuaries of the main deities. Different kings preferred different cities as their capital. The expansionist policies of the Assyrian kings brought enormous revenue but also exacted constant campaigns to re-press rebellions and defend dependent regions from outside aggression. The expansionist imperial regime of Assyria collapsed partly as a result of the kings' own policies, such as the practice of dislocating rebellious popula-tions, and the reliance on punitive campaigns to impose their rule over an ever widening territory. The efforts to maintain control over Babylonia also proved to provoke ever fiercer resistance, and in the end it was a Babylon-ian Median coalition that destroyed Nineveh and the other Assyrian cities and thus brought Assyrian power to an end.

The Babylonians were quick to claim the inheritance of their oppressors and became in turn an imperial state that exercised control over much of the Near East right to the Mediterranean shores. Nebuchadrezzar made Baby-lon into the most dazzling city of the world. But the imperialist phase was of short duration, and the Achaemenid rulers claimed sovereignty over an even larger territory, from eastern Iran to Egypt. Since in Babylonia the col-lective identity was more heavily invested in religious symbols (the cults of the great gods of Babylonia), the tradition of urbanism found that dynasties of foreign origin were tolerated as long as their kings conformed to the cultural norms of Babylonian kingship. The country continued to function and prosper under Persian and later Macedonian rulers. Although most historical accounts take the death of Alexander as the end point of Mesopotamian history, there was no sudden end in 332 B.C. Instead, there was a slow decline in some cities, eclipsed by new foundations and centers of power such as Seleucia, others continued to exist and even flourish, well into the Parthian period. Only when the whole region became marginalized between Rome and Persia did the old cities become deserted and the haunts of jackals and ghosts.

WRITING

Written history in Mesopotamia began in the so-called Early Dynastic period III (c. 2600–2350 B.C.). At this time, the country was divided into a number of individual cities with their surrounding territories. The first inscriptions were little more than the names and titles of men who achieved positions of authority and who dedicated precious objects to the patron gods of their cities. It appears that many of these persons owed their influence and wealth to military success, often at the expense of neighboring cities. Their donations seem to have been partly an attempt to justify their actions to the deities. The written message linked the gift to the donor and his deed and transmitted his name to posterity. Although writing had been invented in the Uruk period (late fourth millennium), it then served only administrative purposes and did not encode speech of any particular language. It was instead a communicative system, rather like the mathematical or chemical formulas of our own time, which are understood rather than read by those accustomed to use them. The archaic writing had served to record economic transactions within a much wider geographical context than southern Mesopotamia—including the Susiana in southwest Iran, southern Anatolia, northeast Syria, and northwest Iran. When this network collapsed at the end of the fourth millennium, the acquired literary expertise was adapted not just to suit bureaucratic control but also to become an ideological tool—able to preserve the memory of individuals whose deeds were giving shape to "history."

Although it appears that the main centers of scribal education were in Mesopotamia and that the primary language referent for cuneiform systems was Sumerian, it could also be used in other linguistic contexts, such as the Semitic language spoken at the Syrian city of Ebla, or the Akkadian used within Mesopotamia itself. In fact, the cuneiform tradition is marked by bilingualism (Sumerian and Akkadian).

Most scribes at all times were employed as clerks to serve the administration of large productive "households" (including temples and palaces), while a much smaller but important sector was engaged in transmitting the arts of writing and to compose works that became the cornerstones of Mesopotamian cultural values: most important, lists of words and signs that composed the conceptual framework and ordering principles of the linguistic and tangible universe.

The memorialization of kings and their deeds was another genre of writing, as were compositions concerning the religious domain—hymns, prayers, myths, and rituals. In time the repertoire expanded to include the recording of divinatory material (from omen collections to astronomical data) and similar "scientific" enquiries (medical texts, technological treatises, etc.). It was a characteristic of Mesopotamian civilizations to foster an awareness of a very long historical continuity "from the days of old" to the "distant days" of the future. The early system of reckoning time by naming a year after a significant event no doubt contributed to this pronounced awareness of history as unfolding in an ordered sequence of dynasties and regnal years. In fact, the chronological system modern historians use is based on such ancient records and chronicles.

The writers of king lists and royal inscriptions, annals, and chronicles throughout the two and a half millennia of Mesopotamian historiography have also bequeathed us a particular view of their past—one in which kings either maintain the status quo or enlarge their territories through military campaigns; found, continue, or challenge dynastic lines; and the main threat to internal stability is the "incursion" of foreigners, most often of nomadic origin. Such were the main themes of official inscriptions, and their ideological purpose was to perpetuate the hegemonic claims of kingship. The problem is also that in difficult and for modern historians "interesting" times, writing almost invariably ceased, and the "other side" (the tribal immigrants) was illiterate.

The best-documented and historiographically richest period was the time when Babylonia and Assyria had intense and controversial relations in the first half of the first millennium. In each country, scribes were at work not only to record the campaigns of kings but to comment on their actions in a critical manner according to their "national" bias. In more recent years, historians have also begun to analyze the vast corpus of administrative texts for their historical relevance. Modern data-processing techniques have been very useful in dealing with such sources, and in the years to come, the seemingly mundane content of economic archives will become important analytical tools for the interpretation and understanding of Mesopotamian history.

CHRONOLOGY

Dating in ancient history remains uncertain and conjectural. It rests on a system of relative chronologies that take into consideration the stratigraphic sequence of archaeological sites, written sources appearing in such contexts, references to astronomical events, and links with later, established chronologies of Greece or Rome. Dates for the first millennium are more reliable because of the regular astronomical observations recorded by Babylonian scholars and because of the Assyrian eponym lists that can be correlated to regnal years of Assyrian kings. All earlier dates are less secure. In fact, there are three different systems that are based on the interpretation of a group of astronomical texts known as the "Venus Tablet of Ammisaduqa," which list first and last visibilities of the planet Venus during the reign of King Ammisaduqa of Babylon. Three dates are possible for his accession to the throne: 1702, 1646, and 1583 B.C. This gives a "high," "middle," and "low" chronology. Although many scholars prefer the high chronology, the middle chronology is used in most of the general historical works, as in the present volume. There is also a fourth chronology that on the basis of pottery evidence dates Ammisaduqa to 1550. Dates for the third millennium are even less clearly established.

The Dictionary

– A –

ABA-ENLIL-DANA (AHIQAR). High-ranking official under the Assyrian kings **Sennacherib** and **Esarhaddon** in the seventh century B.C. Under his **Aramean** name, Ahiqar, he became famous as the author of a series of wisdom texts written in Aramaic.

ABI-ESUH (reigned c. 1711–1684 B.C.). King of **Babylon** in the **Old Babylonian period**, son and successor of **Samsu-iluna**. He had to defend his territories against continuous incursions from **Kassite** groups who had begun to settle in the Middle **Euphrates** region.

ABISARE (reigned 1905–1895 B.C.). King of **Larsa**, successor of **Gungunum**. He won a victory against Larsa's main rival, the city of **Isin**, in his 10th year.

ABI-SIMTI. Wife and queen of **Amar-Sin** (reigned 2046–2038 B.C.) at **Ur**. She was the mother of Shu-Sin.

ACHAEMENID EMPIRE. Persian Dynasty (c. 550–330 B.C.), named after the historically obscure founder Achaemenes. **Cyrus II** (reigned 559–530) laid the foundation of the first Persian Empire. He began by defeating the Median king Astyages, which gave him control over most of Iran. In 593 he conquered **Babylon** and thus took possession of the **Neo-Babylonian** territories (all of Mesopotamia, most of Anatolia, and Syro-Palestine). His son, Cambyses II (reigned 530–522) added Egypt. During the rule of **Darius I**, who conquered parts of northern India, the Achaemenid Empire reached its greatest expansion. However, as famously recorded by Greek historians, his attempts to expand westward into the Aegean were thwarted by fierce opposition. Darius I was also responsible for the relocation of the capital to

1

Persepolis, where he embarked on an ambitious building program. Subsequently, numerous rebellions and internal political rivalry signaled the disintegration of the empire. It was **Alexander** of Mazedon ("The Great") who dealt the final blow. He defeated **Darius III** at Issos in 333 B.C. and thereafter conquered most of the **Persian**-held territories.

ADAD/ADDU/HADAD. North Mesopotamian weather **god**, responsible for the winter rains that ensured a good crop but also for devastating storms. One of his main centers of worship was Aleppo in northern Syria. He was one of the most important deities in **Assyria** where many temples were dedicated to him. At **Assur** there was a double sanctuary for him and his father, **Anu**. He often appears in **royal inscriptions** as a warrior defending the Assyrian **army** and he was also invoked in **curses**.

ADAD-APLA-IDDINA (reigned 1082–1070 B.C.). Eighth king of the **Second Dynasty of Isin**, successor of Marduk-shapik-zeri. According to the New **Babylonian Chronicle**, he was a usurper, although he seems to have been recognized as legitimate and did use the traditional Babylonian royal titles. According to **Assyrian** sources, he was appointed as ruler over **Babylon** by the Assyrian king **Ashur-bel-kala**, whose daughter he married. Although his own inscriptions mention mainly peaceful events, such as temple-building projects, the Babylonian Chronicles record civil unrest caused by **Arameans**. There also seems to have been some military activity by the Assyrians.

ADAD-NIRARI I (reigned 1307–1275 B.C.). King of **Assyria**, son and successor of Arik-den-ili. His reign is historically well documented. His **annals** contain much material about his military campaigns and there are other written sources, such as chronicles, edicts, and letters to other sovereigns. The greatest military achievement of this king was his defeat of the powerful state of **Mitanni** (also known as Hanigalbat), whose ruler Shattuara he took prisoner before he allowed him to return to govern his country as an Assyrian vassal ruler. When the death of Shattuara triggered an anti-Assyrian revolt, Adad-nirari marched against Mitanni, destroyed numerous **cities**, and deported parts of the population. He also extended the southern frontier toward **Babylonia**, defeated the **Kassite** king of **Babylon**, and collected **tribute** from tribes and people in the area. The prosperity and stability of his reign allowed him to engage in ambitious building projects, building city walls and canals and restoring **temples**.

ADAD-NIRARI II (reigned 911–891 B.C.). King of **Assyria**, son and successor of Ashur-dan II. The **Synchronistic History** reports that he defeated the **Babylonian** king Shamash-mudammiq. Hostilities between the two states ceased when a peace agreement was drawn up between Nabu-shuma-ukin I, the new Babylonian king, and Adad-nirari in 891. They also took each others daughters in **marriage**. The good relations between Assyria and Babylonia that this alliance initiated were to last some 80 years.

ADAD-NIRARI III (reigned 810–783 B.C.). King of **Assyria**, son and successor of **Shamshi-Adad V**. A noteworthy feature of his reign is the fact that during his early years on the throne, military campaigns were conducted by his generals, perhaps due to the young age of the king. The first expedition led by Adad-nirari himself (in 805) was directed against Syria, where he collected **tribute** from local rulers. The second took him to **Babylonia**, where he attacked Der, although he seems also to have made efforts to restore peace and order by bringing back Babylonian deportees and statues of **gods** kept in Assyria. Although he maintained the borders of the empire as they had been under **Shalmaneser III**, toward the end of his reign Assyria began a period of decline.

ADAD-SHUM-IDDINA (reigned c. 1222–1217 B.C.). **Kassite** king of **Babylon** during the time of Assyrian domination.

ADDA-GUPPI' (fl. c. 649–547 B.C.). Mother of the **Babylonian** king **Nabonidus**. According to a commemorative stele that her son erected after her death, she was born in the 20th year of **Ashurbanipal** (649) and subsequently rose to a position of influence at the court of **Babylon**, particularly under the kings **Nabopolassar**, **Nebuchadrezzar II**, and Neriglissar. Nabonidus stresses the fact that she was much devoted to the moon god, **Sin** of Harran. This does not prove, however, as often assumed, that she was a priestess of this deity. She lived to a ripe old age of at least 102 years and died in the ninth year of her son's reign.

ADMINISTRATION. The necessity of keeping reliable and durable records of complex economic transactions was the primary motive for the development of **writing** in Mesopotamia. The wide network of exchange relations and central control that characterized the economy of the **Uruk period** (mid–fourth millennium B.C.) led to the formation of bureaucratic structures and systems of bookkeeping. This assigned responsibility of particular sectors to administrative units supervised by "heads of department" within a hierarchical order. In all subsequent historical periods, this fundamental structure of the administration remained the same, although with varying degrees of complexity. All major institutions that engaged in production needed an administrative apparatus to keep track of wages, rations, and other costs incurred for employees, as well as of quantities of goods expended and produced. Hence archaeologists have discovered administrative archives of private estates and "firms," as well as those attached to **temples**, **palaces**, and other forms of state organizations. The more centralized the state's control over resources became, the greater the need for administrative records. The greatest concentration of such sources in the second millennium belongs to the time of the **Third Dynasty of Ur** with its highly developed system of **taxation**.

The **Neo-Assyrian** state **archives** recovered from the imperial capitals also number thousands of tablets and give testimony to the efficiency of Assyrian administration. High officials were often recruited from elite families. In **Assyria** a significant proportion were **eunuchs**.

From the **Neo-Babylonian** period, there are mainly temple archives that give details of agricultural production, as well as those from private companies that sometimes spanned several generations who specialized in loans and investment in various economic sectors.

ADOPTION. Adoption is known from legal contracts and **law** codes dating from the second and first millennia B.C. The most common form was to take an individual to be a son or daughter, but sibling and parental adoption was not unknown. Written documents, duly witnessed, stated the terms and nature of the relationship being entered into, and sometimes the penalties incurred for the repudiation of the contract.

One of the most common reasons for adoption was the desire to secure support in old age and the provision of a funerary cult for the deceased adopter. In exchange, the adoptee could inherit property. Such arrangements were generally conducted between adults. Infants or children could be adopted to legitimize their descent. Sequestered high-status women (such as the *naditu*) who were barred from having children could adopt young women to look after them in old age and to make them independent of the paternal kin group. Legal tablets show that litigation over adoption was not uncommon.

AGRICULTURE. Agriculture formed the basis of the Mesopotamian economy. The first steps toward a managed production of cereals were taken as early as the 10th millennium B.C. in Syria, in the area known as the Fertile Crescent, which receives sufficient natural rainfall for cultivation. Wheat and barley were the earliest domesticated cereals; other plant species used for food were pulses, such as lentils and chickpeas.

In Mesopotamia, the northern area (**Assyria**) that forms part of the Fertile Crescent, crops could be grown in the vicinity of the rivers. Farther south, in **Babylonia**, there was not enough rain to sustain cereal production unless the fields were watered through irrigation, but the rich alluvial soil accumulated by the rivers **Tigris** and **Euphrates** proved to be much more fertile than in other Near Eastern regions. By the seventh millennium B.C., the alluvial plains began to be cultivated, and by the fourth millennium, the first **cities** appeared in response to the need for an efficient agricultural **administration**. The first documents, pictographs written on clay, concerned the allocation of labor for fields, and the distribution of the products. By the third millennium, large institutions, such as **temples** and **palaces**, owned and managed the greatest part of arable land, employing a significant proportion of the urban population who worked for rations or as sharecroppers. By the second millennium and in later periods, private ownership of land was relatively more common.

The most important cereal was the salt-tolerant barley. Oil-rich plants, such as sesame and linseed, were also much used, as were vegetables such as onions and garlic. The date palm was by far the most essential tree, as much for its timber, as for its fruit, which was a vital source of sugars and vitamins.

Fields were planted by teams of oxen (initially two, later four) with a crew of laborers. For the annual harvest in spring, hired hands augmented the labor force. The produce was stored in special granaries and storehouses and distributed as rations, sold, and kept for seed. As long as the fallow principle was maintained, and fields allowed to recover their fertility after having been irrigated and planted, the land was able to yield substantial surplus. These rich grain harvests thus provided the foundation of Mesopotamian urban civilization.

With rising populations and pressure from the central government, too intensive cultivation could drastically affect the carrying capacity of the land, and the weakened fields could only produce a fraction of the normal crop, which was vulnerable to pests and diseases. Famines and epidemics were therefore not uncommon and are described in various literary compositions.

Animal husbandry was more important in those regions that boasted less fertile soil. Sheep and goats could be kept in marginal areas by moving herds from place to place. Cattle and pigs were generally kept in one place. While the former could be profitably managed by **nomadic** and pastoralist groups who moved with their herds in search of pasture, bovines and pigs were raised by special organizations, such as **temples** and **palaces**. During the time of the **Third Dynasty of Ur**, the city of Puzrish-Dagan, not far from **Nippur**, was the livestock center of the state.

All domestic animals were prized because of their wool and hides, as well as for their milk. Meat, rarely consumed by the nomads, formed an important part of the sacrificial repasts in Mesopotamian temples. Various **Sumerian** myths and poems concern the competition between the "shepherd," who is portrayed as uncouth and uncivilized, and the "farmer," who is the quintessential Mesopotamian, refined and urban.

AKALAMDUG (reigned c. 2600–2580 B.C.). King of **Ur**. Although his name does not feature in the **Sumerian King List**, he was identified as king of Ur by an inscription on a seal discovered in the "Royal Graves of Ur," excavated by Sir Leonard Woolley in tomb No. 1050.

AKKAD (also read *Agade*). (1) As a toponym, this refers to the yet undiscovered **city** in northern **Babylonia**, said to have been founded by **Sargon of Akkad**, who made it the capital of the **Akkadian Dynasty**. The city's rise and downfall were the subject of a well-known **Sumerian** literary text that blames the sacking of the city by foreign invaders known as the **Guti** on royal arrogance. Some archaeologists suggest that the remains of Akkad are to be found in the vicinity of Baghdad. (2) As a geographical term (during the late third and early second millennium B.C.), this denoted the northern part of the country, from the point where the **Tigris** and **Euphrates** come closest to the southern part of the Jezirah. It was used in distinction to the southern part, known as **Sumer**. From the time of the **Third Dynasty of Ur**, "*Sumer* and *Akkad*" denoted all of Babylonia.

AKKADIAN. As a modern linguistic term it refers to various Semitic dialects spoken in Mesopotamia over a period of 2,000 years (such as Old Akkadian, **Babylonian**, **Assyrian**). In antiquity, scribes differentiated between texts written in "the tongue of **Akkad**" from those written in the "tongue of the land" (i.e., **Sumerian**). The earliest texts written in Akkadian date from the mid–third millennium B.C. *See also* LANGUAGES; WRITING.

AKKADIAN DYNASTY (c. 2340–c. 2154 B.C.). Dynasty founded by **Sargon of Akkad**. Sargon built on the success of **Lugalzagesi** of **Uruk** in unifying "**Sumer** and Akkad"; having defeated the latter in battle, he established his own capital in the as yet unidentified city of **Akkad**. According to his own inscriptions, he campaigned widely beyond Mesopotamia and secured access to all the major **trade** routes, by sea and by land. His successors, **Rimush, Manishtusu, Naram-Sin**, and **Shar-kali-sharri**, all faced considerable opposition from the **Sumerian cities** that they more or less ruthlessly suppressed. After the reign of these five kings, a period of anarchy and disruption followed, probably caused to a great extent by the **Gutian** invasion. The much reduced kingdom of Akkad enjoyed greater stability under the reigns of Elulu (c. 2198–c. 2195), Dudu (c. 2195–2174) and Shu-Turul (c. 2168–c. 2154).

Various mountain tribes, referred to as the Guti in the **Sumerian King List** and other sources, had established themselves in the vicinity of Akkad, perhaps initially as mercenaries. According to the Sumerian King List, Akkad was destroyed by Ur-nigin of Uruk who established another, short-lived dynasty that was in turn terminated by the "Gutian hordes."

ALEXANDER THE GREAT (fl. 356–321 B.C.). Macedonian conqueror, son of Philip II of Macedon. He set out to challenge the supremacy of the Achaemenid **Persians** in Ionia and ended up with an empire that for the first time in history linked Europe with Western and Central Asia. He achieved this by a series of campaigns with a relatively small but highly disciplined force of fighters in which he provoked pitched battles with the Persian army fielding many thousands of men. He won his first victory at the river Granicus (334), which gave him access to the Cilician Gates. He then confronted the massed forces led by the Persian king **Darius III** at Issos (333) and inflicted another defeat on the Persians. Darius escaped to Babylon while Alexander continued southward to Syria and Palestine, where most of the cities surrendered voluntarily. He then invaded Egypt and was enthroned as pharaoh in 331. Darius had meanwhile assembled a vast army in **Babylonia**. Another battle was fought near Gaugamela, and Alexander triumphed again. He then marched to Babylon, where the satrap Mazeus surrendered. Darius had escaped to Media, and Alexander set out for Persepolis, the dynastic center of the **Achaemenid Empire**, which he looted of its wealth before setting fire to the city.

Darius was assassinated by his own people and Alexander continued his conquest farther east across the Iranian highland and into Bactria, where he married the daughter of the vanquished king in 324. He pressed on into India, reached Pattala in 325, and, while part of his troops returned by sea, marched back to Persia. The return of the fleet and the conquest of India were celebrated at Susa, and he took the eldest daughter of Darius in marriage. Alexander planned the conquest of Arabia and set out for Babylon, where he made the preparations for a sea-borne invasion. On 31 March 323, he caught a fever from which he was never to recover. He died on 10 June, not yet 33 years old. His untimely death sparked intense and prolonged rivalries for his succession and the division of the enormous territories he had conquered. *See also* SELEUCID DYNASTY.

AMARNA CORRESPONDENCE. *Tell el-Amarna* is the modern name for Akhetaten, the city founded by the Egyptian pharaoh Amenophis IV (also known as Akhenaten) who ruled from 1376 to 1379 B.C. Archaeologists discovered an important archive of cuneiform tablets, some with Egyptian glosses, which also included documents from the reign of Amenophis III (reigned c. 1387–1350). The majority are letters and reports, written by local governors and petty rulers of the Levantine coast that was under Egyptian control. Of special interest are the 43 missives sent by kings of independent states, such as **Babylonia**, **Mitanni**, and **Assyria**, which concern the reciprocal exchange of prestigious commodities such as chariots, gold, and various artifacts, as well as princesses.

AMAR-SIN (reigned 2046–2038 B.C.). Third king of the **Third Dynasty of Ur**, son of **Shulgi**. During his nine-year reign, he benefited from the economic and political stability that his father had established. Although his royal inscriptions mention various military campaigns against little-known targets, he gave most of his attention to the building and renewal of sacred buildings, such as the Apsu **temple** at **Eridu**.

AMEL-MARDUK (Biblical Evil-Merodach) (reigned 561–560). King of **Babylon**, son and successor of **Nebuchadrezzar II**. He only reigned for a short time and was deposed by his sister's husband, Neriglissar. According to later sources, such as a fragmentary **Babylonian** epic, he deserved this fate because he had not listened to his counselors and had neglected the Babylonian **temples**.

AMORITES. The word is derived from the **Akkadian amurru**, which designated Semitic-speaking tribal groups, who toward the end of the third millennium B.C. settled in increasing numbers in northern and middle **Babylonia**. Their influx is thought to have contributed to the downfall of the **Third Dynasty of Ur**. Some **tribes** became assimilated and formed chiefdoms and kingdoms in Mesopotamia and Syria in the second millennium B.C. (e.g., **Mari**, Yamhad, Tuttul), others retained a nomadic or seminomadic existence as **pastoralists**. The **First Dynasty of Babylon** was founded by an Amorite. The term *amurru* was also used to designate the language and at later times the western border of **Babylonia**.

AMURRU. (1) Original home of the **Amorites**. (2) Semitic **god** and tutelary deity of the Amorites whose name first appeared in the personal names of people during the **Akkadian** period. He had at least three **temples** in **Babylon**. To assimilate this "man of the desert," he was officially married to a **Sumerian goddess**: one myth describes how he wooed and won the daughter of Numushda, much against the latter's initial misgivings about someone belonging to a people "who do not know bread." In the **Babylonian** tradition his wife was Belet-Seri ("Lady of the Desert").

ANIMAL HUSBANDRY. *See* AGRICULTURE.

ANNALS. A type of royal inscription that was particularly common in **Assyria**, apparently introduced by **Adad-nirari** I at the beginning of the 13th century B.C. Written in a literary style, they were yearly reports of the king's major activities, primarily of military expeditions and building works. Annals are of considerable historical importance as they allowed for greater precision in establishing the chronological sequence of events in a particular reign, although the often stereotyped phraseology of the texts reminds us that they were not considered to be unbiased historical records but served to underpin the ideological basis of **Assyrian** kingship.

ANTIGONUS MONOPHTALMOS (reigned 321–301 B.C.). Macedonian general, chief of cavalry of **Alexander the Great**, satrap of Phrygia and later king. In the aftermath of Alexander's death, he competed with the other generals for a share in the succession. Antigonus managed to dislodge **Seleucus** I from **Babylon** with whom he engaged in bitter warfare for four years (312–308) that ravaged the country. His brutal behavior toward the Babylonian population was described in the **Babylonian Chronicle**. He was finally defeated by Seleucus and killed, 81 years old, in the battle at Ipsus in Phrygia.

ANU (Sumerian: An). Mesopotamian **god** whose written name expresses
the notion of the heavenly deity. The sign dingir could be read as "An"
and function as determinative to introduce the name of any god or goddess. An appears in some **Sumerian** mythical texts as a younger generation demiurge who orders the universe and decrees the fate of gods and
men. He could also form a cosmic union with a female deity of the earth
(Urash, or Ki) and thus become the source of life.

The lists of divine names, which were first compiled as early as the
late fourth millennium B.C., generally begin with An. In many other texts,
he is also seen as the head of the Mesopotamian pantheon as "the great
An" or "Father An." His son **Enlil** eventually assumed some of Anu's
traits and functions, such as the bestowal of kingship.

In the north Anu had affinities with weather gods and hence associations with fertility. The cult of Anu revived in the Hellenistic period at
Uruk, where he had a large temple since the **Uruk period**.

ARABS. Semitic, tribally organized people, subsisting on seminomadic
and **nomadic** pastoralism and **trade**. **Arab** groups were first mentioned
in the first millennium B.C. in **Assyrian** records. Arab contingents, for instance, fought in the great coalition against **Shalmaneser III** in 853. An
Arab queen, Samsi, fought against **Tiglath-pileser III** in 732 but was
forced to pay tribute. Reliefs from **Ashurbanipal's** palace at **Nineveh**
show Assyrian troops doing battle against Arabs on **camels** in retaliation
for their support of the **Babylonians**.

ARAMEANS. A group of peoples speaking a western Semitic language
(Aramaic). They were originally **tribal pastoralists** and emerged in the
middle of the second millennium B.C. to form states in Syria and northern Mesopotamia.

They first appeared as "hordes of Ahlamu" in **Assyrian annals** around
1300 B.C. **Tiglath-pileser I** (c. 1110) defined them as Arameans (**ahlame
armaya**). They were much feared also in **Babylonia**, together with another tribal people known as the Suteans, for raiding and pillaging the
country. Arameans were spread out over large areas of Syria, and divided
into several tribal groupings. They were frequently in conflict with the
Assyrians, either because they raided Assyrian territory or because their
various petty kingdoms had become targets of Assyrian expansion. Some
Aramean groups suffered mass deportation as a punishment.

Nevertheless, their language, Aramaic, became the most widely spoken and understood language in western Asia since the eighth century

B.C. and became the international language of commerce and diplomacy, not only within the Assyrian empire but also under the subsequent empires, until the early centuries A.D. The Arameans adopted an alphabetic form of **writing** in the 11th century that was based on the Phoenician alphabet. Because of the perishable nature of the writing material, few original texts other than those engraved on stone or written on clay bowls and sherds have survived.

ARCHIVES. Because the majority of **cuneiform** documents deal with bureaucratic matters, they were often kept together in the form of archives for future reference. They belonged in the main to the large institutions of Mesopotamia, the **temple** and **palace**, and detail expenditure and income, personnel, hours worked by laborers, as well as legal contracts and correspondence.

From the third millennium B.C. are examples from **Shuruppak**, ancient Fara, that date from the 24th century B.C. The tablets date just from a single year and detail the economic dealings of a large organization involving some 9,660 donkeys and 1,200 men. From about the same time are the archives of **Girsu**, the capital of the city-state **Lagash**, which furnished details about the centralized economy of the city-state. Particularly well known are the palace archives of **Mari** from the 19th century B.C. They entail the voluminous correspondence between the ruler and his various dependants and allies and thus form one of the main sources for the history of the Middle **Euphrates** region of the period.

From the time of the **Third Dynasty of Ur**, temple archives, especially from **Ur** and **Nippur**, as well as from provincial centers such as Puzrish-Dagan, contained often thousands of tablets and reveal the complex workings of these institutions.

With the **Old Babylonian period**, private archives belonging to private entrepreneurs begin to appear, alongside rarities such as the records of the "cloister" at **Sippar**, where unmarried and well-born women lived in seclusion to pray and look after their investments (*see NADITU*).

Of great historical importance are the state archives from **Assyria**, which preserved royal correspondence, especially from the time of the **Sargonids** (seventh century). They contain letters from scholars and diviners, astrologers and exorcists, as well as those pertaining to the **administration** of the empire.

From the **Neo-Babylonian period**, no comparable records survive, but there are important archives from temples such as that of the sun god at **Sippar**.

During the late period of Mesopotamian history, when Babylonia was ruled by the **Persians** and then the **Seleucid** kings, the main **cuneiform** sources come from the archives of large commercial firms, such as the Egibi or the Murashu families, who managed temple land, lent silver, and liaised with the crown. The very last archive collections come from the temple estates of **Uruk**.

ARMY. Information about military organization comes from pictorial and written sources. The earliest visual images, from the **Uruk** period, represent naked men with their arms tied behind their backs. It is not clear though whether such scenes refer to local prisoners or captives of warfare. Depictions of armed ranks in action can be seen on such monuments as the Early Dynastic "Stele of Vultures" (*see* EANNATUM) or the "Standard of **Ur**." They show soldiers protected by leather coats, wearing caps and helmets, and wielding spears. Their leaders ride in wooden **chariots** with solid wheels driven by sturdy donkeys. On the unusual stele commemorating the victory of **Naram-Sin** of **Akkad** over the Lullubi, his men ascend a steep mountain while the enemies are trampled underfoot or fall down the precipice. Naram-Sin carries a large bow.

Much more detailed and numerous are the representations on **Neo-Assyrian palace** reliefs that were meant to impress local and foreign visitors alike with the efficiency and determination of the Assyrian army. Scenes of camp life, with portable kitchens, tents, and baggage trains, showing soldiers at rest, intersperse the more common depictions of an army on campaign, marching across all manner of territories, or setting siege to enemy towns. They represent the different divisions, such as the chariotry, the cavalry, the archers, and the foot soldiers equipped with short and long spears. Some scenes concentrate on the result of victorious battles: smoking ruins of burned towns, heaps of corpses, and clerks taking down the number of casualties from a pile of severed hands. Since wars were also meant to deter insurrections, the palace reliefs served as a reminder of how the Assyrian king could punish rebels; the accompanying texts explained who was flayed or impaled, beheaded, or otherwise mutilated and why.

The written sources of the **royal inscriptions** and **annals** customarily dwell on successful conquests and campaigns that brought fame and wealth to the kings who led them. In the third and much of the second millennium B.C., such campaigns were waged after the harvest, since the king only commanded over a limited number of body guards in peacetime. **Sargon of Akkad**, however, claimed that "5,400 men ate with him daily," which was an unusually large entourage and perhaps constituted the beginning of a standing army.

In the **Old Babylonian period**, numbers of fighting men are sometimes recorded; the **Mari** letters, for example, refer to 10,000 men, and **Shamshi-Adad I** boasts of 60,000 under his command. In the Old Babylonian times fighting men could be conscripted for specific campaigns, or they were part-time professionals who could raise crops on crown land for their services. On campaign they were provisioned by the local population.

Since the army played such a vital role in the **Assyrian Empire**, they were better organized than in earlier periods, with auxiliary contingents from subjugated territories. There were career possibilities in the Assyrian army and senior officers could command a great deal of influence. Some Assyrian generals were **eunuchs**. They could lead campaigns when the king was unable to do so himself. The center of the army since the time of **Shalmaneser III** was a huge building known as the *ekal masarti* (Review Palace) at **Kalhu** (Nimrud). This served as arsenal, training ground, and administrative headquarters. *See also* WARFARE.

ASHURBANIPAL, Assyrian: Ashur-ban-apli (reigned 668–627? B.C.). King of **Assyria**, son and successor of **Esarhaddon**. Despite rich and diverse historical sources it is not possible to establish a generally acceptable chronology of Ashurbanipal's reign. Especially the events of his last years and the date and circumstances of his death remain unclear.

Ashurbanipal succeeded to the throne when his father Esarhaddon died on campaign in Egypt. Moves by the pharaoh Taharka to regain independence had to be repelled by several campaigns that culminated in the fall of Thebes. After this victory over the Kushite rulers Ashurbanipal consolidated the Assyrian hold over the vassal states in Syro-Palestine. In the northeast, he repelled incursions by Mannaeans but maintained friendly relations with a number of buffer states in Anatolia.

Relations with **Elam** and **Babylonia** proved to be more difficult to resolve. While the Assyrian army was occupied with the Egyptian campaign, Elam staged an invasion of Babylonia that was repressed by quickly dispatched troops. When in the following years Elam experienced a dynastic struggle, a rival faction found asylum at the court of **Ashurbanipal**. Hostilities between Assyria and Elam resumed when the new king Teumman invaded the east **Tigris** region. The Elamites were decisively beaten at the banks of the river Ulai, and the decapitated head of their king was sent to **Nineveh**.

The most serious and traumatic confrontation of Ashurbanipal's reign was the rebellion of his brother **Shamash-shuma-ukin**, who had been chosen by Esarhaddon to be king of **Babylon**. The anti-Assyrian faction headed by Shamash-shuma-ukin initiated a bid for independence, supported by Elamites and **Arabs**, as well as troops led by the ruler of the **Sealand**, which led to a four-year war that was eventually won by the Assyrians.

Relations with Elam continued to be problematic. There were several pretenders to the Elamite throne, and Ashurbanipal unsuccessfully backed an Elamite prince who had fled to Nineveh on the throne. In retaliation to a coup by Humban-Haltash, the Assyrian king began a war that was meant to deal with this long-standing enemy once and for all. As depicted on the reliefs from his Ninevite palace, his army stormed one city after the other, finally sacking and despoiling the capital Susa.

Ashurbanipal was also victorious in his other campaigns, especially in battles against the **Arabs**, who had helped Shamash-shuma-ukin.

The final years of Ashurbanipal's reign are still obscure due to a lack of sources from this period. He may have abdicated in 631 and retired to **Harran**, or he may have continued to rule Assyria until his death, possibly in 627. He was succeeded by his son Ashur-etil-ilani.

Despite his shadowy end amid growing internal and external threats to the Assyrian empire, Ashurbanipal was the last great Assyrian soldier-king who also left a considerable cultural legacy, most famously his library at Nineveh. The visual arts under Ashurbanipal reached a high level of refinement, as the numerous sculpted reliefs recovered from the palace at Nineveh testify. They show the king as chief of the victorious armed forces and the hunter of ferocious beasts, as in the famous lion hunt scene.

ASHUR-BEL-KALA (reigned 1074–1057 B.C.). King of Assyria, son of **Tiglath-pileser I**. He undertook numerous punitive expeditions against the raiding **Arameans**, as well as campaigns into Anatolia where the Urartians had become strong. With the Babylonians he concluded a peace treaty that was sealed by his **marriage** to the daughter of **Adad-apla-iddina**, whom he had appointed as king over **Babylonia**. A long inscription on the so-called Broken Obelisk, discovered at **Nineveh**, describes the king's prowess in hunting wild animals, his acquisition of a wide variety of fauna, and his numerous building projects.

ASHUR-DAN II (reigned 934–912 B.C.). King of **Assyria**, son and successor of the undistinguished Tiglath-pileser II, he ended the long period of decline suffered by the country after the demise of **Tiglath-pileser I**.

Royal inscriptions once more become abundant. **Ashur-Dan** began by turning against his neighbors to the north who had inflicted much damage on his border area. In the west he had to take on the ever menacing **Aramean** tribes and restored land and possessions that they had taken from the **Assyrians**. He pacified the eastern border region to secure the **trade** with the Iranian plateau and beyond. Thereafter he made efforts to reactivate the ravaged economy by resettling displaced populations to make uncultivated land productive. Hand in hand with these efforts to secure the **agricultural bases**, he invested in the chariotry and the armed forces. He also undertook various building projects, mainly restoration work on the **palaces**, **temples**, and gates of the capital, **Assur**.

ASHURNASIRPAL (Assyrian Ashur-nasir-apli) II (reigned 883–859 B.C.). King of **Assyria**, son and successor of **Tukulti-Ninurta II**, Ashurnasirpal built on the success of his predecessors to make **Assyria** the dominant power in the Near East. He undertook 14 campaigns, against the north (Anatolia) and the eastern regions of the Zagros Mountains. Westward he traveled to the shore of the Mediterranean Sea and initiated good relations with the economically important Levantine states. In the south he maintained peace with **Babylonia**.

His overall policy was directed less toward further expansion than to the consolidation of Assyrian influence. His mobile and well-equipped **army** could be effectively deployed at short notice to quell insurrections and to punish rebellious vassal rulers. On the other hand, Ashurnasirpal also accepted daughters of local rulers for his royal harem to cement friendly relationships and was ready to defend loyal subjects by lending them military aid. With the huge amounts of **tribute** and **taxes**, he had the resources to finance campaigns and grandiose building projects. In the new capital, **Kalhu** (modern Nimrud), a whole city was built, with **temples**, barracks, and residential quarters, where he resettled people deported from various parts of the empire. The so-called Banquet Stele describes the inaugurating party where he entertained and feasted 69,574 people for 10 days.

ASHUR-UBALLIT I (reigned c. 1365–1330 B.C.). King of **Assyria**. During his lifetime, Assyria's political situation changed significantly, due to the defeat of the neighboring kingdom of **Mitanni** by the **Hittites**. This allowed Ashur-uballit to extend his territory to the east and to grow in importance. He also initiated a close relationship with **Babylonia** by giving his daughter in **marriage** to the Babylonian king.

ASSUR. City in **Assyria**. The site, known as Qalat Sherqat, lies on a lime-stone bluff overlooking the river **Tigris**. It was excavated by the German Oriental Society, directed for many years by Walter Andrae.

A deep sounding at the site of the **Ishtar** temples revealed that it had been inhabited at least since the middle of the third millennium B.C. At the beginning of the second millennium Assur was involved in profitable **trade** with Anatolia, importing and exporting primarily **tin** obtained from western Iran, as well as textiles, in exchange for Anatolian **copper**.

The **Amorite** chief **Shamshi-Adad I** (reigning 1813–1781 B.C.) in-corporated Assur into his kingdom and it became a ceremonial center and thereafter the capital of Assyria until 883 when **Ashurnasirpal II** moved the seat of government to **Kalhu**. The city remained a ritually important place as the seat of the eponymous **god Assur** and served as the burial site for **Assyrian** monarchs. The stone stelae, bearing the names of the "**eponym** officials" (Assyrian limmu), were also displayed at Assur. This formed the basis of Assyrian chronology.

ASSYRIA. The heartland of Assyria lies in the northern area of present-day Iraq, alongside the river **Tigris**, from the Anatolian foothills to the range of the Jebel Hamrin. Other important waterways to the east are the Upper and the Lower Zab, which run from the Zagros Mountains. To the east extends a steppe-like plateau, known as the Jezirah, which reaches toward the Habur Valley. Much of this land was fertile, suited to rain-fed **agriculture** and especially herding. Major **trade** routes, into Anatolia and the Iranian plateau via the Zagros range, as well as southward to **Babylonia** and west to the Mediterranean, went across the country, which contributed toward the development of thriving economies.

In the sixth millennium B.C., it was densely settled, and several im-portant sites produced fine hand-painted pottery in the Halaf culture style. In the fifth millennium, **Nineveh** was a populous **city**; the area was subsequently dominated by the south Mesopotamian **Uruk** culture.

Assyria did not experience the intense urbanization that took place in the south during the third millennium. It was incorporated into the king-dom of **Akkad** and **Naram-Sin** built a temple at Nineveh.

Written sources, using a distinct **Akkadian** dialect known as **Old As-syrian**, only begin in the 20th century, when native kings, such as Ilushuma, established a dynasty. At this time, merchants from Assur be-gan their lucrative trade with Anatolia, exporting Assyrian textiles and **tin** which was obtained from a still unknown source farther east, and importing **copper**. The relevant tablets all come from the Anatolian site Kültepe, near present-day Kayseri.

In the 19th century, an Amorite leader named **Shamshi-Adad I**, exerted his sovereignty over Assyria from his base in the Habur Valley.

During the first half of the second millennium B.C., Assyria was eclipsed by Babylonia. The country saw the influx of peoples from the east, especially the **Hurrians**, and the west, various Semitic speaking tribes, such as the **Amorites**. An Indo-European elite, who ruled the mainly Hurrian population in northeast Syria, formed their own state (**Mitanni**) around 1500 and made the Assyrian kings their vassals. This only changed when the **Hittites** defeated **Mitanni** around 1350 B.C.

From the reign of **Ashur-uballit I** onward, the fortunes of the country began to revive. During the **Middle Assyrian period** (1400–1050), Assyria became one of the great military powers of the Near East. This entailed territorial expansion, mainly toward the north and the west, to form colonial dependencies that furnished **tribute** and manpower to the Assyrian state. Of prime importance for conquest and the maintenance of peace was the **army**, which became one of the best trained and equipped in the world. After the decline of the Hittite empire in the mid–13th century, **Tukulti-Ninurta I** (reigning 1244–1208) engineered the greatest expansion of the kingdom, including the incorporation of Babylonia.

Large-scale invasions and tribal unrest around 1100 contributed to the disintegration of the Assyrian power, and it was only in the 10th century that a new dynasty, with **Ashur-Dan III**, began to prepare the rise of the **Neo-Assyrian Empire** (934–610).

The height of Assyrian power was reached in the seventh century B.C., when energetic warrior kings such **Ashurnasirpal**, **Shalmaneser III**, **Tiglath-pileser III**, **Sargon II**, **Esarhaddon**, and **Ashurbanipal** fought on all fronts to sustain Assyrian pressure. The Assyrian empire included all of Mesopotamia (since Babylonia was under direct rule), most of central Anatolia, Syria including the Levant, and even, for a brief time, Egypt.

The policy of Assyrian kings was to nominate local rulers over their dependencies that had been won by military invasions and impose on them treaties of loyalty. As long as regular **tribute** payments and contingents of auxiliaries were received by the Assyrian authorities, the "vassal" partner was assured of Assyrian protection. Rebellions and treachery, such as joining anti-Assyrian alliances, were severely punished in raids, the leaders being gruesomely executed. Repeated disloyalty could be stopped by incorporating the country into the Assyrian provincial system, which entailed the complete loss of political and economic independence.

A further pacifying method, deployed where the latter option was unfeasible, was to deport a significant sector of the population (the elite and artisans) to other Assyrian-dominated regions. It has been estimated that millions of people were systematically displaced.

Such harsh measures fanned the flame of resistance and the Assyrian kings of the seventh century were forced to campaign relentlessly to keep their huge empire from falling apart. Their demise was swift. A coalition between the Babylonians, who resented Assyrian hegemony with great virulence, and the **Medes**, a new people who had settled in western Iran, spelled the final defeat in 612 B.C. when Nineveh was reduced to ashes.

The Assyrian elite was much influenced by Babylonia. Ever since Tukulti-Ninurta I brought important Babylonian tablet collections to Assur, the Assyrian intelligentsia immersed itself in Babylonian learning. In the seventh century, a number of southern scholars were permanently installed at the royal court.

As far as the visual arts were concerned, Egypt, or rather the traditional Egyptian colonial outposts along the Syria coast, proved more inspirational, as the ivories from Nimrud testify.

The relief sculptures were initially borrowed from the Hittites but the fine, flowing lines of the classic palace orthostats from **Kalhu** and Nineveh are typically Assyrian.

ASSYRIAN. East Semitic dialect, a form of **Akkadian** that was spoken in **Assyria** and rendered in **cuneiform** writing. In accordance with the different historical periods, one distinguishes between Old, Middle, and Neo-Assyrian. The largest number of Assyrian texts excavated so far date from the ninth to the middle of the seventh centuries B.C. *See also* LANGUAGES.

ASSYRIAN KING LIST. A document written in **Assyrian** that consists of a chronologically ordered sequence of 112 Assyrian rulers from the beginning of the second millennium B.C. to **Ashur-uballit II** (died in 609 B.C.), of which several copies exist from the first millennium. It lists the name of the king, his father's name, and the length of his reign, with occasional remarks about particularly noteworthy events. The reliability of the list is doubtful for the early periods, but it still functions as the basis of the modern chronological framework for Assyrian history.

ASTROLOGY/ASTRONOMY. Because all celestial observations in Mesopotamia served divinatory purposes, to discover the hidden meaning of divine messages inscribed in the movements of stars and planets, the two terms are inseparable. The primarily esoteric purpose did not preclude very detailed, regular, and "scientific" measurements and calculations.

Astral and planetary phenomena were only one part of a whole range of observable subjects that included the behavior of animals and human beings, the layout of cities, malformations of organs or fetuses, prices of staple commodities, war, famines, and so forth. The principle was that deviations from a perceived "normality" were inherently "ominous" and had either positive or negative connotations.

The collection and interpretation of such spontaneously occurring omens, as opposed to those solicited in specific rituals, was the task of highly trained **scribes**. They compiled lists of **omens**, in series covering different categories, with a column of text providing the interpretation. To establish astronomical "regularity," planetary and astral data were collected and collated. The scholars aimed to include all possible permutation of phenomena and encoded them in such a way that they could be meaningfully decoded when unusual celestial events occurred.

The earliest celestial series date from the **Old Babylonian period**, from around 1700 B.C. They chart not only unusual astral phenomena but also weather patterns at the time of observation. The collection of data kept growing and was put together in a work called *Enuma Anu Enlil* after its initial words. Copies were found in the library of **Ashurbanipal** at **Nineveh**. The entries concentrate on omens for the king and the country (e.g., "If the sun is surrounded by a halo and a cloud bank lies on the right, there will be a catastrophe everywhere in the country").

Lunar and solar eclipses were considered as particularly ominous. It was crucial for the diviners to predict the timing of an eclipse in time for apotropaic rituals averting any evil influence to be performed. The so-called "Mathematical-astronomical texts," (MUL.APIN "The Plough-Star") from the last centuries of the first millennium B.C. incorporate methods whereby such phenomena could be predicted to a high level of accuracy.

During the **Achaemenid period**, divinatory practices became less popular and individual predictions were solicited, which led to the introduction of the horoscope in the **Seleucid** period, perhaps as a Greek influence. A **Babylonian** invention was the assignment of four groups of zodiacal signs to the Moon, Saturn and Mars.

Astronomical diaries, recording lunar, planetary, meteorological, and economic data were kept well into the Christian era.

– B –

BABA (also known as *Bau* or *Bawa*). **Sumerian goddess** of **Lagash**, called "Mistress of the Animals" and "Lady of Abundance," which marks her as a mother-goddess and patron of life and fertility. She was the wife of the main deity of Lagash, Ningirsu. She shared his **temple** at Lagash and she also had her own sanctuary at Uruku, the sacred precinct of **Girsu**.

BABYLON. Ancient **city** on the river **Euphrates**, south of modern Baghdad. The name is the Greek version of the **Babylonian** *Babili*, which was rendered as "Gate of the Gods," although the original etymology is unclear.

The river used to run through the city but has shifted its course, and the much denuded site was left uninhabited for centuries, while the baked bricks used in the monuments were reused by local villagers for their own shelters. There are several scattered *tells* on an area that used to be enclosed by a wall of some 20 kilometers length. Due to the high water table, archaeological levels lower than those of the later second millennium B.C. are inaccessible. The extensive archaeological site was excavated by the German Oriental Society since 1899, originally led by Robert Koldewey; more recently Iraqi archaeologists have been at work at the sites. The most spectacular remains, such as the restored **Ishtar** Gate with its glazed tile reliefs of sacred animals, are in the Pergamon Museum in Berlin.

Babylon always had the reputation as a sacred site. It was first mentioned in an inscription of the **Akkad** king **Shar-kali-sharri**, but it is unlikely that the city's main **temple**, the Esagil, was founded by **Sargon of Akkad** as a **Babylonian Chronicle** states. It was the seat of a governor during the **Third Dynasty of Ur** but only grew to some importance in the **Old Babylonian period** when Sumu-abum made it the capital of his kingdom. **Hammurabi** enlarged and fortified the city in the 18th century B.C. The **Marduk** temple Esagil and the first **ziggurat** may also have been constructed at this time, although there is no archaeological proof for this.

The **Hittite** king **Mursili I** destroyed Babylon in c. 1595 B.C. It was rebuilt under the **Kassite** Dynasty, who promoted the cult of the venerable Babylonian **gods**. The city suffered another sacking in c.1174 at the hands of the **Elamites**, who also abducted the statues of Marduk and his consort. It was **Nebuchadrezzar I** who vindicated this insult by invading **Elam** and bringing back the stolen gods. In subsequent centuries

Babylon was under foreign influence and occupation, first by Elam and then by the **Assyrians**. While some Assyrian kings wrought havoc in the "sacred city" (e.g., **Sennacherib** in 698) others endowed the sanctuaries lavishly. However, it was during the time when Babylonia had regained its independence and became a powerful empire that the city began to be invested with magnificence. This was largely the work of **Nebuchadrezzar II**. He used the enormous revenue generated from **taxes** and **tribute** to embellish the capital, which became the largest and wealthiest of cities in the Near East.

It was surrounded by a strongly fortified double wall, some 20 kilometers long, pierced by several gates. It was strengthened by huge bulwarks of baked brick at the places where the **Euphrates** entered the city. Nebuchadrezzar built new **palaces** and decorated the throne room with glazed brick wall designs, which have also been partially reconstructed in Berlin.

Of particular importance was the sacred precinct of the god Marduk, with the temple Esagil and the ziggurat, remembered in the Bible as the Tower of Babel, which took 17 years to complete. It incorporated the remains of earlier structures under a casing of brick, some 15 meters thick.

A straight, walled street that served military as well as ritual purposes linked the temple to the western gate. It was used for the annual processions during the New Year **festival**, and glazed bricks lined the walls, showing the symbols of the main deities: the dragon of Marduk, the lion of **Ishtar**, and the bull of **Adad**.

When the **Persians** took political control of Mesopotamia they did not destroy the city. In the **Seleucid period**, a theater was built and a new market, while older temples continued to flourish. Despite the foundation of a new capital, Seleucia-on-the-Tigris, Babylon remained an important urban and especially religious center but declined when **Parthian** rule isolated **Babylonia** from the Hellenized world.

BABYLONIA. As a political term, *Babylonia* became current during the **Kassite period** when it was also known by its Kassite name *Karduniash*. It comprised the area south of the Jezirah up to the marshes of the Persian Gulf, bordered to the east and west roughly by the rivers **Tigris** and **Euphrates** but with no clearly defined boundaries. In modern works, Babylonia is also used as a topographic term, more or less synonymous with southern Mesopotamia, in distinction to **Assyria** or northern Mesopotamia.

BABYLONIAN. Linguistic term for an east Semitic dialect of Mesopotamia since the beginning of the second millennium B.C. There are certain differences between Old, Middle, and Neo-Babylonian. The Babylonian cursives of **cuneiform** tablets can be distinguished from the Assyrian examples by a preference for archaic styles and greater complexity of form. *See also* LANGUAGES.

BABYLONIAN CHRONICLES. Several chronicles were written in **Babylon** from the middle of the second millennium B.C. onward. Chronicle P records the dealings of the **Kassite** Dynasty with their **Assyrian** and **Elamite** neighbors. There are seven **Neo-Babylonian** chronicles from the reign of Nabunasir to the **Persian** conquest in 539 B.C. The Late Babylonian Chronicles follow on after a gap of some 50 years and cover the **Achaemenid** Dynasty, the reign of the successors of **Alexander the Great** (Diadochi), and the period of the **Seleucids**.

The **scribes** who wrote these documents were primarily interested in events at **Babylonia** from a Babylonian point of view and thus often contradict or supplement other sources, like the Assyrian **annals** and **royal inscriptions**. On the other hand, they do not gloss over military defeats or the fact that Babylonia was governed by foreign kings and thus betray a genuine interest in history.

BABYLONIAN KING LISTS. Continuing the framework set up by the earlier **Sumerian King List**, Mesopotamian **scribes** composed similar chronological lists that are not preserved in their entirety. King List A enumerates the kings from the **First Dynasty of Babylon** to the rise of **Nabopolassar** in 626 B.C.

BAZI-DYNASTY (c.1005–986 B.C.). Short-lived and poorly documented **Babylonian Dynasty** featured in **Babylonian King Lists** as springing "from the House of Bazi." Three kings are listed for this period, one of the most difficult and disruptive times in Babylonian history.

BEER. The earliest evidence for the use of beer comes from Godin-Tepe in Central Iran, where remains of beer were found in a fragmentary jar that dates back to the late fourth millennium B.C. In the ancient Near East, beer was part of the basic nutrition and was apparently consumed at all times in large quantities and given out as part of the daily rations to laborers. Since only fresh water was used in its preparation, it was a healthier drink than the often polluted water from the canals and wells, as well as being enriched with protein and vitamins and easily digestible. Its percentage of alcohol is not known. Several myths and narratives describe drunkenness among gods and mortals. One creation myth derives the various defects suffered by people, such as blindness and barrenness, as the result of a competition between two inebriated deities ("**Enki** and Ninhursaga").

Beer was produced mainly from barley. The pounded grain cakes were molded and baked for a short time. These were pounded again, mixed with water, and brought to fermentation. Then the pulp was filtered and the beer stored in large jars. Mesopotamian beer could only be kept for a short time and had to be consumed fresh. The **cuneiform** texts mention different kinds of beer, such as "strong beer," "fine beer," and "dark beer." Other sorts were produced from emmer or sesame, as well as dates in the **Neo-Babylonian** period and later.

Beer was not only part of the rations for workers but offered daily to the **gods**. In the **temple** cult, it was further used at banquets during the major **festivals**.

BEL-HARRAN-USUR. Assyrian official in the eighth century B.C. He was **palace** herald under King **Adad-nirari III** and held several other important offices, such as that of the **eponym** (*limmu*) and governor of Guzana. In a stele discovered north of Hatra, his name appears before that of the king, which demonstrates that his power in the area was greater than the king's. He also mentions in the text that he had founded a new settlement, called Dur-Bel-harran-beli-usur (literally Fort Dur-Bel-harran-usur).

BEROSSUS (Babylonian *Bel-re'ushu*). Babylonian scholar and **priest** of **Marduk**, who lived in the third century B.C. during the reign of Antiochus I. He wrote a "History of Mesopotamia" (*Babyloniaka*) in Greek, of which only fragments survive as quotations in much later Greek and Roman writers.

The work was apparently in three volumes: The first contained a geographical description of **Babylonia** and the origin of human life and civilization, the second was about the 10 kings before the flood and various later dynasties down to Nabu-nasir (eighth century), and the last volume covered the period of **Assyrian** domination to **Alexander the Great**. Later classical tradition also claims that he introduced **astronomy** to the Greeks.

BITUMEN. Latin word for naturally occurring semisolid hydrocarbon (petroleum). Bitumen springs were found in several **palaces** in Mesopotamia, and the substance (*kupru* or *iṭṭu* in **Akkadian**) was used primarily for waterproofing vessels and containers, as well as in construction. It also served to attach ax heads and similar tools to their shafts. Although the Bible reports the Babylonians used "pitch instead of mortar" (Genesis 11:3), this material was only used when protection from rising damp was necessary, such as in buildings near waterways or in large structures such as **ziggurats**. Coatings of bitumen plaster made walls watertight, a practice documented in **Old Babylonian Ur**.

BIT-YAKIN. A **Chaldean** tribe in southern **Babylonia** during the first millennium B.C. They settled in the very south of the country, near the marshes. The tribe grew rich and influential when they began to control the access to the Persian Gulf and thus the maritime **trade** route south.

When Babylonia was under **Assyrian** occupation in the seventh century B.C. the Bit-Yakin made several, at times successful, attempts to challenge Assyrian hegemony. Their most famous leader, who assumed kingship in **Babylon**, was **Merodach-Baladan**, the archenemy of **Sennacherib**.

BORSIPPA. **Babylonian city** (modern Birs Nimrud), southwest of **Babylon**, which early travelers mistook for Babylon. It was investigated in the 19th century by explorer *cum* archaeologists such as Austen Layard, Hormuzd Rassam, and Henry C. Rawlinson, and more recently by an Austrian team.

The site was occupied from the late third millennium B.C. until the Islamic period. The main attraction of the city, especially during the first millennium, was the **temple** of the **god Nabu**, known as Ezida, which **Hammurabi** of Babylon claimed to have restored. Most of the extant archaeological evidence dates from this time. The Ezida precinct then consisted of a temple and a **ziggurat**, both within a walled enclosure. A processional street led from the temple, through the city gates, toward Babylon. This was ritually used in the New Year **Festival** when Nabu, like all major Babylonian deities, assembled at the precinct of **Marduk**.

BOUNDARY STONES (Babylonian *kudurru*). Inscribed stone monuments in the shape of roundly dressed blocks were set up in **temples** and perhaps in special chapels to publicize the donation of land by the king in order to reward loyal subjects.

The earliest example dated from the time of **Manishtusu** (23rd century B.C.), but the word *kudurru* generally denotes boundary stones from the **Kassite** to the **Neo-Babylonian** period (14th–7th centuries B.C.). The legal documentation was given added protection and validity by the carved emblems of deities at the top of the stone, as well as elaborate **curses**.

BRONZE. From the fifth millennium B.C. onward, the use of bronze spread gradually over the Near East and was introduced to Mesopotamia around 3000 B.C. It was first produced as an alloy of **copper** and antimony or lead, later as an alloy of copper and **tin**. It was either made by smelting a mixture of copper ores and tin ores or by melting together metallic copper and tin. Their ratio varied from 6:1 to 10:1 depending on the function of the objects and the raw materials used. Normally the portion of arsenic is rather low in Mesopotamian bronze, but it can rise to 4 percent (arsenic bronze) depending on the copper ore.

Bronze was used for cult objects, tools, **weapons**, and all kinds of everyday items. Several bronze objects such as swords or vessels were found in the Royal Tombs of **Ur**. After 1200 B.C., it was partially and gradually replaced by **iron**. The bronze bands from the **temple** gates of Balawat (Imgur-Enlil) with their depictions of scenes from the military campaigns of **Ashurnasirpal II** and **Shalmaneser III** are of major historical importance, as are the bronze artifacts from **Urartu** and Luristan.

BUILDING INSCRIPTIONS. Since the erection and maintenance of important buildings such as **palaces** and **temples** were the responsibilities of the Mesopotamian kings, they often commemorated their contributions. Inscribed tablets made of metal or stone were placed in a box beneath the foundations or, in the shape of a cone-shaped peg, inserted into the brickwork of the walls. The inscriptions could be short, just containing the name and title of the king and the name of the building, with sometimes the date, such as in which year of his reign the building was dedicated. They could also be much longer and furnish information about important events that took place at the time, such as résumés of military campaigns (especially in **Assyrian** inscriptions).

When a building was renewed, the foundation box was searched for, and a new one could be added to the one discovered. Therefore, many building inscriptions were addressed to "future kings" who are exhorted to treat this document with due respect, and terrible **curses** were heaped on those who would cast them aside or break them.

Building inscriptions are very valuable sources for the reconstruction of historical sequences, especially when other written material is not available, and essential for the identification and dating of an excavated architectural structure.

BUILDING MATERIALS. Because of the geophysical characteristic of the alluvial plains of southern Mesopotamia, the most common building material was clay, in the form of sun-dried mud brick. This was used for vernacular as well as for monumental structures such as **temples**, **palaces**, and **city** walls. The mud could be tempered with organic substances such as chaff and straw, or sand, although in some areas the natural composition of the soils was such as not to need any tempering. The mud bricks were laid in mud plaster, sometimes with additions of lime. **Bitumen** was widely used for damp- and waterproofing in wet rooms and near waterways. Kiln-fired bricks were also primarily used to counteract rising damp and water erosion.

Local trees such as the date palm provided timber for the flat roofs, as well as doorways; for the wider spans in temples and palaces, coniferous hardwood (e.g., cedar) was imported from Syria and the Levant.

In the marshy regions of the south, reeds provided the building material for temporary constructions, such as byres, sheds, and simple dwellings.

Stone, especially limestone, is more commonly found in northern Mesopotamia but did not play a major role in architecture. It was used in **Assyria** for foundations; engineered structures such as bridges, canals, and quays; as well as for door sills and column bases. Stone slabs lining the lower courses of exterior walls (known as *orthostats*) could be found in some palaces in northern Syria and Anatolia. This practice was adapted for interior use by the Assyrians, and many of the carved limestone slabs are now displayed in museums around the world.

The **nomadic** peoples of Mesopotamia lived in tents made from the wool of goats and sheep.

BUREAUCRACY. *See* ADMINISTRATION.

– C –

CAMEL. The home of the one-hump camel (dromedary) was most likely the Arabian peninsula, from where there are indications for its domestication as early as the fourth millennium B.C. Depictions of camels from the Oman Peninsula date back to approximately 3000 B.C.

The two-hump Bactrian camel came from the steppes of Central Asia. Both kinds are mentioned in **Old Babylonian cuneiform** texts. In at least one of them the dromedary occurs as a domesticated animal, but it is not before the middle of the second millennium B.C. that there is evidence for the widespread use of domesticated camels (dromedaries) for transportation and **warfare**. Especially for the stock-breeding **nomads** of the Syrian-Arabian steppe, camels meant greater mobility and independence from traditional pasture areas.

In the overland **trade**, camels opened new caravan routes through territories that had been impassable before due to the lack of water. The oases along these routes—Palmyra, Djuma Djandal, Teima, al-Ula— became important trading places and military posts.

Military expeditions such as **Nabonidus**' conquest of Teima depended heavily on the use of camels. Therefore, they were important items among the booty and **tribute** from the Arabian Peninsula. Wall reliefs from **Nineveh** show **Assyrian** troops pursuing **Arab** fighters mounted on dromedaries. Bactrian camels being presented to the Assyrian monarch are depicted on the famous Black Obelisk of **Shalmaneser III**.

CHALCOLITHIC. An archaeological period (literally "copper-stone" age) that refers to increased use of metallurgy, especially of **copper**, toward the end of the **Neolithic period**. In Mesopotamia, the Chalcolithic lasted approximately from the sixth to the fifth millennium B.C. Pilot sites in the north are Tepe Gawra and Tell Arpachiya, and **Eridu** and Tell Awayli in the south. For southern sites, the term **Ubaid period** is also used; and for the north, Halaf period.

In this phase, all the achievements of the preceding period were further developed; horticulture and **agriculture** spread, and more and more people adopted a sedentary lifestyle. The archaeological evidence points to increased settlement size, and increased specialization, professionalization, and higher labor inputs. All ecological niches and their wild resources (fish, water fowl, game, wild legumes) were exploited, and new cultigens planted in fields and garden, making use of hydrotechnological inventions such as field irrigation.

It also saw the introduction of fundamentally new technologies. Particularly striking is the hand-painted, sometimes glazed **pottery** showing an unparalleled degree of perfection. Pottery sets, found in many grave sites, were probably used in rituals and banquets where status could be displayed.

Metallurgy was less developed in Mesopotamia than in neighboring countries such as Iran. **Gold** was introduced, and arsenic **bronze** appeared in the upper **Euphrates** region in the Ubaid period.

There is some evidence from Tell Awayli of a weaving loom.

Stone was also worked with more sophistication; it was now possible to work stones with a hardness of 4 to 7 on the Moh's hardness scale. The presence of exotic stones, such as lapis lazuli from Badakhshan or turquoise from Central Asia, points to an interlinking supply system. Exchange of goods seems to have been an important factor of Chalcolithic socioeconomics, as was the practice of seals and sealings documents. Some scholars propose that Chalcolithic communities were on the way to forming states ("incipient statehood"), given the whole-scale application of traditional inventions, efforts at maximizing energy output, and increasing full-time sedentarization.

CHALDEAN DYNASTY (626–539 B.C.). **Babylonian** dynasty founded by the **Chaldean** leader **Nabopolassar**, who brought the period of **Assyrian** domination over **Babylonia** to an end. He made an alliance with the **Medes** and successfully launched attacks against the powerful Assyrian cities, destroying **Nineveh** in 612. His successor **Nebuchadrezzar II** fought to win the Syrian and Anatolian provinces for Babylonia and built the **city** of **Babylon** into the most splendid capital of the time.

There were violent **palace** intrigues after Nebuchadrezzar's death, although the situation in Babylonia and the conquered territories remained relatively stable. The last Chaldean king was **Nabonidus**, who spent 10 years in an oasis town in northern Arabia and after his return had to submit to the **Persian** emperor **Cyrus II**, who brought Mesopotamian independence to an end.

CHALDEANS. Semitic-speaking, **tribal** peoples in southern Mesopotamia. The name comes from the Babylonian term for their region, *mat kaldu*. Together with **Aramean** tribes, they entered **Babylonia** between 1000 and 900 B.C. The main tribes were the **Bit-Yakin**, Bit Amukanni, and Bit Dakkuri, all occupying their own territory and having their own rulers. They were prosperous, profiting from the maritime gulf **trade** that passed through their land.

The term *Chaldean* was from then on also used to denote Babylonia, until well into the Roman period.

CHARIOT. The chariot was an important instrument of **war**, particularly during the earlier phases of ancient Near Eastern history. Already for the **Early Dynastic period** (c. 2500 B.C.), the military use of chariots is widely documented. According to visual evidence as on the "Standard of Ur" and the "Stele of Vultures" (*see* EANNATUM), those early chariots were heavy vehicles with two or four solid wheels, drawn by teams of four donkeys. Their personnel consisted of two men, a driver, and a warrior.

In the second millennium B.C., when **horses** were introduced by peoples coming from the Central Asian steppes, chariots were adapted to higher speed by reducing their weight and increasing their maneuverability. This was only possible after the invention of the spoked wheel. The military successes of the **Hittites**, **Kassites**, and **Mitanni** are mainly due to the use of quantities of light horse-drawn chariots for attacks. In Egypt, the two-wheeled chariot was introduced by the Hyksos.

During the first millennium B.C., the military importance of chariots decreased. As an attack force they were replaced by the cavalry, but they remained an important vehicle for the military elite and for the king. **Babylonian** and **Assyrian** monarchs used them on campaigns, during **festivals**, and on hunting expeditions.

CITIES. Mesopotamian **scribes** considered urban life as the only form of civilized communality. A person's civic identity was that of a citizen of a particular city with its suburbs and surrounding countryside. Nonurban sectors of the population defined themselves by tribal allegiance.

Myths describe cities such as **Babylon** to have been created by the **gods** to be their dwelling place. The city was thus intimately connected to a particular deity whose image resided in the **temple**; **Ur**, for instance, was the seat of the moon god Nannar-Suen, **Sippar** of the sun god **Shamash**, and so forth. The fate of individual cities was linked with the prestige and popularity of their main deity. Royal patronage of the cult could sustain a city with a famous sanctuary in periods of economic hardship or ecological problems. A well-developed temple economy, more or less independent from central control, could also contribute substantially to a city's survival. The city of **Uruk**, which boasted two ancient and important shrines, of the goddess **Inanna-Ishtar** and the sky god **Anu**, respectively, owed much of its longevity and prosperity to the religious prestige of the city.

Economically the city functioned as a regional center, controlling the agricultural production of the surrounding fields and organizing the craft and textile manufactory. **Temples** as well as governmental institutions (*see* PALACE) organized the **administration**.

Since the early third millennium B.C., cities competed over land and especially water resources and engaged in intense intercity rivalry that often escalated into **warfare**. As a result, cities came to be surrounded by fortified walls and military commanders could achieve positions of power.

Competing interests of individual cities could be reconciled through alliances and leagues, which ensured cooperation and mutual support. They also prepared the way for centralized state formations that subordinated the control of individual cities to a single political entity, controlled by a king (*see* AKKADIAN EMPIRE; THIRD DYNASTY OF UR). Such centralized control could only be maintained for limited periods since the resentment of city leaders fostered rebellions and resistance. It was the **Kassite Dynasty** that managed to form the first unified state to endure for centuries; this was no doubt to some degree at the expense of cities. Small towns and villages became the dominant settlement form during this time.

The old cities benefited in subsequent periods as centers of production, sacred centers, and political capitals (*see* BABYLON; NINEVEH; URUK). The Babylonian cities survived the demise of the country's political independence under the **Achaemenid** and **Seleucid** regimes.

COPPER. Copper was the first metal humans learned to work with. The earliest evidence comes from Cayönü in southeast Turkey (late ninth or early eighth millennium B.C.) where small items of jewelry were made from cold hammered nuggets. Large-scale copper production is associated with the **Chalcolithic period**. Especially in Anatolia and Palestine, quantities of copper articles were produced in the fifth millennium. Antimony and arsenic were often added to the copper to improve its working properties.

The copper used in Mesopotamia originated from various places, notably Cyprus, Anatolia, Iran, the Levant, Sinai, and Oman.

Copper was melted, cast into easily transportable forms (ingots), and then shipped. From the fourth millennium on, it was made into beads and all sorts of everyday items, later also for objects used in the cult such as statues, musical instruments, or vessels. The coppersmiths fashioned the metal into objects by casting, chasing, hammering, forging, and engraving. One of the most famous copper objects from Mesopotamia is the head of a royal statue found at **Nineveh**. It dates from the **Akkadian pe-**

riod and is believed to depict either **Sargon** or **Naram-Sin** of **Akkad**. For a short time during the **Early Dynastic period**, copper served as standard but was soon replaced by **silver**. Copper was also a raw material in the production of bronze and of glass. In medicine, it was used to cure eye diseases.

COURTS. *See* LAW.

CREATION MYTHS. There is a variety of cosmogonic references in **cuneiform** sources that reflect the different theological themes of individual cult centers. A common theme is the notion that an undifferentiated and watery universe became separated into distinct pairs of opposites. At **Eridu**, home of the water deity **Enki**, the primordial substance was composed of the mingled sweet and salty waters that begat a third creative (female) element, which in turn produced Heaven (Sumerian An) and Earth (**Sumerian** Ki). At **Nippur**, the separation of Heaven and Earth, the **god Enlil** presides over the creation of the heavenly bodies and the organization of the world.

The best-known creation myth is known by its **Babylonian** name as *enuma elish* ("when above"). It builds on earlier cosmogonies and assigns the role of creator to **Marduk**. This text also presents a theme of intergenerational violence that may have been a north Syrian or **Hurrian** influence. The older divine couples are disturbed by the noise of their offspring and plot their destruction. The younger **gods** appoint **Ea** to defend them, but he fails and so they invest the son of Ea, Marduk, with magic powers to meet the challenge. He succeeds to defeat the primeval but now monstrous creator goddess Tiamat. He slices her body in half, fixes the upper part to hold up the sky, and fashions the lower part into the Earth. The rivers **Tigris** and **Euphrates** flow from her eye sockets; her tail becomes a plug to hold back the subterranean waters. Marduk also fixes the planets and stars on the upper heaven and decrees their paths. He fashions man from mud mixed with the blood of Kingu, the general of Tiamat's army. In gratitude, the gods confer on Marduk the **kingship**, and he establishes **Babylon** as his dwelling place on Earth.

The Creation of Mankind in older sources is attributed to mother **goddesses** who collaborate with a divine culture hero (Ea-Enki) who mingles clay with the breath (or the blood) of a god. The destiny imposed on humankind is the service of the gods, especially the backbreaking tasks of maintaining the irrigation system, and mortality.

CUNEIFORM. A system of **writing** in which a cut reed stylus is pressed into soft clay to leave a wedgelike imprint (Latin *cuneus*). It was invented in Mesopotamia in the late fourth millennium B.C. Different versions of cuneiform writing were used to write various Near Eastern **languages**: **Sumerian**, **Akkadian**, Eblaite, **Elamite**, Ugaritic, **Hittite**, and **Hurrian**. It was superseded by alphabetic scripts after the mid–first century B.C.

Archaic cuneiform script had a predominantly pictorial character since most of the signs originally referred to visible entities. Since the soft clay made accurate visual representation very difficult, signs became simplified and individual "strokes" of the stylus replaced curvilinear forms in the early third millennium. Equally, the large number of signs was reduced to some 600.

Different cursive writing styles are associated with different historical periods. The **Neo-Assyrian** style is commonly used in assyriological textbooks because of its comparative clarity.

The original repertoire of logograms (word signs) became extended through the principle of the "rebus," which could isolate the phonetic value of a sign to express syntactic and grammatical relationships that determine the meaning of a sentence. Special signs known as determinatives signaled the context of signs, especially to indicate when they were to be understood as a name (personal, topographical, theophoric, etc.). With the adaptation of cuneiform for several languages within the same culture (Sumerian and the Semitic Akkadian), the system became even more complex as the logographic value of a sign could be "translated" into the Semitic idiom and thereby created further phonetic readings.

Due to this inherent difficulty of the writing system, scribal training was long and arduous, restricting literacy to a relatively small group of persons. The repercussions of cuneiform writing, however, affected the whole population because of the widespread use of writing in the **administration** and the judiciary.

CURSES. Like the **oath**, the utterance of a curse was believed to have the magic powers that could destroy its victim by an inherent force. In the Epic of **Gilgamesh**, the hero Enkidu curses the courtesan who had introduced him to civilization, and only a subsequent, equally elaborate blessing could avert the inevitable actualization of the malediction.

Public monuments could be protected from vandalism, theft, and misappropriation by curses. In such inscriptions, the **gods** are called upon to guarantee the effectiveness of the curse. The most common threat was to have the "seed cut off"—meaning to die without living offspring and to remain "without a name." Royal grants and other publicly displayed legal decrees (*see* BOUNDARY STONES; LAW CODES) had curses that not only safeguarded the stele or actual monument but ensured that the content of the inscribed stipulations were respected for all times.

CYLINDER SEALS. Cylinder seals are short pieces of semiprecious stones or more rarely metal, perforated along the axis so as to be suspended from a string and engraved with a decorative pattern or representational scene, and sometimes an inscription. When the seal was rolled over a flattened damp piece of clay, it left an imprint in high relief. The purpose of such seals was to indicate the authority of the person or institution who applied the seal impression, rather like a signature on a modern document.

The practice originated within the complex **bureaucracies** of the Middle and Late **Uruk period** (in the mid–fourth millennium B.C.). The pictorial scenes that refer to activities such as weaving, attending to domestic animals, hunting, and apparently ritual actions may indicate spheres of administrative competence within the Uruk economy. Thousands of imprints of such cylinder seals have been found on lumps of clay that were attached to door locks, jars, and other containers.

From the end of the second millennium onward, **cuneiform** tablets could also be sealed. The iconography and artistic style of seal engraving naturally changed over time, which allows specialists to assess seals and sealings within a chronological and geographical framework.

CYRUS II THE GREAT (reigned 559–530 B.C.). King of Persia, son and successor of Cambyses I. He was the founder of the **Achaemenid Empire**. Sources for his reign are **Herodotus** and Ctesias, as well as contemporary Babylonian records, especially the **Babylonian Chronicle** and his own inscriptions, such as the Cyrus Cylinder.

Cyrus began his career by defeating the **Median** king, Astyages. Having thus gained control over most of Iran, he set out to extend his dominions farther west. He attacked the Lydian capital Sardis, and within five years he had incorporated most of Anatolia into his empire. He then set out to conquer **Babylonia**. In 539 B.C., Cyrus crossed the Diyala River and took the city of Opis on the **Tigris**, after he had vanquished the defending Babylonian troops. Soon afterward, **Sippar** surrendered and **Babylon** was taken by his commander, Gibryas, on 12 October. **Nabonidus**, the king of Babylonia, was taken prisoner and deported to Persia.

Cyrus entered Babylon on the 29th. He declared his son Cambyses II to be "King of Babylon," while he himself took the traditional Mesopotamian title "King of the Lands."

According to the Old Testament Book of Ezra, he issued the decree that allowed the deported Jews to return to Palestine and rebuild the temple in Jerusalem.

Cyrus made efforts to extend his realm farther east, and it is likely that he controlled most of Afghanistan and south-central Asia. Within 30 years, he had turned a small kingdom into a vast empire. He died, probably on the battlefield, in 530 B.C., while fighting against a Central Asian tribe. His body was taken to Pasargadae, his new royal foundation, and buried in a stone-built tomb. A funerary cult continued there until the end of the Achaemenid Empire.

– D –

DAGAN. West-Semitic weather **god** who was worshipped especially in the middle **Euphrates** region within the zone of rain-fed **agriculture**. He was the chief deity at **Ebla** and of great importance in **Mari**. He was introduced to Mesopotamia by the kings of **Akkade** in the third millennium. During the **Third Dynasty of Ur**, the cult of Dagan was centered at the livestock center Puzrish-Dagan near **Nippur**. He also had a temple at **Isin** during the **Old Babylonian period**. Eventually Dagan merged with other weather gods, especially **Adad**.

DAIIAN-ASHUR. Field marshal of the **Assyrian army** under **Shalmaneser III** (reigned 858–824 B.C.). He was also an **eponym** official for many years. In the royal **annals** of this period, he is often mentioned as conducting campaigns in the king's name.

DARIUS I (reigned 522–486 B.C.). **Achaemenid** king. Darius seems to have acceded to the throne in mysterious circumstances and had to repress internal dissent and quell rebellions in the **Persian** provinces. His rock inscription recording his eventual triumph in a cliff face at Behistun was written in Old Persian, **Elamite**, and **Babylonian**. It proved an invaluable source for the decipherment of **cuneiform**.

Darius much enlarged the territories of the empire toward the east. In the west, he faced revolts by the Ionian cities in Asia Minor and was

beaten by the Greeks at Marathon. He also built a new capital at Persepolis, as well as **palaces** at Susa.

DARIUS III (reigned 336–330 B.C.). **Achaemenid** king who was defeated
by **Alexander the Great** and lost the **Persian** Empire to the Macedonian conqueror. Although he escaped from the battlefields at Issos and
Gaugamela, he was killed by one of his own generals.

DEITIES. *See* GODS.

DUR-KURIGALZU (modern 'Aqar Quf). **Babylonian city**. The name
means "Fortress of Kurigalzu" since it was **Kurigalzu**, a **Kassite** king,
who built his residence there in about 1400 B.C. It served as the capital
of the Kassite Dynasty until their demise in the mid–14th century. Kurigalzu surrounded the city, which covered some 225 hectares, with a fortified wall. Some of the colorful murals that decorated the walls of the
royal **palace**, as well as a number of statuary and small ornaments, have
been discovered in its ruins. Kurigalzu also built a **temple** and a large
ziggurat (69 by 67.60 meters) that still stands to a height of 57 meters
today.

In 1170, the city was put to the torch by the **Elamites** and thereafter abandoned until it became inhabited once more during the **Neo-Babylonian**
period.

DUR-SHARRUKEN (modern Khorsabad). **Assyrian** capital, inaugurated
by **Sargon II** in 707 (the name means "Fortress of Sargon"). Sargon decided to move the center of Assyrian **administration** and the royal
palaces from **Kalhu** to a brand new site. The **city** was therefore planned
from the beginning.

A massive wall of mud brick (14 meters thick and 12 meters high) surrounded the rectangular outline of the city, enclosing an area of 300
hectares. There were seven gates, each dedicated to an Assyrian **god**. Within
a separate enclosure stood the palace and the administrative complex
known as the "Palace without Rival." According to the French excavators,
it contained more than 210 rooms, grouped around three courtyards. The
portals were guarded by colossal human-headed and winged bulls made of
stone, and the walls of the palace were lined with relief-covered limestone
slabs that showed the triumph of the Assyrian **army** and the deeds of Sargon. Numerous administrative tablets have also been found. There were
several sanctuaries at Dur-Sharruken, the most notable was dedicated to the

god **Nabu** and decorated with glazed tiles. The city was destroyed in the final cataclysm of the Assyrian empire around 612 B.C.

DYNASTY OF E (c. 979–647 B.C.). Little-known **Babylonian** dynasty at a time when tribal unrest, famine, and general disorder characterized Mesopotamian history. Most kings ruled only for a few years at the time, and **Assyria** dominated the political fate of the country, insofar as most kings occupied the throne on the behest of Assyrian rulers if they did not proclaim themselves direct rulers of **Babylonia**, such as **Tiglath-pileser III, Sargon II,** and **Esarhaddon**.

– E –

EA. **God** of the underground waters and the magic arts, the **Babylonian** equivalent of the **Sumerian** god **Enki**, whose main sanctuary was at **Eridu** in southern Mesopotamia. Being the wisest among the gods, he was also the patron of craftsmen, artisans, and exorcists.

In various **Akkadian** myths, Ea is sought out for his advice and cunning; he alone realizes that the gods need the services of mankind and therefore helps his protégé Atra-hasis to escape the flood. Likewise, he knows how to resurrect the **goddess Ishtar**, who was doomed to remain in the underworld.

Ea was one of the most important Mesopotamian gods throughout history, as the many personal references (e.g., "Ea is my protection") testify. From the mid–second millennium B.C. onward, he was primarily appealed to as a protector against evil demons.

EANNATUM (reigned c. 2454–2425 B.C.). **Early Dynastic** ruler of the city-state **Lagash**, brother of his successor Enannatum I. Eannatum was probably his official throne name; he was also known as Lumma, an **Amorite** name. According to his inscriptions, he fought against other **cities**, such as **Kish**, **Ur**, and **Mari**, and also campaigned in **Elam**. Eannatum is best known for his victory over **Umma**, the neighboring **city** that had a long-standing conflict with Lagash over the control of fields along their respective boundaries. He had a large stone monument put up, the so-called Stele of Vultures, which depicts the victorious **army** of the Lagashites trampling over the fallen foes, while vultures pick their bones. The text describes the history of the dispute and how the victory was granted by the will of the **god** Ningirsu, the patron deity of Lagash.

EARLY DYNASTIC PERIOD. Archaeological term referring to levels of Mesopotamian sites from the end of the **Jemdet-Nasr period** (c. 2900 B.C.) to the reign of **Sargon of Akkad** (c. 2330). There are three subdivisions: Early Dynastic (ED) I (2900–2750), ED II (2750–2600), ED III A (2600–2500), and ED III B (2500–2330).

The first historical records appeared in Early Dynastic III A, brief inscriptions from **Kish**, **Ur**, and **Uruk**. Other texts, mainly of **administrative** purpose, were discovered at Abu Salabikh and Fara (ancient **Shuruppak**).

The Early Dynastic period saw the emergence of several important city-states and a marked trend toward urbanization. There was much competition between individual **cities**, not only for power and influence but for water rights and territorial boundaries. The documents found at Fara refer to large institutional organizations that could command thousands of men for various civic and military tasks. There may also have been coalitions of cities, as the still poorly documented "Kengi-League." Toward the end of ED III, Uruk had achieved prominence under the leadership of **Lugalzagesi**.

EBLA (modern Tell Mardikh). **City** in the Orontes Valley in Syria, a land well known for the fertility of its fields and rich pasture. The history and economy of Ebla are unusually well known, due to the voluminous **archives** discovered by Italian archaeologists. The cuneiform texts were written in a Semitic language, now simply called Eblaite.

Ebla had been first inhabited during the **Chalcolithic period** (Mardikh I 3500–3000). This is followed by Level II, subdivided into phases A, B1 and B2.

The most illustrious period was II B1, when the Royal **Palace** (with the **archives**) was built. The palace was the main institution of the Old Ebla kingdom, it employed some 4,700 people, entailed numerous workshops, such as smithies and textile manufactories. The city was destroyed in c. 2250, probably by an **Akkadian** ruler. Ebla revived after an interval (Mardikh III A and B) in the **Old Babylonian period** and was finally destroyed in c. 1600. Sources for this period are far fewer.

ELAM. Region in southwest Iran, presently known as Khuzistan. Its geographical position, at the edge of the Iranian plateau and within the alluvial plains of the rivers Karun and Karkeh, tributaries of the **Tigris**, gave this area access to the central Iranian highlands, as well as the Persian Gulf and the southern Mesopotamian plains. During the prehistoric period in the fifth and fourth millennium B.C., there were strong cultural links with southern Mesopotamian sites.

The inhabitants of Elam called themselves *haltami* (*elamtu* in **Akkadian**). They spoke a **language** that is not connected with any other known language (Elamite) that they began to write in **cuneiform** in the mid–third millennium.

The country is first mentioned in **Sumerian** inscriptions from the **Early Dynastic period**; **Eannatum**, for instance, reports that he conquered Elam (in the 25th century B.C.).

There were several dynasties in Elam, one, dominated by the city Awan, defeated **Ur** and thus was included in the **Sumerian King List**. **Sargon of Akkad** (reigned 2340–2284 B.C.) incorporated the Susiana into his empire where he appointed his own governors. **Naram-Sin**, (reigned 2260–2223 B.C.) concluded a treaty with the king of Awan, which was preserved in the temple of the Elamite **god** Inshushinak.

According to an Elamite king list, the dynasty of Awan was followed by that of Shimashki, a city in the mountains of Luristan. The southern part (Susiana) was under the control of the **Third Dynasty of Ur** until c. 2004, when Kindattu, a king of Shimashki, invaded **Ur** and took **Ibbi-Sin** prisoner. Kindattu called himself "king of Anshan and Susa."

The next phase is known as the period of the *sukkalmah* (the title of governors during the Third Dynasty of Ur) (c. 1970–1500). At that time Akkadian was adopted as the official language although few documents survive.

The so-called Middle Elamite period (1500–1100) saw the rise of Elamite power. Under the Igehalkit Dynasty, Elamite became once more the main written language. King Untash-Napirisha (reigned 1275–1240) built a new capital, Dur-Untash (modern Choga Zanbil). His grandson Kiden-Hutran (reigned 1235–1210) raided **Babylonia**, where he destroyed a number of **cities**. From then **Elam** was closely involved in the history of Babylonia.

A new dynasty (the Shutrukides) was founded by Hallutush-Inshushinak (c. 1205–1185). The kings continued their raids against **Kassite** Babylonia, and **Shutruk-Nahhunte I** sacked and plundered **Babylon** in 1185. Among the booty were several ancient Mesopotamian monuments, such as the stele of **Hammurabi**. This success only spurred further campaigns against Babylonia that resulted in the demise of the **Kassite Dynasty** in 1155. The most important Elamite king of this dynasty was Shilhak-Inshushinak (reigned 1150–1120), who enlarged the territories to the north and the northwest. The Babylonian king **Nebuchadrezzar I** (reigned 1126–1105) launched a successful attack against Elam, where he recovered the abducted statues of the gods **Marduk** and his divine consort Sarpanitum.

Elamite history for the next few centuries is obscure due to the almost total absence of written sources.

During the last phase, the Neo-Elamite period (eighth–seventh century B.C.), Elam became closely implicated in the conflict between **Assyria** and Babylonia. Elam took advantage of Babylonian weakness by invading its territories but it also joined in anti-Assyrian coalitions with Babylonia. They gave asylum to **Sennacherib**'s archenemy **Merodach-baladan** and even kidnapped (and probably killed) the Assyrian crown prince whom Sennacherib had put on the throne of Babylon (c. 692). When they also assisted **Shamash-shuma-ukin** in his revolt against **Ashurbanipal**, the Assyrian king vowed vengeance against Elam. The Elamite king Tepti-Humban-Inshushinak (Teumman in the Assyrian **annals**) invaded Assyrian territory; Ashurbanipal pursued them and won a decisive victory near the river Ulay. He then ravaged the Elamite countryside and destroyed Susa, returning with enormous booty.

The final years of the Neo-Elamite period are not well documented; internal intrigues and coups continued to upset the political balance as in the preceding generation.

The **Medes** finally put an end to Elamite independence around the mid–seventh century B.C.

ENHEDUANNA. Daughter of **Sargon of Akkad**. An inscription on a small limestone disk found at **Ur** records her dedication as *entum* priestess of the moon **god** Nannar-Suen at Ur. She may have been the first of a long line of royal princesses who held this prestigious position. Enheduanna also appears as the author of several literary works, such as the "Sumerian Temple Hymns" and an enigmatic text known as *nin-me-šar-ra* that seems to relate to the political tensions between Ur and **Uruk** during her period of office.

ENKI (Akkadian Ea). Sumerian god of the "Deep" (Abzu) whose main sanctuary was at **Eridu**. He was one of the most important deities, together with **Anu**, **Enlil**, and **Inanna**, and mentioned in prominent place in the earliest god lists. He was the son of An and the old mother goddess Nammu.

Enki plays a prominent role in Sumerian mythology. On the one hand, he represents the potential fertility of the groundwater; the "water" of his penis is said to have filled the **Tigris** and **Euphrates**, and his copulations with a succession of nubile **goddesses** led to the extension of fertility on the primordial land "Dilmun." His superior intelligence is the subject of other narratives; he knows how to rescue the doomed Inanna and advises other heroes in distress. On the other hand, his weakness for drink results in the loss of the *me* (divine prerogatives and powers) to Inanna and in the creation of abnormal human beings.

ENLIL (**Akkadian** Ellil). **Sumerian god**, one of the most important Mesopotamian deities since the early third millennium B.C. His name is usually taken to mean "Lord (of the) Air/or Wind" and denotes that his domain was the earth, above that of the "below" (Abzu) ruled by **Enki**. Enlil controlled the weather and hence the fertility of the land by wind and rain. As such, he has characteristics of the weather gods that feature so prominently in those regions where **agriculture** depended on annual rainfall.

In **Sumer**, Enlil also played a more political role, as the "leader of the gods" who presides over the "divine assembly." It was he who conferred legitimate **kingship** on a **city** and its ruler; this was known as *ellilutu*, "Ellil-ship," since the **Old Babylonian period**.

His main **temple** was the Ekur at **Nippur**, one of the most important sanctuaries in Mesopotamia. In the myths he is described as the one "who controls the fate" and who is in possession of "Tablets of Destiny," the seducer of the young goddess Ninlil, who became his wife, and the god whose repose is continually disturbed by humankind's clamor. In the flood myths, it is always **Enlil** who decides to eradicate all human beings.

In **Babylonia**, he came to be eclipsed by **Marduk** who assumed most of Ellil's prerogatives and powers.

ENLIL-NADIN-AHI (reigned c. 1157–1155 B.C.). Last king of the **Kassite Dynasty** in **Babylon**. According to an inscription on a **boundary stone** and later historical chronicles, he led a campaign against **Elam** and suffered a crushing defeat by Kudur-Nahhunte, which brought the Kassite Dynasty to an end.

EPONYM CHRONICLES. These were lists drawn up of the names of **eponyms** who gave their name to a year, augmented by a brief comment on specific events during the year, such as eclipses. The earliest extant Eponym List only enumerates the officials' names and covers the years before and during the reign of **Shamshi-Adad I** (c. 1813–1781 B.C.). Another fragmentary texts lists eponyms from about 1200. A consecutive listing covers the years 910–649. Eponym chronicles, together with the royal **annals**, form the backbone of **Assyrian** historiography.

EPONYMS. In **Assyria**, since the **Old Assyrian period**, there was a dating system in which years were named after an important official (Assyrian *limmu*). Lists were then kept that enumerated the sequence of eponyms (*see* EPONYM CHRONICLES). In the **Middle Assyrian** period, kings held the office in their second regnal year; it then passed on to senior officials of state in a regular pattern, including provincial governors. After a reign of 30 years, the king became eligible once again, and the cycle began a second time. While this sequence was fixed, individual candidates still had to be chosen. Apparently this was done by some random decision-making process, such as the rolling of dice.

ERESHKIGAL. **Goddess** of the Underworld. Her name "Lady of the Great Place" refers euphemistically to the Land of the Dead, which the Mesopotamians also dubbed "Land of No Return." According to the myths, she was the older sister of **Inanna**, the "Lady of the Heavens," who desired to extend her influence also "below." **Ereshkigal** punishes Inanna's incursion into her domain with death but is tricked to surrender her corpse to the flattery of some transsexual creatures.

In the **Old Babylonian period**, Ereshkigal lost her sovereignty to the male deity **Nergal**. A myth describes how the lonely goddess gladly surrendered her old independence to rule the underworld with Nergal. Her main sanctuary, and also that of Nergal, was at Kutha.

ERIDU (modern Abu Shahrein). South Mesopotamian **city**, regarded by the **Sumerian scribes** as the oldest city in the world, where "**kingship** came first from heaven." The kings of Eridu, according to the **Sumerian King List**, all ruled for phenomenally long periods, the first Alulima for 28,800 years, the second for 36,000 years.

In historical times, it was never the seat of a dynasty. Eridu's importance was religious rather than political, as the site of the main sanctuary of **Enki**. Numerous Mesopotamian kings contributed to the buildings at the site that reached its greatest size during the time of the **Third Dynasty of Ur**. It became deserted in the 18th century B.C. The cult of Enki continued to be maintained at other shrines, notably at nearby **Ur**.

The archaeological excavations by the Iraqi Department of Antiquities revealed a long sequence of buildings, one above the other, which began in the **Ubaid period**, around 4900 B.C. There are altogether 18 building levels of what came to be known as the Eunir, the temple of Enki.

ESARHADDON (Assyrian Ashur-ahhe-iddina) (reigned 680–669 B.C.). **Assyrian** king, son, and successor of **Sennacherib**, who had been assassinated in a palace coup. According to Esarhaddon's own inscriptions, his father had destined him, though the youngest, to be his heir in view of the fact that his eldest son had died in **Elam**. In the ensuing fight for the throne, Esarhaddon prevailed and was crowned at **Nineveh** on the eighth of Adar 681.

The main event of his career was the invasion of Egypt, which had changed its policy from being pro-Assyrian to fomenting revolts. In 671, after an abortive first effort three years before, he crossed the desert of Sinai with the help of **Arab camels** carrying water for the troops and fought three victorious battles against the Egyptians. He seized Memphis and took the son of pharaoh Taharka prisoner.

Esarhaddon had to repress numerous rebellions, such as that of Sidon in 677. He also had to campaign in Anatolia, where nomadic tribes from the east, the Cimmerians and Scythians, caused a good deal of trouble in Assyrian provinces. Toward **Babylonia** he pursued a policy of appeasement and began a program of reconstruction and redevelopment, resettled exiled inhabitants, and restored to them their property. Esarhaddon also rebuilt the **temple** precinct of **Babylon** that had been destroyed by Sennacherib.

Wary about the difficulties of a peaceful transition of power to his sons, he drew up a document affirming the succession of his younger son **Ashurbanipal** that stipulated that the older brother and crown prince **Shamash-shuma-ukin** was to be king of Babylon. All his vassals and the Assyrian nobility were sworn by **oath** to honor this proclamation. It was to be the cause of a bloody war between the brothers that devastated Babylonia. In 669, Esarhaddon died on campaign on the way to Egypt.

ESHNUNNA (Tell Asmar). Mesopotamian **city** in the Diyala Valley in the east **Tigris** area. The site was inhabited since the fourth millennium B.C. and grew in importance in the **Early Dynastic periods** II and III. Eshnunna experienced its greatest growth between 2000 and 1800 during the **Isin-Larsa period**. After the fall of the **Third Dynasty of Ur**, it became the capital of a small independent kingdom called Warum. According to the **archives** found at **Mari**, the kings of Eshnunna also engaged in the armed rivalries for supremacy that characterize this age. An interesting document from the last king of Eshnunna, Dadusha, is a collection of laws regulating commercial activities and social relations. The same king was eventually defeated by **Hammurabi** of **Babylon** in c. 1763 B.C.

EUNUCHS. Eunuchs played a significant role in most ancient Near Eastern **administrations**, although the scholarly debate over the meaning of terms denoting "eunuch" (Sumerian *LÚ.SAG*; **Akkadian** *ša reši*) is still going on.

In the textual material from Mesopotamia, eunuchs are attested from **Old Babylonian** times on in various positions, ranking from high **palace** officials to servants in private households. The most significant and complex evidence comes from **Assyria**, and it is no surprise that the classical tradition attributes the origin of eunuchs to the legendary **Assyrian** queen **Semiramis**. From the Middle Assyrian laws, we learn that the penalty for adultery and homosexuality was "to turn him into a eunuch." The Assyrian Palace Edicts from the same time show that eunuchs had access to the royal court and harem. In the texts from the **Neo-Assyrian** empire, eunuchs and "bearded ones" are mentioned side by side as terms for state officials, and they occur without beards on the Assyrian palace reliefs.

As in other civilizations, eunuchs probably came from the elite families and were chosen already at an early age for a court career. They became high-ranking officers in the Assyrian **army**. The "Chief of the Eunuchs" sometimes even led the whole Assyrian army on a campaign (e.g., Mutarris-Ashur under **Shamshi-Adad V**). Others held important offices in the central and the provincial administration. Outside the palace administration, eunuchs occupied various professions, such as **scribes**, musicians, actors, and so forth. It is not known whether all of them were **slaves** or whether there were free men among them.

EUPHRATES. Together with the **Tigris**, the most important river that defined the borders of Mesopotamia. The Euphrates has its source in the mountains of Anatolia, which receive substantial amounts of snowfall in the winter. The river was called *purattu* in **Akkadian**, a name that survives in the Arabic form Firat. Its main tributaries are the Balikh and the Habur. Farther south, the alluvial plains begin, the gradient of the land becomes very low, and the Euphrates carved out a number of subsidiary beds and side arms. It was an important means of communication by boat and less turbulent than the Tigris.

While the upper reaches of the Euphrates were situated in the "Fertile Crescent," where rain-fed **agriculture** was possible, south of present-day Baghdad began the dry zone. The Euphrates was one of the main sources of water that was channeled into numerous man-made canals. While most Mesopotamian **cities** were situated on side arms of canals, some lay directly along the main watercourse of the river, such as **Nippur** and **Babylon**. Because of the low gradient of the plains and the soft soil, the river was liable to change courses, sometimes drastically, and nowadays neither city lies in the vicinity of the stream.

– F –

FAMILY. The basic constituent of Mesopotamian society was the patriarchal family. The **administrative** documents from the major sites recorded people's names and affiliation, but it is still difficult to get a clear picture of the family sizes and patterns of residence at any given period.

From the archaeological record, it appears that extended families, including several generations and more than one couple with children, were common in later prehistoric periods (*see* CHALCOLITHIC; URUK PERIOD). This can be deducted from the size of habitations, the number of fireplaces, and the number of individuals buried beneath the floor of houses. Such extended families formed productive units, pooling their labor and sharing resources. On the other hand, nuclear families, consisting of a couple with their (young) children, also existed, especially within larger groupings. There is no doubt that the several forms of family organization developed early, in response to different subsistence activities and social configurations. They persisted into later, historical periods. There is evidence from the **Early Dynastic period** that large households (*oikos*) were common (*see* SHURUPPAK), which included not only the members of the family but also servants and slaves. They could generate substantial revenues from enterprise, both commercial and agricultural. The land held by such a household could only be sold if all the male adults agreed, as sale contracts from the **Akkad** period document.

The large state organizations (*see* PALACE) and the temples employed people of all ages and gender. **Women** and their children would work together in the manufactories of the **Third Dynasty of Ur**, for instance, producing textiles. Small family units could work on plots assigned to them by these organizations for a fixed percentage of the harvest. When a family experienced crop failures and could not meet their obligations, they had to take loans of **silver** or grain at often usurious rates. If the loans could not be paid either, the head of the family could pledge his own labor, and/or that of any of his children or his wife, or, in a more desperate move, sell them into slavery to raise capital.

Excavations at **Nippur** have shown how in the **Old Babylonian period** wealthy, professional families lived in spacious houses, with domestic slaves, which in later more difficult times partitioned up and were occupied by poorer, more numerous families.

In the **Neo-Babylonian** period family firms, such as the Murashu or the Egibi, could conduct lucrative banking and investment business that continued for several generations. Such a practice can also be observed in the early second millennium import-export family businesses at Ashur.

Some literary texts as well as proverbs allow some insights into the emotional comfort of family life. In the Old Babylonian version of the **Gilgamesh** epic, the "innkeeper" called Siduri advises the hero to seek solace in the embrace of his wife and delight in the presence of his children. The 12th tablet of the epic describes the unhappy fate of the dead who have no children to offer libations for them, and it praises the lucky father of many sons who has an exalted position in the netherworld. Proverbs warn of the disruptive presence of pretty slave girls in the house and admonish the young to show respect for their elders.

FESTIVALS. Feasts and festivals are celebrated in all cultures; they are defined by their reason or purpose, their rituals, and whether they are celebrated at regular intervals of time or occasioned by special events. Furthermore, there is a difference between feasts that are (1) personal and private (rites of passage such as weddings or funerals), (2) public and royal (enthronement of kings, victory celebrations), or (3) religious. Overlaps between these categories could occur in Mesopotamia, where religion permeated all aspects of daily life there were no purely "secular" feasts.

1. Private feasts. **Sumerian** poetry and myths allude to the preparations and celebrations of marriages. The groom was to ask the bride's parents for permission to wed. He then brought wedding gifts according to his station. The bride, having bathed and adorned herself in the wedding finery, was received with music into the house of her groom's family where the feast was celebrated. There are also a number of reliefs from the third millennium B.C. that show people seated on low chairs and drinking beer together through a straw. Whether such scenes illustrate special occasions or daily conviviality is not clear. Coming-of-age ceremonies are not attested in Mesopotamia, and there were no age group associations.

2. Victory celebrations and enthronement are also known from literary sources. Especially the myths associated with the **god Ninurta** describe the awe-inspiring march of the victorious troops toward the main **temple**, where the spoils of war were dedicated to the gods. **Assyrian** inscriptions refer to splendid feasts for the official opening of a new **palace** or royal residence; Ashurnasirpal II famously invited 69,574 to the inauguration part at **Kalhu**. Other public festivals related to the agrarian cycle, such the preparation of the fields, or bringing in of the harvest.

3. A large number of religious feasts were held in Mesopotamia. The names of many festivals are known, as well as the expenses they incurred, but the written sources say very little about their purpose or the rituals performed since such knowledge was taken for granted. However, texts such as the **Neo-Sumerian** offering lists provide some information about the main religious festivals organized by the temples. Some were fixed and some were variable, and they often concerned the movement of the divine statue from one temple to another. The timing of feasts could depend on their agrarian significance (many of the journeys of divine statues coincided with important seasons), the lunar, the solar, or the Venus cycle. Processions outside the temple, or between temples, accompanied by musicians and dancers, and the clergy in their specific paraphernalia, were the most visible manifestation. The distribution of extra food and drink allowances to the personnel and/or the citizens at large, were also important factors.

The best-known festival that originated in **Babylon** was the New Year Festival, which lasted 12 days. It was mainly performed in the huge temple of **Marduk** called Esagil. The king's presence was of vital importance as he guaranteed the divine order decreed by the gods. He may have played an active part in the playing out of the main events of the Epic of Creation (*see* CREATION MYTHS), such as the battle between Marduk and Tiamat. The king had to make a negative confession ("I have not sinned, I have not been negligent of your godhead, I have not destroyed Babylon . . .") and was struck across the face hard enough to cause tears. Another important aspect was the arrival of all the major **Babylonian** deities. On the ninth day began the public phase of this festival, where all the assembled gods and **goddesses**, led by the king holding the hand of Marduk, processed with great pomp along the Festival Way and embarked on boats to reach the Festival House that was located beyond the city walls. The New Year Festival was a public holiday for all Babylonian citizens who could watch the processions, complete with the display of war booty and prisoners, and partake of the banquets. It arose from the traditional barley harvest celebrations of early spring and the rituals served to confirm the divinely decreed order of the universe after the potentially dangerous liminal period between the ending of one year and the beginning of the new.

The New Year Festival was also celebrated in **Assyria**, where the god Ashur played the role of Marduk.

FIRST DYNASTY OF BABYLON (c. 1894–c. 1595 B.C.). A historical period in which the **city** of **Babylon** first became the political center of Mesopotamia. The dynasty was founded by Sumu-abum, an **Amorite**; hence, it is also sometimes referred to as the Amorite Dynasty.

At the beginning, the rulers of Babylon only controlled a small territory around the city since there were several competing political configurations in Mesopotamia, such as **Larsa**, **Isin**, **Eshnunna**, and **Assyria**. It was the sixth king, **Hammurabi** (reigned 1792–1750 B.C.), who triumphed over all these rivals. Babylon became the capital of a powerful kingdom with roughly the same borders as that of the **Third Dynasty of Ur**. The **administration** of the state was modeled on the one set up by **Rim-Sin** of Larsa. There was a widespread use of literacy, and the king was kept informed about all manner of governmental details. It was a characteristic of Amorite kings to remain approachable to their subjects and to rule more in the manner of a traditional sheikh than an exalted king. They were also much concerned with the promulgation of **laws** and legal statutes and that justice was upheld in the land. The final legal instance was the king himself.

The **Babylonian** state was less highly centralized than that of **Ur** during the Third Dynasty. It employed private middlemen to ensure the collection of revenue rather than bureaucrats. Some documents of the time also mention a special category of semifree citizen, the *muškenum*, whose status was neither free nor that of a slave and who were possibly persons tied to the **palace**.

The most important rulers of the First Babylonian Dynasty were Hammurabi and his successor, **Samsu-iluna**, who ruled for 37 years (1749–1712 B.C.). During the latter's reign, the territorial integrity of the kingdom disintegrated; the south became independent under the leadership of the **Sealand** (c.1742), and a new people from the east, the **Kassites**, settled in increasing number in the northern and northeastern regions of Babylonia. Economic problems, due to the deteriorating ecological situation in the south, the loss of access to the sea, and tribal unrest, contributed to unstable conditions that affected some cities more than others. Royal edicts, releasing public and private debts, indicate that many people were affected by the inability to meet debt payments.

The demise of the First Babylonian Dynasty resulted from a surprise raid by the **Hittite** king Mursili, who marched down the **Euphrates** and attacked Babylon. The date of this event is traditionally given as 1595 B.C., although more recently a revised date of 1499 has been proposed.

FIRST DYNASTY OF ISIN (c. 2017–c. 1794 B.C.). After the fall of the **Third Dynasty of Ur**, the center of power shifted farther north to the city of **Isin**, where the erstwhile **Ur** governor **Ishbi-Erra** founded a new dynasty to carry on the traditions of Mesopotamian **kingship**. Although the territory controlled by Isin was much smaller than that of the Ur kingdom, it preserved the institutional structure and the ideological basis of the former state. One of its rulers, Enlil-bani (reigned 1860–1837 B.C.), was originally a gardener who was appointed as "substitute king" during an inauspicious time for the incumbent king who happened to die during this period. It was at this time that the **Sumerian King List** received its final form. Throughout the history of the Isin Dynasty, it vied for supremacy with the city of **Larsa**. Eventually, Isin's importance declined until it was swallowed up in the new state founded by **Hammurabi** of **Babylon**.

FOOD. The people who lived in Mesopotamia during the prehistoric periods (*see* CHALCOLITHIC; NEOLITHIC) enjoyed a very varied diet procured from hunting the still plentiful wild sheep and other mammals, fishing, fowling, and the gathering of legumes, nuts, and wild as well as domesticated cereals.

Once a predominantly settled and later urban lifestyle was adopted, this diversity declined, and people relied predominantly on cereal staples (mainly barley), in the form of porridge or bread. The vitamin and mineral content of this monotonous diet could be enhanced by vegetables such as lettuces, gourds, onions, garlic, and pulses that were grown in smaller plots near the city. Of particular importance as a source of energy and vitamins was the date palm, which flourishes in the south Mesopotamian climate. Regular meat consumption (beef, mutton, pork, and game) was the preserve of the wealthy; the poorer members of society consumed fish for protein, widely available in dried form. A fermented fish sauce was the most popular condiment in Mesopotamian kitchens.

Dairy products such as clarified butter, cheeses, and fresh and fermented milk were also available, either produced on the great estates of temples or brought to the market by **pastoralists**.

Sesame and linseed were used for oil, both for cosmetic and culinary purposes.

The most popular and nutritious drink was **beer**, which was available in different strengths. The wealthy imported wine from Syria and the Levant.

Sweet dishes were prepared with concentrated date syrup, usually translated as "honey." Mesopotamians were also fond of fruit, such as medlars, apples, apricots, and grapes, as well as nuts.

A cooking manual by a **Babylonian** master chef has survived from the 17th century B.C. This makes it clear that the preparation of meals in elite households (and temples) was a complex task. Meat was sautéed, broiled, and stewed, sometimes undergoing all these stages for one dish. Sauces were as important as in classic French cooking, being composed of several different kinds of meat, bones, vegetables, and condiments, boiled, strained, and reduced. The final presentation involved dumplings and dough crusts, fresh herbs and onions, with the meat being served separate from the sauce and vegetables.

FORTIFICATIONS. Since the purpose of fortifications is the protection of inhabitants and goods inside a building or a settlement, the most durable materials available were chosen for their construction. In most areas of the ancient Near East, this was stone. In the alluvial plains of Mesopotamia, mud brick was used but in sufficient thickness to make attacks difficult. Urban installations were vulnerable because of their stored grain and other valuables. As early as the **Uruk period**, towns in the more exposed regions were surrounded by rectangular defensive walls, with towers and gates. In the **Early Dynastic period** when rivalries between cities in Mesopotamia became widespread, such installations became a common feature of all cities. The best known is the city wall of **Uruk**, which was nearly 9.5 kilometers long.

The **Sumerian** text "**Gilgamesh** and the Agga of Kish" describes the conflict between Uruk and **Kish** and the psychological stratagems used to win access to well-defended cities.

In the Iron Age, technologies of **warfare** became more advanced as the machinery and tools for attack became more durable than the earlier

bronze weapons. As a result, the fortifications became stronger, with regularly spaced watchtowers and projection bastions, crenellations, and gate towers with lateral guard chambers. In the more rocky regions (e.g., **Assyria**), fortifications were built on stone outcrops and steep hillsides (e.g., at **Assur**). In the mid–first millennium, **Nebuchadnezzar II** built the famous walls of the capital **Babylon**, an undertaking made even more challenging by the fact that the river **Euphrates** ran right through the city. The walls close to the water had be constructed of baked brick, in places up to 25 meters thick. According to the descriptions of **Herodotus**, the walls were wide enough for two teams of horse-drawn **chariots**.

FUNERARY AND BURIAL PRACTICES. In the prehistoric periods, a great variety of burial practices existed side by side: inhumation of the whole skeleton, partial inhumation and possible secondary burial after exposure of the body, and cremation. Bodies could furthermore be buried singly or in groups, in a common plot or cemetery, or beneath the floor of habitations. Cemeteries are believed to reveal a special claim that a particular group of people could make of a territory and its resources. The more or less equal treatment of the mortal remains may reveal an egalitarian social system, while the burial of children in special plots may point to elite formation.

Bodies in earth or stone graves could be accompanied by sets of tools, such as flint knives, or personal ornaments, such as beads. Traces of red color is also frequently found on bones, indicating some color symbolism. In the **Ubaid period**, the graves at **Eridu** contained rich grave gifts, such as exquisite miniature pottery sets, anthropomorphic clay figurines, joints of meat, and jewelry. Some people had been buried with a dog that was given a bone.

In historical times, the variety of burial practices declined. Inhumation of the whole skeleton became the norm for Mesopotamia. Intramural burials continued to be popular but populous **cities** also had cemeteries outside the city walls, such as at **Ur**. In early periods, people were placed flat on the back, with their hands folded across the chest; later a flexed position, with knees drawn up, became more common. Clay and terra cotta coffins contained the mortal remains.

The most controversial graves were discovered by Sir Leonard Woolley at Ur. They date form the **Early Dynastic period** and contained high-ranking, possible royal personages, surrounded by fabulous gold and in-laid funerary gifts. The **chariots** and the oxen used to transport the dead were also kept in the stone-constructed burial chambers. The presence of a number of other skeletons, predominantly female, holding musical instruments and golden goblets, was interpreted by Woolley as evidence for ritual sacrifice or collective suicide. It has since become clear that these bodies were manipulated after death and are to be considered as secondary burials; the association of their bodies to the main personages was probably a matter of prestige or of some other significance that eludes us. Few other royal graves are known; the hypogeum tombs at Ur did not contain any remains. **Assyrian** monarchs were buried at **Assur**, and a richly equipped tomb of a queen has recently been found by Iraqi archaeologists.

Cuneiform texts refer to funerary rites and beliefs. The dead were thought of as dwelling in the underworld, a gloomy and overcrowded place. Those whose remains were left unburied, and had had no rites performed for their souls, were doomed to haunt the living as ghosts. **Nomads** were also held in contempt by the urban population because they had no grave cults. Of particular importance were libations of water, which the eldest male of a household poured out for the ancestral spirits on the family altar. The myth "**Inanna**'s Descent into the Underworld" makes it clear that mourning ceremonies were expected, which involved the temporary disfigurement by ashes and the donning of mourning clothes. Inanna's lover, Dumuzi, is banished to the Underworld for failing to behave in the proper way. The Mesopotamians did not have eschatological beliefs of a Last Judgment, nor did they expect to enjoy some form of eternal life as the Egyptians. They did not expend vast sums on their tombs, nor did they practice embalming. Their best expectation was to have peace of mind after a customary burial and to have raised enough offspring to bring libations to stave off the thirst of death.

– G –

GILGAMESH. (1) **Sumerian** king of the **Early Dynastic period** who appears in the **Sumerian King List** as a king of **Uruk**, son of **Lugalbanda**. There is as yet no contemporary evidence for his reign, but Gilgamesh is mentioned among the deified rulers in the **Shuruppak** tablets from the 25th century B.C. (2) Eponymous hero of several Mesopotamian literary compositions, the best known of which is the Epic of Gilgamesh (*see* next page).

One Sumerian narrative that was not incorporated into the Epic concerns Gilgamesh's fight against Agga of **Kish**, whose historicity is assured by a short inscription on a vase discovered at Kish.

The forerunners to the epic are preserved in four Sumerian versions:

- "Gilgamesh and the Land of the Living" describes the journey Gilgamesh undertakes with his servant Enkidu. They go to the Cedar Forest, which is sacred to the **god Enlil** and protected by a demonic creature called Huwawa. The heroes cut down the cedar trees and kill the captured Huwawa.
- "Gilgamesh and the Bull of Heaven" is only preserved on fragments. The goddess **Inanna** proposes **marriage** to Gilgamesh. When he rejects her offer, she sends the mighty Bull of Heaven to avenge the insult, but the beast is killed by Gilgamesh.
- "Gilgamesh, Enkidu and the Netherworld" begins with an account of the sacred *huluppu* tree that Inanna had planted in her garden at Uruk. She wants to use its wood to fashion a bed and a throne from it but is unable to fell the tree. Gilgamesh manages to drive out its demonic squatters (a snake, a lion-headed eagle, and a female demon), and as a token of gratitude the goddess gives him two magical objects made from the timber. These objects happen to fall into the underworld, and his servant Enkidu offers to descend in order to retrieve them. He is given detailed advice as how to behave in the underworld, but he fails to adhere to it and is therefore doomed to remain there forever. Gilgamesh manages to persuade the god **Enki** to summon the shadow of his servant, who tells him of the conditions in the underworld. Those who have many sons fare well, but those whose bodies lie unburied have no rest (*see* FUNERARY AND BURIAL PRACTICES).
- "The Death of Gilgamesh" is very fragmentary, and it is not clear whether Gilgamesh's or Enkidu's death is described.

The oldest version of the Epic of Gilgamesh dated from the **Old Babylonian period**. Numerous fragments and excerpts have been discovered from later periods, in many different parts of the Near East, from Palestine to Anatolia. The most extensive source is the so-called Ninevite version, discovered in the archives of **Ashurbanipal**'s royal **palace**. It contains some 1,500 lines and is divided into 12 tablets. Most of the themes of the Sumerian versions (except for the Agga of Kish story) have been worked into the epic, as well as other narratives, most notably that of the flood.

Gilgamesh is portrayed as two-thirds man and one-third god, endowed with supernatural strength. He oppresses the citizens of Uruk so much that they pray to the sky god **Anu** to help them. Anu responds by ordering the mother **goddess** to create Enkidu, a wild man who roams the uncultivated lands in the steppe where he runs with the animals and frees them from the hunter's traps. News of this strange and entirely hairy being are brought to Gilgamesh, who sends a prostitute to charm him. Her mission is successful since after a week of ardent love-making Enkidu tastes human **food** and finds himself alienated from his former companions, the animals of the steppe. He follows her to Uruk, where he meets Gilgamesh who had portentous dreams about him. After a bout of wrestling, they become the best of friends. Then follows the story of the expedition into the Cedar Forest, more or less as told in the Sumerian narrative of the Land of the Living, where they cut down the cedars and kill the demon Humbaba (= Huwawa).

When they return in triumph to Uruk, the goddess **Ishtar** appears and invites Gilgamesh to become her consort. As in the Sumerian tale, he rejects her offer with frivolous taunts. The Bull of Heaven, sent down to avenge her wounded pride, is killed by the heroes. Enkidu now falls sick and dies, which deeply affects Gilgamesh: He is so overcome with grief and fear of his own death that he renounces the exercise of **kingship**.

Dressed only in a lion skin, he roams the wilderness, hoping to find Utnapishtim, the man who survived the flood and whom the gods had granted eternal life. He passes mountains and strange lands and eventually arrives at a garden of precious stones, where the ale wife Siduri lives. He tells his story, and although she advises him to abandon his futile quest and enjoy the simple pleasures of human life, she tells him how to proceed.

Gilgamesh arrives at the river where he finds a ferryman, who after some pleading agrees to ferry him across. Utnapishtim then tells him the story of the flood, which only he and his wife survived. He puts Gilgamesh to a test to refrain from sleep for seven nights. The hero falls fast asleep. Utnapishtim gives him clothes that won't wear out, and Gilgamesh decides to return to Uruk, accompanied by the ferryman. As a final gift, he presents them with a plant that makes the old young again. It so happens that a passing serpent eats the plant, shedding its skin as it slithers away. With empty hands Gilgamesh returns to Uruk. He makes the ferryman climb the ramparts of the city and survey his domain. The 12th tablet adds the story of the encounter between Gilgamesh and the spirit of Enkidu, who tells him about conditions in the underworld.

GIRSU (modern Tello). Important city in southern Mesopotamia during the third millennium B.C. It was initially thought to be the site of **Lagash**, but it became clear that Girsu was some 20 kilometers to the north.

During the **Early Dynastic periods** I and II, Girsu may have been the political center of Lagash. In later periods, it had a primarily religious role since it housed the **temples** of Ningirsu and Bau. Archaeological excavations by French teams have yielded important **cuneiform archives**, numerous **cylinder seals**, and statuary, among them the Stele of Vultures by **Eannatum** and the statues of **Gudea**.

GODS AND GODDESSES. As in all polytheistic religions, a great number of deities were worshipped in Mesopotamia throughout the ages. Most people had names composed with that of a god or a goddess. This serves as a useful indication of the popularity of a particular deity at a given time. To what extent the theomorphic element of a person's name allows conclusions about his or her ethnic affiliation is less clear.

Already in the **Early Dynastic period**, **scribes** attempted to bring some order into the confusing number of known deities by compiling lists of divine names. They also introduced a ranking order by beginning the lists with the major gods, such as **Anu, Ea, Enlil**, and **Inanna/Ishtar**, and ending with more obscure ones. A great number of these names is only known from such lexical lists that preserved the most ancient entries while adding new ones.

Each Mesopotamian **city** had its own patron deity. They resided in their "homes on earth," the **temples**, and received daily offerings of **food**, drink, incense, and other gifts, such as textiles and jewelry. The deity did not live in isolation in the temple but enjoyed a **family** life. Divine couples shared a bed chamber, while their children and servants were accommodated elsewhere. The statues were also taken on regular outings, touring the country and visiting each other's shrines, especially during the time of the **Third Dynasty of Ur**. Larger cities also had temples of other gods; **Babylon** was known to have had hundreds of temples at the time of the **Neo-Babylonian period**.

Most of the great gods had a particular area of responsibility and expertise. Anu was the patriarchal head of the pantheon and was the lord of the heavens. Ea-Enki was the god of water, also known for his wisdom and creative potential. Nannar-Suen (or **Akkadian Sin**) was the moon god who was associated with the fertility of cattle, while the sun god **Shamash** was the "judge" and safeguarded justice and fairness on earth. There were also mother goddesses, blessing fields and **women** with fertility and protecting women in childbirth, healing gods to ward off evil influences and speed up recovery, and weather gods who brought storms and rain.

Mesopotamian attitudes to the gods were often ambiguous; they were feared as much as loved, since gods were considered to be fundamentally unpredictable and even capricious. Enlil could send just the right amount of rainfall or cause devastating floods; Ishtar could enhance sex appeal but also cause impotence. Inversely, a god of pestilence and fever could also be invoked to combat such afflictions. Many rituals and incantations, especially from the late second and first millennium B.C., were devised to soothe the hearts of "angry gods" and to harness their divine powers in the constant battle against malevolent influences.

During the **Old Babylonian period**, the notion of a "personal god" developed, who like a guardian angel was responsible for a particular human being. He (or she, for women) would intercede with higher-ranking gods and plead the case of the patron. On the other hand, the personal deity was adversely affected by his or her charge's ritual impurity or sinfulness.

Some deities had strong connections with **kingship**. In the third millennium B.C., Enlil legitimized the control over the country; in the second and first millennium, this was **Marduk** in **Babylonia** and **Ashur** in **Assyria**. The goddess Ishtar was also often quoted as lending invaluable support to a king of her choice (*see* SARGON OF AKKAD).

Foreign deities could easily be integrated in the Mesopotamian pantheon; they could be equated with a similar divine figure (as happened when the Semitic Eshtar merged with the **Sumerian** Inanna) or married to an existing goddess (as in the case of the **Amorite** god Martu).

In the **Seleucid** and later **Parthian** period, some Babylonian gods, notably **Nabu** and Bel (another name for Marduk), continued to be worshipped. Only the advent of Islam in the seventh century A.D. brought about the final demise of the ancient Mesopotamian gods.

GOLD. In Mesopotamia gold ornaments first appeared in **Ubaid period** sites (fifth millennium B.C.). Like all metals, it had to be brought into the country from far afield, such as Eastern Anatolia, part of a loose network of exchange for high-status luxury commodities. It was usually alloyed with **silver** in varying proportions.

In the **Early Dynastic period**, the wealthy **city**-states of Mesopotamia could command a whole range of such articles, and gold plays a prominent part in the **funerary** gifts discovered at the "royal tombs" at **Ur**.

Gold objects include not just rings and other items of jewelry but cups, plates, ceremonial daggers, and wiglike headdresses. The metal had been hammered in thin sheets before being shaped and cut.

Workers of the "shining silver" (KÚ.BABBAR in **Sumerian**) were distinguished from other craftsmen working in metal. Their services were also needed for the fashioning of cult statues that could be covered with gold foil.

In the mid–second millennium, Egyptian gold came to be imported, initially as a high-level exchange between pharaoh and the **Babylonian** kings, in return for richly worked textiles, inlaid furniture, and war **chariots** (*see* AMARNA CORRESPONDENCE). For a while gold was so plentiful then that it replaced silver as the standard of exchange.

GUDEA (reigned c. 2141–c. 2122 B.C.). **Sumerian** ruler of **Lagash**. Gudea is best known as a patron of the arts and as the builder of a new **temple** at **Girsu**. Among the ruins of this temple were found a number of life-size statues of diorite stone, representing Gudea. Some of these statues have lengthy inscriptions that refer to the circumstances of the temple project. He commanded enough resources to furnish the building with sumptuous materials that had to be procured from far afield. There is no indication that Lagash was subservient to any other city-state at that time. Gudea kept peace with his neighbors but undertook raids to Anshan and **Elam** which yielded substantial booty. The literary style of his inscriptions counts as the epitome of classical Sumerian.

GULA. **Babylonian** healing **goddess**, identified with the **Sumerian** Nin-isina. Her main sanctuary was at **Isin**, and her symbol was a dog.

GUNGUNUM (reigned 1932–1906 B.C.). King of **Larsa** ("whose name sounds like the beat of a battledrum," according to Georges Roux). He attacked the kingdom of **Isin**, took **Ur** and with it the control over the access to the Persian Gulf, and gradually extended his influence in southern Mesopotamia to the detriment of Isin.

GUTI. **Tribal pastoralists** who inhabited the mountainous regions of the Zagros and the upper valleys of the Diyala River. This northeastern region was known as Gutium throughout Mesopotamian history.

The Guti (or Gutians) were always described in negative terms in the **cuneiform** sources, mainly as the "hordes of Gutium," "numberless like locusts," invaders, and raiders of **cities** and countryside. They first appear in the royal inscriptions of **Shar-kali-sharri** around 2200 B.C., who reports to have captured their "king." On the other hand, Guti mercenaries also served in the **Akkadian** armies.

According to the **Sumerian King List**, it was the Guti who brought the **Akkadian Dynasty** to an end, and they are said to have furnished 21 kings. The sack of the capital is also blamed on them in the literary composition "The Curse of Akkade." Just how much territory the Guti controlled is uncertain. There is no evidence of destruction in other **cities** or of a cultural break. It is most likely that the Guti rulers commanded not much more than the area around the Diyala River.

Around 2120, they were defeated by Utu-hegal, a king of **Uruk** who reports that he slew the "Gutium, the dragon of the mountains, enemy of the gods, who had carried of the **kingship** of Sumer to the mountains." The Guti remained the archetypical enemy of Sumerian civilization, at least in literature, as, for example, in the "Lamentation over the Destruction of Ur."

– H –

HAMMURABI OF BABYLON (reigned 1792–1750 B.C.). King of **Babylon**, the sixth ruler of the **Amorite** or **First Dynasty of Babylon**. Initially, Hammurabi controlled only a rather small territory around the **city** of **Babylon**, including **Kish**, **Sippar**, and **Borsippa**. He gradually extended his control, gaining possession of some important southern cities such as **Uruk** and **Isin** and forming alliances with other powerful rulers in the region. At the same time, he built up a centralized **administration**, invested in irrigation projects to extend land for cultivation, and strengthened city walls. After 30 years, he was ready to deal a decisive blow to his greatest rival, **Rim-Sin** of **Larsa**, who had ruled over most of **Babylonia**. A year later he also gained control over **Eshnunna** and thereby the eastern **trade** routes leading to Iran and beyond. In 1761 B.C., he conquered **Assyria**. **Mari**, hitherto an ally of Babylon, was taken in 1760. By 1755, Hammurabi was the undisputed ruler over all of Mesopotamia.

Numerous letters and administrative documents from his reign are known. It appears that he built on bureaucratic structures and practices set up by his predecessors, especially Rim-Sin of Larsa. The redistribution of new crown land that resulted from conquest was strictly controlled under the so-called *ilku* system.

Hammurabi is widely known for his "law code," inscribed on a large stone stele (*see* LAW). At the top it bears a scene of the sun god **Shamash** investing the king with the insignia of royal power. The lengthy prologue and epilogue describe the king as the protector and shepherd of his people, upholder of justice and peace. Although it is not proven that the laws were ever implemented, they were much admired in antiquity and often copied on clay tablets. Hammurabi's letters and **royal inscriptions** also became standard works, and subsequent generations of **scribes** copied them assiduously.

Hammurabi remains one of the great kings of Mesopotamia, an outstanding diplomat and negotiator who was patient enough to wait for the right time and then ruthless enough to achieve his aims without stretching his resources too far. After his death, the power of the Babylonian state began to decline.

HANIGALBAT. *See* MITANNI.

HARRAN. **City** in the northern plains of Upper Mesopotamia, in present-day southeastern Turkey, near Urfa. It was an important **trade** center, at a crossing of routes, as its name (KASKAL, *harranu*) implies, which means simply "road."

The city was first mentioned in the **cuneiform** tablets found among the merchant **archives** at **Kanesh** from the 19th century B.C. The **Assyrians**, who called it Huzirina, incorporated Harran into their empire in the eighth century. After the destruction of **Nineveh** in 612, it became the last Assyrian capital. Two years later the **Medes** conquered and sacked the city.

Harran was also famous as a religious site, the seat of the moon **god Sin**. His **temple**, the Ehulhul ("House of Rejoicing"), was rebuilt several times by various Assyrian monarchs and finally, with vast expense, by the **Babylonian** king **Nabonidus**. No archaeological evidence of the temple has been found so far.

HERODOTUS (fl. c. 484–420 B.C.). Greek traveler and historian. He was born at Halicarnassus in Asia Minor, was exiled to Samos, lived in Athens, and died in Sicily. He wrote nine books of *Histories* that chronicle the wars between the Greeks and the **Persians**.

He was interested to show the historical antecedents of the **Achaemenid** empire and thus included accounts about **Assyrians**, **Babylonians**, Egyptians, and Syrians. It is not clear how many of the places he actually visited in person, although some descriptions are lively and almost ethnographic reports. His sources about Mesopotamian history are relatively poor; he often confuses Assyrian and Babylonian places and personages and includes much fictional material that served to demonstrate the cultural superiority of the Greeks.

HITTITES. A people speaking an Indo-European **language** who formed a powerful state in central Anatolia in the second millennium B.C.

Having penetrated into Asia Minor by several routes since the late third millennium, they took the name of an indigenous people, the Hatti, whose main land lay around the bend of the river Halys (Kizilirmak). A Hittite king called Anitta is mentioned in the tablets found at **Kanesh** (19th century), although a Hittite source from the 16th century says that a certain Labarna was the first king of Hatti.

The expansion of the Hittite kingdom began during the reign of Labarna's successor, Hattushili I (around 1680). He moved the capital to the rocky hillsides of Hattusa and began a series of incursions into north Syrian territories. They were intensified by his son **Mursili I**, who took Aleppo and made a surprise raid down the **Euphrates**. He sacked **Babylon** and returned with much booty.

During the reign of his successors, the Hittite kingdom was extended westward, at the expense of the **Hurrian** state, and northward into the territory of the Kaska who inhabited the Pontic region.

The stability of the Hittite state was precarious due to frequent **palace** intrigues and assassinations until Telepinu issued an edict around 1525 to regularize the royal succession. Despite his efforts, the Hittites were not major players until the reign of **Suppiluliuma I** (reigned c. 1370–1342). He succeeded to incorporate the fertile and wealthy north Syrian region and to subdue the Hurrian state of **Mitanni**. He conducted an alliance with the **Kassite** kings of **Babylon** and married a **Babylonian** princess. However, the Hittite expansion into Syria was much resented by the Egyptians, who had long controlled the Syrian coastal regions. This conflict eventually led to a military confrontation in the Orontes Valley near Qadesh (c.1265) that resulted in a bilateral treaty.

The Hittite Empire was enlarged further by Tuthaliyas IV, who conquered Cyprus. His successors were forced to make alliances at the expense of territory in order to hold onto their power, which was increasingly threatened by the old enemy, the Kaska people.

In the 12th century B.C., the Hittite Empire collapsed in the turmoil of various invasions and unrest that engulfed Anatolia and all of Syria. Descendants of the Hittites continued to survive and eventually to prosper in southern Anatolia, where a number of small kingdoms retained a precarious independence in the first half of the first millennium, in the face of **Assyrian** pressure.

The main **languages** spoken in the Hittite kingdom were Hittite (called *neshili* by the Hittites after the city of Nesha) and Luwian, another Indo-European language. The Hittites wrote their language in **cuneiform**; later they developed a hieroglyphic system of **writing**.

HORSES. While donkeys and other short-legged equids were present in the ancient Near East since the Paleolithic period, horses were introduced form the Central Asian steppes not before the late third millennium B.C. Their foreign origin is reflected in the **Sumerian** term *ANŠE.KUR.RA,* which means "donkey of the mountains."

At the beginning, horses were primarily used to pull **chariots**; the reins were connected to a ring through the nose. With the influx of peoples from the east, who were more familiar with horses (e.g., the **Kassites**), technologies improved. Since the 16th century, true bits worn in the horse's mouth and made of **bronze** were introduced, and this much improved the handling of the animals. They became an important part of the armed forces as cavalry and to pull **chariots**. While earlier mounted warriors had to ride in pairs, allowing one of them to use his bow while the other controlled both horses, improved reins and bridles could be secured, leaving the hands free. Saddles and stirrups were unknown, but horses could wear breastplates and various ornaments.

In the beginning of the first millennium B.C., the **Assyrians** owed their rapid rise to power to their efficient cavalry units. The Assyrian uplands were suitable for horse breeding, and part of their conquests were motivated by the need to secure a reliable supply of horses and riders for their **army**.

The chariotry initially represented a prestige unit; costly chariots constituted a noble royal gift. Only in the first millennium did lightweight chariots become an integral part of the military organization.

Cuneiform archives from the Kassite period, from Nuzi and **Assyrian** sites, contained manuals on horse breeding, horse terminology (replete with foreign words), and training methods. One text from Ugarit concerns veterinary matters.

HURRIANS. A people originating from the south Caucasian region who settled along the northeastern borders of Mesopotamia and southern Anatolia in the last quarter of the third millennium B.C. Their **language** is not related to any of the other known group of languages. It was agglutinative, which means that chains of suffixes and infixes were added to generally monosyllabic stem words to create meaning. It is not well known, since only relatively few texts were rendered in a **cuneiform** system of writing, either in **Hittite** or Mesopotamian contexts.

Hurrian personal names were already recorded in the texts from the **Akkad** period, and Hurrians were present in all parts of the Near East for most of the second and first millennia, especially in southeast Anatolia, northern Mesopotamia, and eastern Iran. They achieved the greatest political importance between 1500 and 1200, within the framework of a kingdom called **Mitanni** where an Indo-European elite exercised political control. After the demise of Mitanni, smaller Hurrian principalities survived for a while in the Upper Mesopotamia.

Hurrian influence was particularly strong in religious matters. They are also thought to have brought various Mesopotamian ritual practices to the Hittite realm, where Hurrian magicians enjoyed high esteem.

Most of the information concerning their social practices and legal norms come from **archives** discovered at the site of the city of Nuzi.

– I –

IBBI-SIN (= Ibbi-Suen) (reigned c. 2026–c. 2004 B.C.). Fifth and last king of the **Third Dynasty of Ur**. His reign is well documented by **royal inscriptions** and letters sent and received by the court that illustrate the volatile political situation of this period. Several important Mesopotamian **cities** rebelled against the supremacy of **Ur**, and from the west **Amorite** tribes poured into the country. Despite these problems, Ibbi-Sin secured his hold on power for some 20 years, by force as well as by diplomatic means.

This policy produced a measure of relative stability until the downfall proved inevitable. This was probably precipitated by a major flooding of the **Euphrates** and ecological problems in the south that led to severe food shortages in the capital. One **Ur** governor, a certain **Ishbi-Erra**, had gained control of **Nippur** and **Isin** and held Ibbi-Sin to ransom over shipments of grain. Finally, the eastern states of **Elam** and

Shimashki attacked and devastated the **city** of Ur and many other towns of Mesopotamia. The king was taken captive and died on alien soil.

INANNA. The foremost **Sumerian goddess**, patron deity of **Uruk**. Her name was written with a sign (mùš) that represents a reed stalk tied into a loop at the top. This appears in the very earliest written texts from the mid–fourth millennium B.C. She is also mentioned in all the early god lists among the four main deities, along with **An**, **Enki**, and **Enlil**. In the **royal inscriptions** of the **Early Dynastic period**, Inanna is often invoked as the special protectress of kings. Also, **Sargon of Akkad** claimed her support in battle and politics. It appears that it was during the third millennium that the goddess acquired martial aspects that may derive from a syncretism with the Semitic deity **Ishtar**.

Inanna's main sanctuary was the Eanna ("House of Heaven") at **Uruk**, although she had **temples** or chapels in most cities.

During the time of the **Third Dynasty of Ur**, Inanna's ritual **marriage** to the king was much celebrated in poetry. In the context of the Ur royal ideology, Inanna does not appear as the "Lady of the Battle" as in **Akkadian** inscriptions but as the "Lady of Voluptuousness." The king is said to be "worthy of her holy loins." Her lover in many songs is the "Shepherd" Dumuzi, and the king of Ur identified himself with this role.

Inanna was the subject of a great number of literary compositions, hymns, songs, and prayers. Many of these depict Inanna as the embodiment of sexual drive and allure in all its ambiguities; she could "turn men into **women**," and in her entourage appear transsexuals and transvestites. She was the patron of prostitutes and said to haunt the taverns in search of male partners. Without her, life cannot continue; one myth recounts that when she was kept captive in the Underworld, all copulation (and hence reproduction) came to a sudden end.

Although it was Inanna's sister **Ereshkigal** who ruled over the Underworld, Inanna, too, had destructive and dangerous qualities. She doomed her lover Dumuzi to be her substitute in the Underworld and tricked the normally wise god **Enki** into relinquishing many of his divine powers.

Inanna as the "Queen of Heaven" was associated with the planet Venus.

INHERITANCE. Although it is not possible to make generalized statements about the extent of "private property" in Mesopotamia at any one period, one must bear in mind that the economy of the country depended on surplus production and astute managerial control over labor expenditure and investment on seed and equipment. Therefore, large institutions such as **temples** or the **palace** appear as controlling a considerable share of arable and/or otherwise productive land. The majority of the population worked as laborers or sharecroppers. They received rations or kept a percentage of the yield. Land could also be leased or rented. In some periods, the king distributed large parcels of land to trusty individuals that then became theirs "forever," as the **kudurru** documents specify.

However, it has also become clear that households, clans, and **families** could own or at least control access to **agricultural** land, as early as the **Early Dynastic period**. In such case the land was collectively owned. From the **Old Babylonian period** onward, privately owned land was divided into equal shares after the death of the father. Brothers could pool their shares, buy one another out, or simply accept this practice. It could also lead to litigation, as court cases report. Some far-seeing patriarchs issued inheritance contracts to avoid such disputes. Daughters did generally not receive a share of paternal property since they were given a dowry upon **marriage**. An exception to this rule were the *naditu* **women** of the Old Babylonian period, who did not marry and who were given a share of the paternal estate to manage during their lifetime, after which it was meant to revert to the family holding. Some of these women, however, adopted younger *naditu* to be their heirs, which was not infrequently challenged by their male siblings.

The **laws** of **Hammurabi** attempt to regularize inheritance in the case of children from secondary **marriages**.

Inheritance documents are almost always the preserve of the wealthy. Poorer families could not afford to pay **scribes** for their services, but court cases involving ordinary citizens give some idea of the chattels that could be passed on to the next generation.

Not just land could be inherited but real estate, draught animals, donkeys, wagons and boats, as well as other craft or professional equipment. Items of personal use, such as jewelry, **cylinder seals**, clothes, mirrors, and other valuable objects were mentioned. Some lucrative positions at the temple, for instance, so-called prebends, could be passed on, again a preserve of the rich. **Slaves** were a prized commodity and also inherited, along with "cash" (**silver** or **gold**).

Women received furniture, especially beds and stools, as well as cooking implements made of expensive materials (**copper**, **bronze** cauldrons, grinding stones, pestles and mortars), although men sometimes got the largest metal objects among the household goods.

IRON. Iron ore deposits occur in Anatolia and northwest Iran. The metal was probably first worked as a by-product of **copper** smelting, and rare small iron objects have been found in Mesopotamian graves since the fourth millennium B.C. Iron was worked as wrought iron and tempered by cooling and reheating. It was the **Hittites** who mastered the technology and produced the first tools and **weapons**.

In Mesopotamia, iron implements and arms were not used in significant quantities before the **Assyrians** introduced them in the eighth century B.C. They procured their iron weapons and tools by exacting them as **tribute** from their Anatolian provinces. The Iron Age therefore arrived later in Mesopotamia than in the Levant and Anatolia and coincides with the **Neo-Assyrian** and the **Neo-Babylonian periods**.

ISHBI-ERRA (reigned c. 2017–c. 1985 B.C.). King of **Isin**. Ishbi-Erra, an **Amorite**, served as an officer in the **army** of king **Ibbi-Sin** of the **Third Dynasty of Ur**. He was entrusted with the command over Isin and managed to assert independence from **Ur** by exploiting the unrest caused by the **Amorite** invasion into **Babylonia** and the renewed aggression of **Elam**. He helped to foster resistance against the supremacy of Ur within Mesopotamian **cities** and formed alliances with Ur's other enemies. Firmly entrenched at Isin and in control of the neighboring **Nippur**, he profited from the destruction of the capital Ur by the Elamites and presented himself as a legitimate successor of the Ur kings. The **Sumerian King List** thus presents Ishbi-Erra as the founder of a new dynasty, the **First Dynasty of Isin**.

ISHTAR. An originally Semitic **goddess** associated with the planet Venus, the Mesopotamian Ishtar owes much of her personality as described in myths and hymns to the **Sumerian** goddess **Inanna**, with whom she was identified as early as the mid–third millennium B.C. Like her, she embodies libido and sexual love without being a mother goddess. Only the topic of the king as lover and even husband of the goddess disappeared from the repertoire of **Babylonian royal inscriptions**. In the Epic of **Gilgamesh**, the hero goes so far as to express his revulsion at the idea of **marriage** to the goddess. Ishtar's masculine traits as a warrior goddess are perhaps more pronounced in the **Assyrian** royal inscriptions than in

the Babylonian texts, where her exalted position in Heaven is empha-
sized more. Her main symbol became the star and the rosette, and her sacred animal was the lion.

ISIN (modern Ishan-al-Bahriyat). **City** in southern **Babylonia**, 20 kilometers south of **Nippur**. Archaeological excavations show that the site was
already occupied in the **Ubaid period** in the fifth millennium B.C. Isin
was well known for its temple dedicated to the healing **goddess** Ninisina
("Lady of Isin"), who was later identified with the **Babylonian** goddess
Gula.

The **city** had some importance in the **Early Dynastic** and **Akkadian**
periods, but the name *Isin* does not appear in texts before the time of the
Third Dynasty of Ur. Most of the extant structures date from the second millennium. The city came to prominence after the fall of **Ur** in c.
2004, when **Ishbi-Erra** founded the **First Dynasty of Isin** in c. 2017.
Isin's supremacy was continuously contested by other cities, especially
its arch rival **Larsa**, which eventually conquered the city in c. 1794.

The **Kassite** kings promoted the cult of **Gula** and invested in the
restoration and enlargement of her **temple**. When the Kassite rule was
brought to an end by the Elamites who then exercised control of most of
central Babylonia, Isin's position in the south provided relative auton-
omy. The **Babylonian King List** credits an Isin with exercising legitimate **kingship** as the **Second Dynasty of Isin** (1158–1027). There are
few sources from this period apart from those of the reign of its most
prominent king, **Nebuchadrezzar I**, who undertook a successful campaign to **Elam** and restored national pride.

– J –

JEMDET-NASR PERIOD (c. 3200–c. 3000). A prehistoric period named
after the site Jemdet-Nasr in southern Iraq, which is mainly manifested
by distinct cultural artifacts (pottery, **cylinder seals**, **cuneiform** tablets)
in southern Mesopotamian sites. The term is not generally used for
northern Mesopotamian archaeological sequencing.

This phase in the south is distinct from the previous **Uruk period** levels and shows a degree of cooperation between several southern **cities**
whose seals are preserved on the tablets.

– K –

KADASHMAN-ENLIL I (reigned c. 1374–1360 B.C.). **Kassite** king of **Babylonia**. He is best known from the diplomatic correspondence with the Egyptian pharaoh Amenophis III (*see* AMARNA CORRESPONDENCE). One of Kadashman-Enlil's daughters was given to the pharaoh as a wife and seems to have pleased him enough for him to demand another. The **Babylonian** king complains in his letters that "his brother" did not return the favor of sending him one of his princesses and that his gifts of **gold** were disappointingly meager.

KALHU (modern Nimrud). **Assyrian city** some 30 kilometers south of present-day Mosul on the river **Tigris**. Although excavations have shown that the place had been inhabited in prehistoric times, it only became a site of some importance when **Shalmaneser I** (reigned 1274–1245 B.C.) began to build there. Kalhu became the capital of the Assyrian Empire under **Ashurnasirpal II** (reigned 883–859), a role it played for some 150 years until **Sargon II** moved the seat of government to **Dur-Sharruken** (Khorsabad).

In its heyday, Kalhu had a population of up to 100,000 people. Ashurnasirpal feted the inauguration of the city with a huge banquet. He and his successors built vast **palaces** and **temples** and surrounded the city with a wall of 7.5 kilometers. British archaeological teams have unearthed not only architectural vestiges but also **archives** containing royal correspondence and **administrative** documents from the time between **Tiglath-pileser III** and Sargon, as well as the famous "Nimrud ivories" that used to decorate furniture and architectural elements in the palaces. The city was destroyed by the **Medes** and **Babylonians** between 612 and 614, although parts of the site, which measured originally some 360 hectares, continued to be inhabited by villagers into the Hellenistic time.

KANESH (Kültepe). Anatolian **city** in Cappadocia, near Kayseri. Turkish excavators discovered the remains of a pre-**Hittite** city that had been inhabited since the mid–third millennium B.C. It seems to have been the center of a wealthy kingdom that benefited from the **trade** routes crossing near the site. Around 2000 B.C., kings with Indo-European names appear in the **cuneiform** tablets discovered at the nearby **Assyrian** trade colony. Kanesh was called Nesha by the Hittites, who incorporated the city in their kingdom. It was continuously occupied throughout the second millennium and was an independent city during the Neo-Hittite period (10th–8th centuries). Thereafter, Kanesh was conquered and destroyed by the Assyrians.

Kanesh is of importance to historians of Mesopotamia because of the cuneiform **archives** found in the *karum*, as the trade colony was called. These archives detail the commercial activities of Old Assyrian merchants who in a time between c. 1920 and 1742 B.C. conducted a lucrative business of importing **tin** and Mesopotamian textiles in exchange for **silver** and **gold**. The *karum* was destroyed by fire several times and rebuilt again, until the unstable situation after the death of the Assyrian king Ishme-Dagan made business impossible and the colony was abandoned.

KARDUNIASH. The name for **Babylon** and **Babylonia** during the **Kassite** period. It appears as such in the **Amarna archives**.

KASSITE DYNASTY (c. 1595–1150 B.C.). According to the **Babylonian King List**, the Kassite Dynasty comes after the **First Dynasty of Babylon** and before the **Second Dynasty of Isin**. Thirty-two kings are listed, but the first three (Gandash, Agum I, and Kashtiliash) reigned before the end of the Babylonian Dynasty and were thus contemporary with the last **Babylonian** kings. Most but not all of the kings had **Kassite** names. There are few historical sources from the first 200 years.

According to the Babylonian King List, there were 36 Kassite kings who ruled some 500 years. It was a king named Ulam-Buriash who was credited with the unification of **Babylonia** after he defeated the king of the **Sealand**. The best-knowm Kassite rulers were **Kadashman-Enlil I** (reigned c. 1374–c. 1360) and **Kurigalzu II** (reigned c. 1332–c. 1308).

The Kassite kings were responsible for a reorganization of the country into a strongly centralized state. Although they were most scrupulous to endow the ancient cult places and rebuild **temples**, the old **cities** lost some of their importance during this period as the countryside became more densely inhabited and smaller political units, such as villages and towns, proliferated. The Kassite kings donated large tracts of land in perpetuity to private individuals. Such donations were recorded on large, cone-shaped stones known as *kudurru*.

The Kassites made few attempts to enlarge their territory by invading other countries and generally presided over a peaceful and prosperous period; for a while, **gold** rather than **silver** became a medium of exchange.

Like other elites of the time, the Kassites were very interested in the breeding of **horses** and the new technology of **chariots** that was to transform military strategy. Generally, the Kassite elite did not impose their cultural traditions on their Babylonian subjects. They were keen to demonstrate their respect for the local customs and religious practices. They encouraged scribal activities, and it was under Kassite kings that Babylonian became the *lingua franca* for the whole of the ancient Near East.

KASSITES. A people of unknown origin who entered Mesopotamia from the east, across the Zagros Mountains. They spoke a **language** that is not related to any other known language. It is only poorly known from a few phrases and personal names in **cuneiform** documents.

The Kassites were first mentioned by the **Babylonian** king **Samsu-iluna** (reigned 1749–1712), and they appear with some frequency as a menace to the rural population in many **Old Babylonian royal inscriptions**. They penetrated into Mesopotamia and were concentrated in the region around **Sippar**. Many Kassites remained tribally organized even when they became sedentary. When the Hittite king **Mursili I** raided **Babylon** and thus terminated the **First Dynasty of Babylon**, a Kassite ruling elite achieved power over North Mesopotamia, which was gradually extended to include the whole country with the victory over the **Sealand** by Ulam-Buriash in c. 1595 (*see* KASSITE DYNASTY). When the Kassite Dynasty came to an end in c. 1155, the Kassites continued to live as a distinct group in Mesopotamia. Some occupied important posts in subsequent kingdoms, while the tribal groups in the eastern hills were still feared as a warlike people at the time of **Alexander**'s conquest.

KIDEN-HUTRAN (reigned c. 1235–1210? B.C.). **Elamite** king who launched two invasions into **Babylonia**, which at that time was ruled by local puppet kings appointed by the **Assyrian** monarch **Tukulti-Ninurta I**. In the first attack, Kiden-Hutran conquered **Nippur** and the city of Der. Several years later he took **Isin** and Marad.

KINGSHIP. According to Mesopotamian belief, "kingship came down from heaven" and was therefore a divinely decreed institution. The notion that kings were chosen for their office by the **gods** of the land is expressed in the **royal inscriptions** of all historical periods. There were special rituals of coronation that confirmed the ruler's responsibility toward the deities and his subjects whose "shepherd" he was meant to be. Kingship was hereditary in the male line, thus forming dynasties, but persons could also accede to the throne by violent means or usurpation of the throne.

Some kings of the **Early Dynastic period** and those of the **Third Dynasty of Ur** also fulfilled important religious offices, as did the **Assyr-**

ian kings, but they did not hold a supreme priestly office. The **Akkadian** kings (e.g., **Naram-Sin**) and those of **Ur** assumed the status of a deity; at least their names were written with the determinative sign that was usually reserved for divine names. In the third millennium B.C., there was also a cult for the statues of living and deceased kings.

Babylonian kings during the second millennium B.C. saw themselves as arbiters of justice. Especially the **Amorite** rulers were keen to show an interest in the affairs of all their subjects, while the **Kassite** and **Neo-Babylonian** rulers were more remote. During the annual **New Year Festival**, the Babylonian king had his ears pulled and his face slapped by a priest to remind him that he, too, was a subject of the gods.

Assyrian monarchs saw the defense and enlargement of their country by military means as their primary duty.

Much of the Babylonian divinatory sciences was dedicated to safeguard the country and its king. Especially the Assyrian kings surrounded themselves with learned advisers skilled in the arts of interpreting the "signs," and the king had to undergo a lengthy ritual of purification to avert evil portents (*see* ASTROLOGY/ASTRONOMY). In some cases, a "substitute king" could be officially appointed for a limited period of time so that any misfortune might befall him rather than the real king (*see* ISIN).

KISH. City in central Mesopotamia, some 15 kilometers east of **Babylon** (several sites: **Tell** Oheimir, El-Khazneh, El-Bender, and Ingharra). One of the oldest cities, it was continually occupied from c. 5000 B.C. to the sixth century A.D.

According to the **Sumerian King List**, "**kingship** came down from heaven again at **Kish**" after the Great Flood to begin the First Dynasty of Kish. The text lists 23 kings at Kish with very long reigns (a total of 24,510 years). The penultimate ruler, Mebaragesi, is historically documented by an inscribed vase that bears this name and title.

The Second Dynasty of Kish, listed after that of Awan, had eight kings reigning for 360 years. None of these kings are known from written sources that have preserved the names of other kings of Kish who are not mentioned in the Sumerian King List; the most important of those is Mesalim of whom several inscribed objects survive.

During this time, the **Early Dynastic period**, there were several independent city-states; Kish was one of them, although the title "king of Kish" began to imply sovereignty over all of **Sumer** and **Akkad**, and it was borne by **Sargon** and his successors during the **Akkadian period**. The Third Dynasty of Kish (c. 2450–2350) is said to have been founded by a woman, the "innkeeper" Kubaba. Again according to the Sumerian King List, she was defeated by a ruler of Akshak, but her son Puzur-Sin regained power and initiated the Fourth Dynasty of Kish, which was brought to an end by **Lugalzagesi**, who was captured by Sargon. Thereafter, the city was never the seat of kingship again, but it remained an important center of learning, as it had been since the Early Dynastic period.

The main archaeological discoveries were Early Dynastic houses and graves from the Early Dynastic period in Ingharra, as well as the terraces of large **ziggurats** from the same period. There were also the remains of a **palace** and an **administrative** building. At Tell Oheimir the **temple** complex of the **god** Zadaba dates from the **Old Babylonian period**, and in "mound W" a **Neo-Assyrian** tablet collection from the seventh century was discovered.

KIZZUWATNA. A country in southeast Anatolia with a large **Hurrian** population, which became part of the **Hittite** Empire in the mid–second millennium B.C.

KUDURRU. In the **Kassite** period the word *kudurru* designated a monument of a dressed stone or clay boulder that recorded land donations by the king to individuals. They were kept in **temples**, but sealed copies of the wording were kept in **archives**. Some had elaborate decoration with divine symbols or the plan of the estate, and powerful **curses** were addressed to anyone who would obliterate the monument or act against the agreed stipulations.

KÜLTEPE. *See* KANESH.

KURIGALZU II (reigned 1332–1308). **Kassite** king of **Babylon**. According to a **Babylonian Chronicle**, Kurigalzu was put on the throne by the **Assyrian** king **Ashur-uballit I** to replace the usurper Nazi-Bugash. This did not stop him from attacking **Assyria** in later years, an enterprise that did not succeed and resulted in the loss of Babylonian territories. A campaign against **Elam**, however, resulted in victory. Kurigalzu is also known for his architectural projects, such the restoration of the **temple** of **Inanna** at **Uruk** and especially the foundation of the Kassite royal city **Dur-Kurigalzu**.

– L –

LAGASH. Important **Sumerian** city-state in the third millennium B.C. It had several urban centers: Lagash itself (modern Al-Hibba), **Girsu**

(modern Tello), and Nin-Sirara (modern Zurghul). Girsu, excavated by the French archaeologist Ernest de Sarzec, in the 1880s, was the first Sumerian **city** to be discovered. No important architectonic structures were detected at the time but the team found a large number of **cuneiform** tablets, artifacts, and statuary, which provided valuable information on the **Early Dynastic** and **Neo-Sumerian periods**.

Lagash does not feature as a seat of **kingship** in the **Sumerian King List**, but according to the inscriptions of its rulers (who always bore the title *ensi*), it enjoyed periods of political independence and prosperity. The inscription by an *ensi* called Enhegal dates from the Early Dynastic period III, around 2570 B.C. Best known is Ur-Nanshe (c. 2494–2465), who recorded his many building projects, such as the **temples** of Nanshe, **Ningirsu**, and the mother **goddess** Gatumdug, as well as the city walls of Lagash. He fought wars against **Ur** and especially with **Umma**. His grandson **Eannatum** (reigned c. 2452–2425) won the famous victory over Umma. Ur-nanshe's dynasty ended with **Uruinimgina** (previously read as Urukagina) (reigned c. 2351–2342), who was defeated by **Lugalzagesi**.

Little is known of what went on in Lagash during the **Akkad** period, but while the **Gutians** held sway in the north, the city-state enjoyed another period of prosperity and expansion, especially during the reign of **Gudea** (reigned c. 2141–2122). It became part of the unified state created by the **Third Dynasty of Ur** and began to decline in the **Old Babylonian period**.

LANGUAGES. Numerous different languages were spoken in Mesopotamia throughout the ages, although not all of them are represented on written documents. It appears that the simultaneous presence of several linguistic groups contributed significantly to the success of urbanization and the richness of the intellectual culture.

Nonclassifiable languages are **Sumerian**, which has an agglutinative structure and was spoken in southern Mesopotamia throughout the third millennium B.C.; **Elamite**, current in southwest Iran from the **Early Dynastic** until the **Persian** period; **Hurrian**, spoken in Upper Mesopotamia and southern Anatolia; and **Kassite**, the language of the political elite in the second millennium B.C., which they did not render in **cuneiform** except for some technical terms and personal names.

The second group are Semitic languages: generally known as **Akkadian** in cuneiform sources, which include the different historical stages of **Babylonian** and **Assyrian**. Akkadian includes numerous loan words from Sumerian. Immigration from the west brought in people speaking West

Semitic languages, such as **Amorite** and **Aramean**. They were widely spoken in Mesopotamia in the late third and second millennia B.C. The written form of Aramaic, using an alphabetic system, became current side by side with Babylonian and Assyrian, in the first millennium B.C.

Indo-European languages had comparatively less currency in Mesopotamia. They were spoken by foreign elites, such as the **Mitanni** or the **Persians**. **Hittites**, **Medes**, and **Parthians** also spoke such Indo-European languages.

There has been some speculation about the pre-Sumerian and pre-Akkadian language substratum in southern Mesopotamia, which seems to have left traces in place names, but the evidence is too scant and vague to allow any conclusions as to what type of language it may have been.

LARSA (modern Tell Senkereh). A **city** in southern Mesopotamia, some 20 kilometers southeast of **Uruk**. The site had a long history of occupation, from the **Ubaid period** in the fifth millennium B.C. to the **Parthian** periods (to 224 A.D.).

The earliest architectural remains belong to a **palace** built by Nur-Adad who reigned c. 1865–1850 B.C. The city remained independent after the disintegration of the **Third Dynasty of Ur** and vied with **Isin** for supremacy. The king lists record the names of the kings of Larsa, from Naplanum (reigned 2025–2005) until **Rim-Sin** (reigned 1822–1763), who was defeated by **Hammurabi** of **Babylon**. It was **Gungunum** (reigned 1932–1906) who had put an end to the supremacy of Isin, campaigned against **Elam**, conquered **Ur**, and took on the ancient title "king of **Sumer** and **Akkad**." This marks the apogee of Larsa's power.

Gungunum's successors, Abisare and Sumuel, also built canals to extend and improve **agricultural** exploitation. Long-distance **trade** flourished. The reign of the last king, the **Amorite** Rim-Sin, lasted for 60 years. He put in place an **administrative** network that was to benefit his rival Hammurabi.

Larsa was an important religious center, and its main **temple**, the Ebabbar ("Shining House"), belonged to the sun **god Shamash**. It stood in the middle of the city and was already in existence during the **Early Dynastic period** III. The temple was then substantially rebuilt by **Ur-Nammu** around 2100 B.C. and continued to function well into the **Neo-Babylonian period**. The temple also had a **ziggurat**, and the main priestess of the Sun (**Akkadian** *entu*) had her own residence, the Giparu, within the sacred precinct. Other temples were dedicated to **Ishtar** and **Gula**.

LAW. The Mesopotamian justice system relied primarily on customary law that was upheld by the assembly of elders or town official or courts. Judges could be chosen from the local community or be appointed by the king. Affected parties represented their own case and brought witnesses as appropriate. Proceedings, or at least the verdicts, were written down, and numerous tablets have been preserved from most historical periods. In the absence of witnesses, the accused could be referred to an ordeal, such as being thrown into a river or canal. The innocence was proved when the "river refused" the culprit. Defendants and plaintiffs were made to swear an **oath** on the divine emblems, such as the sun disk, which represented the **god** of justice, **Shamash**.

As kings were seen as the upholders of law and order, they often issued legal reforms, debt releases, and decrees that were recorded in writing and are often referred to as law codes, although there is no evidence that courts ever referred to such edicts. The earliest known royal edict is by the **Sumerian** ruler **Uruinimgina** of **Lagash** (c. 2351–2342), who abolished a number of malpractices such as officials overcharging for **funeral** services. Then follows the Code of **Ur-Nammu** (c. 2100), of **Lipit-Ishtar**, of **Eshnunna**, and of **Hammurabi**, all from the early **Old Babylonian period**. They are all introduced by the clause "if this and this happens," followed by the verdict.

The Code of Hammurabi is the longest extant collection of laws. It was published toward the end of his reign and represents the first known effort to produce a coherent set of abstract legal precepts for the whole country, incorporating diverse local practices and traditional law. There are several main sections (family law, including subsections on adultery, incest, divorce, and **inheritance**; property law and restitution; loan and hire agreements; and setting standards on charges and wages). It differentiates fines and punishments according to a person's legal status: free, **slave**, and a category in between called *muškenum*. In contrast to earlier legal practices, Hammurabi's Code favors the so-called talionic principle ("an eye for an eye") rather than monetary fines, which may express a preference for tribal customary practice.

The **Middle Assyrian** laws from the 12th century B.C., among other matters, regulate the behavior of **women** and **palace** staff. There is only a fragmentary code from the **Neo-Babylonian period**.

LIPIT-ISHTAR (reigned c. 1934–c.1923). Fifth king of the **First Dynasty of Isin**. He is primarily known for his legal and fiscal reform contained in the "Code of Lipit-Ishtar," which regulates the participation of the populace in public work projects and tries to deal with the then increasingly widespread practice of debt enslavement. Otherwise, his inscriptions mainly record building activities. He restored the Giparu, the residence and chapel of the *entu* priestess at **Ur**, a high office to which he had appointed his daughter.

LUGALBANDA. Legendary **Sumerian** king. He is mentioned in the **Sumerian King List** as the third king of the First Dynasty of **Uruk**. There are no historical records to substantiate this claim, but Lugalbanda, like his father Enmerkar, appears as the heroic king in a number of literary works written in Sumerian. On the other hand, he is also listed as a **god** in lexical lists and received a cult during the **Old Babylonian period** at **Nippur** and Uruk. In the **Gilgamesh** epic he appears as the father of Gilgamesh and the husband of the goddess Ninsun.

LUGALZAGESI (reigned c. 2341–c. 2316). He appears in the **Sumerian King List** as king of the Third Dynasty of **Uruk** with a reign of 25 years. According to his own inscriptions, he was initially the ruler (*ensi*) of **Umma**. In the long-lasting conflict between Umma and Lagash, he inflicted a serious defeat on the rival **city** and went on to win supremacy over the whole country as king of Uruk. He was in turn defeated by **Sargon of Akkad**, who brought him as captive to the **temple** of **Enlil** at **Nippur**.

– M –

MAGAN AND MELUHHA. Geographical terms for regions in the distant south and southeast of Mesopotamia. Both names first appear in **royal inscriptions** of the **Akkad period**; ships from Magan and Meluhha were said to have brought goods to the quays of **Akkade** and other cities. It has been proposed that Magan referred to the coast of Oman along the Persian Gulf, rich in **copper** and dates, and Meluhha in the Indus Valley. In **Neo-Assyrian** texts of the first millennium B.C., Magan and Meluhha probably designated the African coast of the Red Sea (Upper Egypt and Sudan).

MAGIC. Religion and magic cannot be distinguished as separate concerns in the context of Mesopotamian attitudes to the "supernatural." The great **gods** were all invoked to combat destructive and malevolent forces by lending efficacy to spells and apotropaic rituals. **Ea** and **Marduk**, for instance, were seen as "master magicians" whose divine powers were harnessed for the combat against evil.

Human beings were under constant threat of falling victim to harmful influences; any accident, misfortune, illness, or death could be interpreted as a demonic attack, witchcraft, or even the "anger" of one's personal god. Magic protection, in the form of amulets, unguents, or special invocations (prayers) acted as a prophylactic.

Once the harm was done, however, and sickness and ill luck would not go away, the afflicted person would seek professional help from a magician-healer. The king and the elite could afford to avail themselves of the services of experienced specialists (*ašipu*) who had spent many years of apprenticeship and training, while the less well-off had to be content with "unlicensed" amateurs. Before any treatment could begin, the cause of the affliction had to be determined. This was a lengthy process that involved divination to aid diagnosis—to identify which evil spirit or demon was to be blamed. Then followed the exorcism to expel the offending agent and thereby rid the patient of his torments. Since sinfulness and ritual pollution could also attract demonic attacks or cause divine anger, purification rituals could be added for good measure.

Especially the king was in grave danger from evil influences. They had to undergo time-consuming and uncomfortable ritual treatment to ward off danger or reverse an ill-fated course of events. The correspondence between some **Assyrian** kings (e.g., **Esarhaddon**) and their diviners and magician-priests show that there were rivalries between different royal advisers and often a lack of unanimity.

There is a great amount of **cuneiform** literature on the subject: incantations and spells, as well as instructions for the accompanying ritual actions and which materials and substances had to be used, how and at what stage of the proceedings. They are difficult to understand since they were written for persons with insider knowledge and must have relied on oral commentaries.

The earliest magic spells date from the **Akkadian period** and concern love magic. A **Sumerian** incantation series that was also translated into **Akkadian** (*uttukki lemnuti*) tried to address all evil spirits and find the right formula to banish them. The most famous Babylonian magic series are *Maqlu* and *Surpu* (both mean "Burning"), which concern witchcraft. The texts refer to a seven-day-long ritual combat and cosmic trial of the "witch" in the widest sense, by a divine assembly. It involved the burning of specially prepared effigies.

MANISHTUSU (reigned 2275–2261 B.C.). **Akkadian** king, son of **Sargon of Akkad**. Although, like his predecessor and brother **Rimush**, he had to suppress widespread rebellions against his rule, he also conducted long-distance **trade**, as with **Magan**, and engaged in building activities. Later, tradition credited him with the foundation of the **Ishtar temple** at **Nineveh**. According to some "historical" **omens**, Manishtusu was killed by his courtiers with their **cylinder seals**.

MAR-BITI-APLA-USUR (reigned 985–980 B.C.). The only king of the so-called Elamite Dynasty. He may have had **Elamite** ancestry although his name is **Babylonian**.

MARDUK. **Babylonian god**. The origins of this god are obscure, and even the etymology of his name is unclear, a matter that already occupied the minds of Babylonian scholars in antiquity. In later time, his symbol was the hoe, which may reflect some agrarian connections. More was made though of a possible solar aspect, as reflected in the popular form of writing his name as *AMAR.UTU,* which can be translated as "the bull calf of the Sun." Although Marduk's name appeared in god lists of the **Early Dynastic period**, he only became a major Mesopotamian deity in the time of **Hammurabi** (reigned 1792–1750 B.C.). This can be seen in the literary texts of this period that allocate Marduk a prominent place at the expense of **Enlil**. Many people in the **Old Babylonian period** and thereafter bore names composed with Marduk.

Together with **Ea** and the sun god **Shamash**, Marduk had great powers against all kinds of evil forces and is frequently invoked in incantations and **magic** rituals. In the **Kassite** period, the cult of Marduk was also much promoted, and by the time of the **Second Dynasty of Isin**, he had become the "lord of the gods" and the "national" deity of **Babylonia**.

Marduk and even to a greater extent his son **Nabu** (the god of **Borsippa**) were also introduced to **Assyria**, where chapels and **temples** were built for them in all the major **cities**.

The vicissitudes of Marduk's statue, which was stolen first by the **Elamites** in 1185 and then again by the **Assyrians** in the seventh century, echo the political fate of Babylonia. The restoration of the divine statue and its secure presence in the temple Esagila at **Babylon** was regarded as a manifestation of security and stability. This intimate connection between Marduk, the city of Babylon, and the whole of Babylonia was also the major theme of the New Year **festival**. The grandiose restoration

works at his temple at the time of **Nebuchadrezzar II** further empha-
sized the vital links between Babylonia's economic prosperity and its
status as the greatest power in the Near East to the unrivaled position of
Marduk as the head of the Babylonian pantheon.

Various myths and other literary works describe the rise of Marduk as
the most courageous of the younger gods, who defeated the forces of
chaos and designed and built the universe (*see* CREATION MYTHS).
One text, known as the Erra epic, elaborates on the disastrous conse-
quences of Marduk's absence from his shrine.

MARDUK-APLA-IDDINA II. *See* MERODACH-BALADAN.

MARDUK-NADIN-AHHE (reigned 1100–1083 B.C.). **Babylonian** king,
the sixth of the **Second Dynasty of Isin**. He was the brother of the famous **Nebuchadrezzar I** and acceded to the throne after the brief reign
of his young nephew, Enlil-nadin-shume, whom he may have deposed.
Marduk-nadin-ahhe pursued his brother's policy of extending Babylonian influence. While the latter had made successful campaigns against
Elam, Marduk-nadin-ahhe targeted **Assyria**, which was then ruled by
the energetic warrior-king **Tiglath-pileser I**. For the first 10 years, the
Babylonians had the upper hand, then followed a period in which attack
was followed by counterattack but eventually Tiglath-pileser launched a
massive invasion of Babylonia, capturing **Dur-Kurigalzu**, **Sippar**, Opis,
and **Babylon**, where he destroyed the royal **palace**. The final years of
Marduk-nadin-ahhe were made even more troubled by the incursions of
Aramean tribes and a severe famine in his 18th regnal year. The circumstances of his death are not known; according to Assyrian sources,
he "disappeared."

MARI (modern Tell-Hariri, in southeast Syria). Important **city** on the middle **Euphrates**, excavated by French archaeologists since 1933. It is of
special importance for the reconstruction of historical events at the beginning of the second millennium B.C., which the rich finds of
cuneiform tablets at the site have made possible. The occupational levels of the city go back to the early third millennium. According to the
Sumerian King List, it was the seat of the 10th dynasty "after the
flood," between those of Adab and **Kish**, and was said to have lasted 136
years. The names of the kings are not preserved, but there is some archaeological evidence from **Early Dynastic Mari**, mainly **temples**, the
remnant of a **palace**, and several inscribed statues of dignitaries.

Mari was destroyed by the ambitious **Lugalzagesi** and subsequently incorporated into the **Akkadian** Empire. Then followed a period of independence under the rule of another dynasty, the so-called Shakkanakku (originally the title of Akkadian military governors).

Mari was subject to **Ur** during the **Third Dynasty of Ur**, but then began its most illustrious period, when the city enjoyed its greatest prestige, from c. 2000 to 1800 B.C. Much of its wealth derived from its improved irrigation schemes around the river; good relations with the surrounding **pastoralist** tribes, which provided wool for flourishing, **palace**-based textile workshops; and control over riverine and overland **trade**.

Mari became a much coveted target of political ambition and **Shamshi-Adad I** (reigned c. 1813–c. 1781), the **Amorite** king of **Assyria**, managed to dislodge the local ruler Sumu-yaman, and appoint his own son Iasmah-Addu, as governor of Mari.

Eventually **Zimri-Lim** (reigned c. 1775–1761), the son of the dislodged Mari king Iahdun-Lim who had found exile in Aleppo, defeated the Assyrians and assumed kingship. Zimri-Lim maintained complex relations with tribal leaders and other rulers such as **Hammurabi** of **Babylon**.

He ordered the complete rebuilding of the palace on a vast scale, covering some 2,500 hectares. Such a huge edifice was not just a royal residence but comprised the center of **administration** and textile workshops. The walls of some official rooms were decorated with painted murals, the courts were paved with baked brick, and the whole edifice was drained by a complex system of underground water pipes. The walls of this palace are unusually well preserved, up to a height of four meters because of the sudden and violent destruction it suffered at the hands of Hammurabi's soldiers in around 1760 B.C. The city continued to be inhabited, but on a much reduced scale, into the first millennium B.C.

MARRIAGE. The social structure of Mesopotamian society was patriarchal, but **women** were not considered the legal property of males. They could own property and engage in business in their own right. Marriage in Mesopotamia was the socially sanctioned cohabitation between a man and women for the purposes of procreation. Great value was placed on female fertility, and barrenness constituted grounds for divorce or for the husband inviting another women to the household to bear him offspring. According to the **law** code of **Hammurabi**, a childless wife should take it upon herself to supply such a secondary wife.

The groom's family would begin negotiations with that of the prospective bride. The girl was given a share of her father's wealth as a dowry

(Old Babylonian *šeriktum*). According to his status, this could range from a few items of clothing and simple jewelry, as well as household items such as kettles and mortars, to substantial amounts of **silver**, furniture, and, in some cases, **slaves**. Land was not usually part of a dowry except in cases where there were no male heirs. Dowry lists, of generally more prosperous women, have survived, especially from the **Old Babylonian period**. The husband could not lay claim to this dowry; it was passed onto the women's children (*see* INHERITANCE).

The groom presented the father of the bride with the bride-price. Since virginity was rated highly, it warranted a greater amount than if the bride had been married before. The groom's family also contributed to the marriage in the form of a gift (*terhatum*) (mainly victuals) for the wedding feast. The husband could also make a personal present (*nudunnum*) to his wife, which became her legal property. The marriage was made legal by a contractual agreement between the parties. In wealthy families, this was drawn up in writing, but oral agreements before witnesses were equally valid.

The wedding feast held at the husband's father's house concluded the marriage.

Although the general pattern of marriage was monogamous, men could take secondary wives in case of barrenness or residence in another country (as the **Assyrian** merchants did in Anatolia). They could also take concubines whose status was below that of the main wife. Numerous clauses in **law** codes deal with the inheritance implications of such polygamous situations.

Divorce was possible on the grounds of maltreatment by husbands (at least according to the Code of **Hammurabi**), infertility of the wife, or simply loss of affection by the husband. It had to be ratified before a court, which made sure that the repudiated woman had some means of survival and could force the husband to return her dowry.

Diplomatic marriages, arranged by kings to cement political alliances, are well attested in Mesopotamia, especially during the second millennium. It was a popular method used by **Zimri-Lim** of **Mari**, whose daughters were married off to various local rulers as virtual spies. Letters of these unhappy women have been found among the Mari archives. The **Kassite** rulers also gave their princesses to foreign potentates, notably the pharaohs of Egypt.

MEDES. The Medes were a people of Indo-European origin who migrated into Iran toward the end of the second millennium B.C. By the eighth century, they had consolidated themselves into a kingdom with the capital

Ecbatana (modern Hamadan). They became instrumental in the downfall of the **Neo-Assyrian empire** in the late seventh century when they joined **Babylon** in an anti-Assyrian alliance that resulted in the sack of **Nineveh** in 612 B.C. They were to take most of the former **Assyrian** provinces and dependencies in eastern Anatolia and northwest Iran. The Medes were in turn overrun by other **Persian** groups led by the **Achaemenid** king **Cyrus II** around 550 B.C. Although they lost their independence, the Median elite continued to exercise much influence at the new court.

MERODACH-BALADAN (biblical form of the name Marduk-apla-iddina II) (reigned 721–710). King of **Babylon**. The career of Merodach-baladan, originally a tribal leader of the **Chaldeans** in southern **Babylonia**, is unusually well documented, due to his long struggle against **Assyrian** supremacy. In the Assyrian records, he is depicted as an archenemy and "terrorist" *avant la lettre*; he was especially loathed by **Sennacherib**. According to the **Babylonian** sources he was a "good" Babylonian king who maintained the privileges of the cult **cities**, invested in irrigation, restored **temples**, and fought against Assyrian oppression. According to the Bible (II Kings 18 and Isaiah 39), he sent a delegation to the Judean king Hezekiah, perhaps in the hope of gaining support against Sennacherib.

Merodach-baladan is first mentioned as the "king of the **Sealand**" in the **annals** of **Tiglath-pileser III**, who fought a campaign against the rebellious southern tribes. Profiting from the internal problems in Assyria following the death of Shalmaneser V in 722, he established himself as king of Babylon. **Sargon II** was determined to win back Assyrian control over Babylonia and launched a series of attacks that were meant to dislodge the Chaldean king from Babylon. He inflicted defeats on the Babylonian forces and declared himself king of Babylon, while Merodach-baladan went to **Elam** to ask for military assistance against the Assyrians.

By the time Sargon died in 705, Merodach-baladan had assembled a formidable alliance and challenged the new king Sennacherib on two fronts. The Assyrians managed to defeat the Babylonian allies, and Sennacherib entered Babylon, where he took captive the wives of Merodach-baladan. He had these women transported to Assyria, together with other Babylonian nobles and much treasure.

Sennacherib sought to safeguard Assyrian interests by placing a puppet ruler on the Babylonian throne, which he replaced in 700 with his own son and crown prince, Ashur-nadin-shumi.

Sennacherib launched a final attack against the south, where Merodach-baladan had taken refuge in the marshes. However, he was not to succeed; Merodach-baladan had escaped to the Elamite coast, and in the counterattack mounted by Elam, Sennacherib's son was kidnapped and probably killed. Merodach-baladan's end is not known, but he evaded capture by the Assyrians.

METALS. *See* BRONZE; COPPER; GOLD; IRON; SILVER; TIN.

MIDDLE ASSYRIAN PERIOD. The term Middle Assyrian has two connotations: (1) It is a linguistic term used to refer to the **language** of documents written in "Middle Assyrian" as opposed to Old or Neo-Assyrian. (2) In a historical context it circumscribes the period between c. 1400 and c. 1050 B.C. that saw the rise of a new **Assyrian** state after a long period of decline following the breakup of the **Old Assyrian** kingdom in c. 1741. This new era of Assyrian growth happened at a time of great international competition for political and economic supremacy in the Near East and the struggle for the control of the fertile valleys of Syro-Palestine. Egypt, the **Hittites**, and **Mitanni** were involved in this rivalry. Assyria only became one of the major players when Mitanni was in the throes of a disastrous civil **war**.

Ashur-uballit I (reigned 1365–1330) emerged as an able and determined king who soon sent rather cocky letters to the pharaoh, with princely gifts of **horses** and **chariots**, to initiate a royal gift exchange. He was also keen to establish good relations with the **Kassite** kings of **Babylonia** and a friendship treaty was sealed by the **marriage** of the Assyrian princess to the son of the Babylonian king Burnaburiash. The Assyrians duly intervened when a usurper dislodged the son from their union.

Relations between Assyria and Babylonia continued to be tense, and it was in the Assyrian interest to push the northern frontier of Babylonia farther south (it had been not far from the **city** of **Ashur** at the time of Ashur-uballit). Due to the more expansionist dynamics of Assyria, they succeeded to enlarge their territory progressively.

Adad-nirari I (reigned 1307–1275 B.C.) pushed westward, conquering the Hittite vassal state Mitanni, and took its ruler prisoner to Assur. The Assyrian presence in the Habur and Balikh Valleys was strengthened by fortified towns and the setting up of permanent administrative control.

During the reign of **Tukulti-Ninurta I** (c. 1243–1207), the Assyrians consolidated their control of the northern and eastern borders by setting up garrisons and pacifying nomadic **tribes**. When the Babylonian king

Kashtiliash IV tried to recapture some towns held by the Assyrians, Tukulti-Ninurta moved his forces southward, inflicted a defeat on the Babylonians, and assumed Assyrian control over the country that was to last for some 32 years. Tukulti-Ninurta was assassinated by one of his own sons, which resulted in a political turmoil and the loss of territory, including Babylonia.

The situation improved with the accession of **Tiglath-pileser I** (reigned 1115–1076). He was able to capitalize on the collapse of the Hittite Empire and established a strong Assyrian presence in Anatolia. He led systematic but not altogether successful campaigns against various tribal groups, especially the **Arameans** in Syria who proved a serious threat, and invaded Babylonia, which was at that time ruled by **Nebuchadrezzar I**.

In the 11th century, persistent guerilla warfare by the Aramean and Sutean tribes weakened Assyrian military power; there were rebellions in most of the previously conquered territories, and Assyria was reduced to its "heartland" around Ashur, **Nineveh**, and Arbela. After about 1050 B.C., all documentation ceased, and the end of the Middle Assyrian state remains unrecorded.

MIDDLE BABYLONIAN. This is primarily a linguistic term to differentiate the **language** from the earlier **Old Babylonian** and the later **Neo-Babylonian**. It comprises texts written between c. 1600 and 900 B.C.

MITANNI. A kingdom in northern Syria, centered around the Habur Valley. It was called Hanigalbat by the **Assyrians** and Naharina by the **Babylonians**. The population of Mitanni was predominantly **Hurrian**, but the ruling elite were Indo-European warriors who called themselves *Mariannu* and worshipped deities with Vedic names such as Indar, Uruwana, and the collective Devas. This elite was to intermarry with the local population as the names of their children testify.

Not much is known about the historical circumstance of the early Mitanni kings of the 16th century B.C., such as Kirta, Shuttarna, and Barratarna. Shaushtatar (fl. around 1430) was a major figure who greatly extended the territory of Mitanni by his conquest of Alalakh, Nuzi, **Assur**, and **Kizzuwatna** (Cilicia).

The Mitanni kings were in direct competition with Egypt's pharaohs of the XVIII Dynasty over the fertile lands in western Syria. Tuthmosis III defeated the Mitanni forces at Aleppo and Karkemish, but his successors preferred to make treaties with the Mitanni kings; Tushratta's daughter Taduhepa was given in **marriage** to Amenophis III. This established a balance of Mitanni and Egyptian influence.

Trouble came from within, when a civil **war** broke out over the succession of Shuttarna, who had been assassinated. A usurper acceded to the throne but was soon dislodged by Shuttarna's younger son Tushratta (II). The **Hittite** king **Suppiluliuma I** backed another descendant of the murdered king, Artatama II, and later his son Shuttarna III, while the sons of Tushratta went to find support from Egypt. Suppiluliuma's forces invaded the north of Mitanni, plundered the capital Washshukanni, and Tushratta was murdered by his own son.

The **Assyrians** who had by this time become a new political player under their king, **Ashur-uballit I** (reigned 1365–1330 B.C.) also concluded a treaty of mutual support with Shuttarna III. These rival factions, backed by military support from their allies, plunged the country into internal warfare and political chaos.

In the end, it was the Assyrians who gained from this situation; **Adad-nirari I** (reigned 1307–1275) marched against Washshukanni, took King Shattuara I prisoner to Assyria, and quelled a subsequent revolt by destroying various towns and deporting parts of the population. Mitanni was reduced to vassal status, and during the reign of **Tukulti-Ninurta I** (c. 1243–1207) it became an integral part of Assyria as the province of Hanigalbat.

MITHRIDATES I (reigned 171–c.139 B.C.). **Parthian** king who expanded the Persian control over Media and conquered Mesopotamia in 141 despite fierce opposition by the **Seleucid** ruler Demetrios II.

MURSILI I (reigned c. 1620–1590 B.C.). **Hittite** king who greatly enlarged the power base of the Hittite kingdom by his campaigns in northern Syria, where he captured the city of Aleppo. He also fought against the **Hurrians**. His most famous exploit was the surprise attack on the city of **Babylon**, which brought the **First Dynasty of Babylon** to an end.

– N –

NABONIDUS (Babylonian Nabu-na'id) (reigned 555–539 B.C.). **Babylonian** king. He was not of royal blood and claimed descent from a scholar and courtier, Nabu-balatsu-iqbi. His mother, **Adda-guppi'**, had spent many years at the Babylonian court. Her devotion to the moon god **Sin** was shared by **Nabonidus**.

Nabonidus had been a prominent citizen and an experienced soldier, and he was no longer young when he became king. It is not quite clear under what circumstances he acceded to the throne, in the aftermath of assassination of the designated crown prince.

In his first regnal years, he had to assert Babylonian authority in southern Anatolia and Syria, and his campaigns there resulted in rich booty that he used to repair **temples** throughout the land. He then moved to Arabia, where he set up Babylonian strongholds in an effort to impose control over the nomadic population and the lucrative incense **trade**. From his headquarters from the oasis **city** Teima, he was able to direct the project of rebuilding the temple of Sin at **Harran**. During his absence from **Babylon**, which was to last some 10 years, his son, Belshazzar, was entrusted with the running of the state.

Nabonidus returned to Babylon in c. 543 B.C. and duly celebrated the New Year **festival**, which had not been performed while he was at Teima. He managed to inaugurate the completed temple at Harran and other building projects, but by 539, his reign came to an end when the **Persian** king **Cyrus II** invaded **Babylonia**. Nabonidus, who had marched to meet his adversary, was beaten in battle near Opis and surrendered. The Persians entered Babylon freely, and Cyrus declared himself king. Nabonidus was moved to Carmania in southern Iran, where he died. He was the last indigenous king of Babylon.

NABOPOLASSAR (Babylonian Nabu-apla-usur) (reigned 626–605 B.C.). **Babylonian** king. The first ruler of the so-called **Third Dynasty of the Sealand**. He was an official appointed by **Assyria** when he began his career, but during the troubled period after the death of **Ashurbanipal**, he declared himself king of the **Sealand** and rallied **Babylonian** troops around him to fight off Assyrian control. Having defeated the Mannaeans, allies of Assyria, he made an alliance with the **Median** king Cyaxares, whose daughter married Nabopolassar's son **Nebuchadrezzar (II)**. When the Assyrian king Sin-sharra-ishkun attacked Nabopolassar, the alliance moved against **Nineveh** and took the city after a three-month siege in 612 B.C. The allies then pushed on to **Harran**, the then Assyrian capital, and drove out the last Assyrian government in c. 610. Nabopolassar became king of Babylon.

He himself campaigned in east Anatolia and just before his death (in 605 B.C.). Nebuchadrezzar defeated an Egyptian army that contested Babylonian control over Syria, thus securing large parts of the former Assyrian empire for Babylonia.

NABU. Babylonian god, whose main shrine, the Ezida **temple**, was at Borsippa, near **Babylon**. He was introduced to the Babylonian pantheon around the beginning of the second millennium B.C., at the same time that **Marduk** became prominent. He was first called the "scribe and minister of Marduk"; later he was known as the son of Marduk. Nabu became the patron of **scribes** and the scribal arts, and his symbol was the stylus. Beautifully written **cuneiform** tablets were popular offerings to this learned god.

Nabu's cult was introduced to **Assyria** in the 13th century, when **Tukulti-Ninurta I** built him a **temple** at **Assur**. He endured when other gods, who had been more closely identified with political power (e.g., Marduk), had lost popularity. In the late Babylonian period, he assumed many traits of other deities, such as wisdom and associations with water and fertility. Nabu's cult lasted well into the Roman period.

NADITU. **Babylonian** term for a group or institution of **women** during the **Old Babylonian period** who occupied special quarters known as *gagum* (the locked house). The best-known naditu women were those serving at the temple of the sun god **Shamash** at **Sippar** due to the voluminous **archives** that have been discovered at the local *gagum*. The etymology of the word *naditu* is not very clear; translations such as "barren" or "fallow" have been proposed. It appears that these women lived in relative seclusion (the **laws** of **Hammurabi** are especially severe against them visiting taverns) and that they were not permitted to have children. Married naditu could provide their husband with a secondary wife to father progeny. They were given a dowry upon their entrance to the institution that they were free to administer at their discretion.

The surviving business documents show that naditu women came from affluent families, including royal daughters, and that they were actively engaged in business ventures, such as **trade** enterprises, or indeed the ownership of profitable taverns. It was expected that their dowry returned to their paternal families after their death, but some women preferred to **adopt** younger naditu in order to secure support in their old age. As a result of their childlessness and isolation, the life expectancy of naditu was considerably higher than that of ordinary women of the period.

Little is known about the cultic duties of the naditu. They were expected to contribute to the daily sacrifices, appear at certain cult services, and, according to some surviving letters, their main function was to pray for the well-being of the relatives. The main focus of their devotion was not Shamash but his spouse Aya.

The institution did not survive after the Old Babylonian period but was revived briefly by the **Neo-Babylonian** king **Nabonidus**.

NANNA(R). Sumerian moon **god** whose main **temple** was the Ekishnugal at **Ur**. His cult was particularly prominent at the time of the **Third Dynasty of Ur**, when his temple and the **ziggurat** were rebuilt. He was especially associated with the fertility of cattle whose horns look like the new moon at the latitude of Mesopotamia.

NARAM-SIN (reigned c. 2260–2224 B.C.). **Akkadian** king, grandson of **Sargon of Akkad**. Like his predecessor **Manishtusu**, he had to repress rebellions by the main **cities** within his realm to assert his centralized control over the country. He then called himself "king of the four quarters (of the universe)" and began to write his name with a sign generally only used for **gods**.

Naram-Sin campaigned widely in all parts of his empire, from the east (where he famously subdued the mountainous tribes as depicted on a stele now at the Louvre), the north, and the northwest, where he fought the **Amorites**. He even ventured as far south as **Magan** on the Persian Gulf.

In the later literary tradition (*see* OMEN LITERATURE), Naram-Sin was depicted as an unlucky ruler, whose arrogance angered the gods. It appears, however, that his long reign brought stability rather than disruption to the country.

NEBUCHADREZZAR I (Babylonian Nabu-kudurru-usur) (reigned 1126–1105 B.C.). **Babylonian** king of the **Second Dynasty of Isin**. He secured his place in the Babylonian historical tradition by a decisive victory over **Elam**, which had been a major threat to **Babylonia** for some generations. He not only defeated the Elamite king Hutteludush-Inshushinak but also recovered the statues of the **god Marduk** and that of Marduk's wife Sarpanitum, which had been taken to Susa. The triumphal return of these statues may have given rise to the composition of the **creation myth** *enuma elish*. Nebuchadrezzar utilized booty from the Elamite campaign to rebuild sanctuaries in several Babylonian **cities**.

NEBUCHADREZZAR II (Babylonian Nabu-kudurru-usur) (reigned 605–562 B.C.). **Babylonian** king, son of **Nabopolassar**. Before his father's death, he had managed to defeat the Egyptians at Charchemish. He went to **Babylon** to be crowned but quickly returned to Syria. He fought there for some eight years to enforce Babylonian dominion over the Levant and

Syria, including Damascus, Tyre, and Jerusalem. He also campaigned in the east, against **Elam**, and had to repress rebellions within Babylonia. Eventually, he managed to secure Babylonia's succession over most of the territory's once held by **Assyria** and began to reap the economic benefits.

Much of the enormous revenue was spent on beautifying and protecting the capital **Babylon**. He built new **city** walls, double in construction and with a moat, a new bridge over the **Euphrates**, new **palaces**, and the splendidly decorated Processional Street, which was used for the ceremonies of the New Year **festival**. He also rebuilt and enlarged the precinct and **temple** of **Marduk** and began work on the huge **ziggurat** Etemenanki.

Nebuchadrezzar's royal inscriptions contained primarily detailed descriptions of his architectural projects. According to biblical records, he went mad in his later years, but there are no Babylonian sources to deny or substantiate this claim.

NEO-ASSYRIAN. The **language** of the documents written in the **Neo-Assyrian period**, which has certain linguistic features that distinguish it from **Old** or **Middle Assyrian**.

NEO-ASSYRIAN PERIOD (934–610 B.C.). This historical phase derives its name from a linguistic category of the **Assyrian language** as expressed in the documents of the time. According to the **Assyrian King List**, there was no break between the rulers of the mid–second millennium and those of the first millennium.

The first phase (c. 934–745) was marked by the resurgence of Assyrian assertiveness after the political turmoil associated with the **Aramean** invasions in the 12th and 11th centuries. Kings such as **Adad-nirari II**, **Tukulti-Ninurta II**, and **Ashurnasirpal II** were primarily concerned to regain control over the old Assyrian-held territories in northeast Syria and Upper Mesopotamia; local rulers were forced to submit to Assyrian authority and treated as subjects of the king. They also began to expand gradually northward into southern Anatolia to secure a hold over the **metal** resources that were traded in this region. Equally important were the foothills of the Zagros in the east—prime **horse**-breeding country and straddling the **trade** routes from and to the Iranian Plateau.

Ashurnasirpal II (reigned 883–859 B.C.) and **Shalmaneser III** (reigned 858–824) were to consolidate the Assyrian presence in all those regions. They initiated their systematic exploitation for their resources: manpower, horses, raw materials, and provisions for the Assyrian **army**, as well as regular **tribute**. Treaties assured the exclusive rights over trade commodities. Much of the revenue was used to construct and embellish new residential and administrative centers. Ashurnasirpal founded a new capital, **Kalhu** (ancient Nimrud) and Shalmaneser III concentrated on fortified provincial control points in northern Syria.

Relations with **Babylonia** were generally good; the two countries were allied by treaties and fought a common cause in subduing troublesome **nomads** in the western fringes of their realms. Babylonia lent support against various internal revolts that shook Assyria in the late ninth century.

This pattern only changed when **Shamshi-Adad V** (reigned 823–811) challenged the succession of Baba-aha-iddina. He invaded and ravaged the country, which plunged it into chaos for the next 10 years. The situation in Assyria remained difficult. There were rebellions in the provinces, and kings had to rely on the compliance of their (native) governors.

In the time between 745 and 705 B.C., the Assyrian Empire took shape. This was the result not only of renewed military expansion but of new **administrative** structures that ensured much tighter political and fiscal control. When **Tukulti-Ninurta II** (reigned 744–727) acceded to the throne, Assyria's prestige in Syria had weakened, and there was a new powerful state in eastern Anatolia, that of **Urartu**, which contested Assyrian influence in Anatolia and the Zagros foothills. In Babylonia, **Chaldean** chieftains were asserting their independence and allied themselves with **Elam** against the Assyrians. Tukulti-Ninurta III campaigned in all these areas. He defeated Urartu, took direct control of Babylon, and one by one coerced the Syrian polities to submit.

The empire now consisted of the heartland of Assyria, the provinces in Upper Mesopotamia, northern and southern Syria, with a further ring of client states ranging from southern Anatolia to the borders of Egypt, with tight control over the eastern trade routes. Tukulti-Ninurta III was succeeded by Shalmaneser V (reigned 726–722), who is chiefly known for his conquest of the Israelite capital Samaria.

He was soon ousted by **Sargon II** (reigned 721–705), whose accession was widely contested in Assyria. This triggered a concerted effort among the imperial dependencies to launch a collective revolt, led by the ruler of Hamath, which Sargon managed to defeat. He also had to counter the renewed threat of Urartu and to contend with the challenge of **Merodach-baladan** in Babylonia. By means of incessant campaigns, Sargon succeeded in holding Tukulti-Ninurta's empire together; he defeated the

Urartians and their Mannaean allies and drove Merodach-baladan into exile. He even had time to build another vast palatial complex at **Dur-Sharruken** north of **Nineveh**. He was killed on a campaign against the Cimmerians in Anatolia.

The reigns of his successors—**Sennacherib**, **Esarhaddon**, and **Ashurbanipal**—were also dictated by the need to quell numerous insurrections, police the frontiers of the empire, and confront coalitions by the enemies of the Assyrian imperial state. Although their military machine was the most formidable in the whole of the Near East, they could not be employed simultaneously in many different places.

Sennacherib (reigned 704–681) concentrated his efforts on solving the Babylonian problem in a long drawn-out **war** that ended in the destruction of Babylon. Esarhaddon (reigned 680–669) had to counter Egyptian interference in the Levant and even mounted a successful campaign into the Egyptian heartland that culminated in the sack of Memphis.

His policy of trying to secure the succession of his younger son **Ashurbanipal** to the Assyrian throne proved calamitous when the latter became embroiled in a war against his older brother **Shamash-shumu-ukin**, whom Esarhaddon had appointed as king of Babylon. Ashurbanipal was to prevail in this conflict, and he was also successful in annihilating the power of Elam, whose provocative and opportunistic policies toward Assyria had long been a thorn in his side. However, serious problems beset his later reign; it is not clear when and under what circumstances he died, and the empire received its mortal blow by a combined onslaught of **Median** and Babylonian forces between 612 and 610 B.C. when the cities of Nineveh, Assur, and the last capital, **Harran**, were conquered.

NEO-BABYLONIAN. A linguistic term that characterizes the **language** of texts written in the first half of the first millennium, from c. 900 to 500 B.C.

NEO-BABYLONIAN EMPIRE (605–539 B.C.). It was founded by the **Babylonian** king **Nabopolassar** (reigned 626–605 B.C.), who with the help of the **Medes** brought the **Neo-Assyrian empire** to its knees by destroying **Nineveh** and other major **Assyrian cities**.

His son **Nebuchadrezzar II** (reigned 605–562), an able military commander, managed to ward off Egyptian claims on the western former Assyrian provinces in Syria and the Levant, and he maintained control over the central south Anatolian regions as well. The Iranian regions remained under **Persian** rule.

The Babylonian empire was thus the heir to the Assyrian empire and reaped the economic rewards that were primarily invested in reconstructing the ancient Babylonian **cities**, especially **Babylon**. The empire weathered the serious internal political problems after Nebuchadrezzar's death; his son Amel-Marduk was assassinated by his brother-in-law Neriglissar, who only ruled three years, leaving a minor on the throne, which triggered further bloody intrigues.

Nabonidus (reigned 555–539 B.C.) emerged victorious from the fray, and, perhaps in anticipation of Persian ambitions under their new **Achaemenid** Dynasty, he moved westward to Arabia, where he built up a strong Babylonian presence before returning to Babylon. In any event, his efforts were fruitless. He faced **Cyrus II** in battle and was defeated. The Persian king then took possession of Babylon and assumed the Babylonian throne. This was the end of Babylonian independence.

NEO-SUMERIAN. The **language** used primarily in the documents from the **Third Dynasty of Ur**, which differs in some respects from that used in older material.

NEO-SUMERIAN PERIOD. This is another way of referring to the time just before and during the **Third Dynasty of Ur**, when **Sumerian** became once more the **language** of written documentation in private as well as administrative contexts.

NEOLITHIC PERIOD (c. 9000–5000 B.C.). Literally this term means "new stone age." The most prevalent tools were still made of stone, such as flint and other hard rocks. However, in many other respects the Neolithic period in the Near East has justly been associated with technological "revolution," especially the intensive exploitation of the ecological niches, increasing sedentarization, the invention of **pottery**, and, most important, the beginning of **agriculture**. The most important pilot sites in Mesopotamia are Jarmo, Umm Dabaghiyah, Tell Hassuna, and Choga Mami, all in northern Mesopotamia.

All these sites were within reach of montane valleys where wild cereals, species of wheat and barley, grew naturally. Early settlers had access to these zones and brought back seeds that were planted in the river plains, producing new cultivated species, such as six-row cultigens, with shatter-resistant seed heads. Even artificial irrigation was already employed at this stage. The investment of labor in such projects tied people more securely to one place and made them rely more heavily on a relatively limited diet.

Skeletons show that teeth were worn down more than in the preceding period and that the heavy work, especially the carrying of loads on the back, deformed neck and vertebrae. Nevertheless, the new food-procuring system allowed for greater population expansion and permanent settlements.

The domestication of wild animals was another Neolithic achievement. The dog already accompanied Paleolithic hunters; now sheep and goats, bred out of their wild ancestors, appeared. The first domesticated cattle emerged in the sixth millennium B.C. Most of these animals still showed a high degree of variability, most likely a result of the mobility of herding groups who would come into frequent contact with other groups. Hunting, too, became more professionalized, especially that of gazelles and onagers, which need coordinated group efforts. Gathering activities also continued, making use of periodically available wild resources, such as mushrooms, nuts, and wild fruit.

Neolithic craftsmanship is marked by the invention of pottery, hand shaped rather than wheel turned, but with exquisite painted designs and increasingly well fired. There is evidence of specialization in craft production (e.g., Umm Dabagiyah had a center of stone tool production).

Generally speaking, the Neolithic people had a "broad-spectrum economy," making use of a variety of subsistence strategies (agriculture, food collecting, herding, hunting) without any visible bias to a particular kind of exploitation. It is also increasingly evident that there was still a high degree of mobility; people could move from one site to another in a form of transhumance, inhabiting one ecological sphere for part of the year and moving on to the next site (winter and summer camps). Such movements also explain the rapid exchange of ideas and technologies over a wide area, as well as the exchange of goods. This led to the adaptation to different geographical conditions and to more intense contact between different groups and lifestyles.

The Neolithic society can be characterized as basically egalitarian and kinship based, possibly patrilocal and patrilinear.

NERGAL. Babylonian god of the underworld whose main cult center was at the as yet unidentified city of Kutha. He first appeared in the **Akkadian** period, and, by the second millennium B.C., he had supplanted the previously female chthonian deities, such as **Ereshkigal**. He was both a god of death and epidemics as well as of fertility and vegetation.

NINEVEH (ancient Ninua). **City** in **Assyria**, on the left bank of the river **Tigris**, now on the outskirts of the modern city of Mosul. The ancient site comprises the ruin fields of Kuyunjik and Nebi Yunus. It was first discovered in the mid–19th century A.D. and excavated by French, British, and recently Iraqi teams of archaeologists.

Nineveh is one of the oldest cities in Mesopotamia, but the prehistoric levels are only known from deep soundings that have revealed successive layers of **pottery** since the seventh millennium B.C. The first excavated architectural structure, a **temple** dedicated to the goddess **Ishtar**, dates from the predynastic period. It was rebuilt in c. 2260 by the **Akkadian** king **Manishtusu**. The **Amorite** ruler **Shamshi-Adad I** also left records of his building activities at the temple some 450 years later. The temple of Ishtar was thus the main attraction of the city, despite the fact that some **Middle Assyrian** kings built **palaces** there.

Nineveh only became a capital when **Sennacherib** (reigned 704–681 B.C.) decided to abandon **Dur-Sharruken** and moved his residence and **administration** to Nineveh. He surrounded the city, planned generously on 750 hectares with double walls 12 kilometers long, pierced by 15 gates. He was particularly concerned to secure an adequate water supply to the gardens and parks of the city and built for this purpose a series of ingenuous canals and aqueducts. His successors **Esarhaddon** and **Ashurbanipal** remained at Nineveh and built additional palaces lavishly decorated with wall reliefs. The royal **archives**, which were recovered from Ashurbanipal's palaces at Kuyunjik, have yielded some 24,000 tablets.

Nineveh, with its heterogeneous population of people from all over the Assyrian Empire, was one of the most beautiful cities in the Near East, with its gardens, temples, and splendid palaces. The city was besieged by the **Medes** and **Babylonians** in 612 and fell after a three-month siege after a desperate struggle. Thereafter, only small areas remained occupied until Roman times.

NINGAL. **Sumerian goddess**, wife of the moon god **Nanna(r)/Sin** and mother of the sun-god **Utu/Shamash**. Together with her husband, she was worshipped at **Ur** and in the Upper Mesopotamian **city** of **Harran**. She was also a goddess of dream interpretation.

NINURTA. **Sumerian god**, well known since the **Early Dynastic period**. He was originally an **agricultural** and rain deity and was called "the farmer of **Enlil**" who "lets the barley grow." His main **temple** was the Eshumesha at **Nippur**. By the end of the third millennium B.C., he had become more of a warrior, "the right arm of Enlil," and some myths describe him doing battle against the "hordes of the mountains." Ninurta was replaced by **Marduk** as the "champion of the gods" in the **Old Babylonian period**. He continued to enjoy great popularity in **Assyria**, where he was both a storm god and a warrior.

NIPPUR (modern Niffar, some 150 kilometers southeast of Baghdad). **Sumerian city** with a long history of occupation reaching back to the seventh millennium B.C. It was never the seat of a dynasty, although in the third millennium, Nippur seemed to have had an important role in confirming a dynasty's legitimacy. Its most important structures were **temples**, especially the Ekur (the temple of **Enlil**) and the **Inanna** temple. There were many other smaller temples and chapels in the city. Many Mesopotamian kings throughout history honored the **gods** of Nippur by endowing and repairing its sanctuaries and depositing votive gifts. It also had a reputation as a center of learning, and most of the extant copies of Sumerian literary works from the **Old Babylonian period** were discovered in the Nippur libraries, which belonged to private individuals rather than institutions.

The city suffered a major environmental crisis in the 18th century B.C., precipitated by the shift westward of the **Euphrates**, which originally ran right through the town. Nippur revived in the **Kassite** period, after a break of almost 300 years. A **palace** from this time has been found. In 1224, Nippur was attacked and destroyed by the **Elamites**, and most of the population left, leaving only the priests to maintain the cult of Enlil.

After centuries of near abandonment, the city prospered once more in the first millennium B.C. **Ashurbanipal** rebuilt the temple, and the city regained its ancient privileges and its importance in the **Neo-Babylonian period** and thereafter under the rule of **Achaemenids** when it was a center of commercial activity and especially banking, as documented by the archives of the Murashu family.

NOMADS. Much of the land in and around Mesopotamia was unsuitable for **agriculture** because of the scarcity of waterways and insufficient rain but provided enough seasonal grass for transhumant herding. The most important animals for pastoralism were sheep and goats whose growth period coincides with the renewal of vegetation in the winter months. The social structures of seminomadic or fully nomadic pastoralism developed to ensure maximum mobility for herds and people while maintaining internal cohesion. Little is known about these configurations in antiquity due to the fact that the settled population held nomads in contempt. It appears, however, from documents such as the **Mari** archives, that they were tribally organized, patrilinear, and patriarchal.

The relations between the **city** dwellers in Mesopotamia and nomadic groups were generally described as problematic in the **cuneiform** documents, especially at times when waves of nomadic tribes pushed into the rural districts, which were normally controlled by the state. Such forceful occupations were met by military resistance or even the building of defensive walls, but neither proved effective. Nomadic immigrations into Mesopotamia came mainly from the west, the Arabian peninsula and southern Syria, and to a lesser degree from the Iranian Plateau and the Caucasian Mountains. The best-recorded periods of tribal incursions were those of the **Amorites** in the late third millennium and those of the **Arameans** in the 12th and 11th centuries B.C.

Such large-scale and violent incursions were not symptomatic for the relations between nomads and those settled in Mesopotamia. Mutually beneficial contacts were the norm; the nomads were allowed to graze their herds on the stubble after the harvests, thus loosening and fertilizing the soil; after planting, the animals could nibble off the first shoots and thus render the plants more hardy and encourage growth. The markets of the cities supplied the necessary articles such as **weapons**, tools, and jewelry for **women**. There was an ever ongoing process of gradual sedentarization for some tribal members who would maintain social contact with their kin groups and relay new modes of thinking and living. Mesopotamian civilization was thus continuously enriched by the absorption of tribal people.

Camel nomadism only developed in the first millennium, after the domestication of the camel.

– O –

OATHS. A solemnly sworn oath was the most binding of all agreements or testimonies. It was thought to be irrevocable, and the oath breaker would automatically be destroyed by the divine power of the oath. As such, they were only undertaken in serious cases. In Mesopotamian **law** courts, defendants had to swear an oath or undergo an ordeal when there was no reliable witness or any other proof of their innocence. In property disputes, litigants could choose between paying a fine or taking the oaths, most of whom preferred the latter. Oaths were sworn on emblems of **gods** who were thus witnesses and protectors of the agreement. International treaties and vassal treaties were also concluded by oaths; here the parties swore on the deities of their own countries. They often include self-imprecations detailing what dreadful events should befall those who will act contrary to any of the clauses of the treaty.

OLD ASSYRIAN. The **Assyrian language** of documents written in the first few centuries of the second millennium B.C., especially those discovered in Cappadocia (*see* KANESH). The inscriptions of **Shamshi-Adad I** in contrast were written in **Old Babylonian**.

OLD ASSYRIAN PERIOD (2000–1500 B.C.). According to the **Assyrian King List**, the first 17 Assyrian kings "lived in tents," which means that they were little more than **tribal** leaders or sheikhs who dominated the region around the **cities** of **Nineveh** and **Assur**. One of these, Kikkiya, was said to have built a wall around Assur (around 2000 B.C.).

Little historical information exists from the early period, and most documents concern mercantile enterprises outside **Assyria**. Assur became the base for a network of commercial activities that centered on the import of **tin** from the east (via intermediaries) and an intense import-export business with central Anatolia (**trading** Mesopotamian textiles against **silver** and **copper**).

There was a break in the succession of Assyrian kings after the reign of Erishum II when the **Amorite** leader **Shamshi-Adad (I)** (reigned c. 1813–c. 1781), who originated from the west of Assur, acceded to the throne, having deposed Erishum. During his long reign of 32 years, he greatly enlarged his territory by attacking **Babylonian cities**, such as **Sippar** and **Babylon**, seizing control of **Mari** and the Habur Valley with Shubat-Enlil. He controlled all the Assyrian cities, such as Ekallate, Nineveh, and Assur, and the **Tigris** Valley right up to the Zagros and farther south toward **Elam**. After his death, most of the conquered territories were lost, and Assyria remained a small north Mesopotamian kingdom until it became reduced to the state of a vassal to the powerful **Mitanni**, following a raid by king Shaushtatar around 1500 B.C.

OLD BABYLONIAN. Linguistic term to classify the **language** of **Akkadian** documents written during the **Old Babylonian period**.

OLD BABYLONIAN PERIOD (c. 2000–1600 B.C.). On the basis of linguistic rather than historical criteria, this period begins with the fall of the **Third Dynasty of Ur** when documents began to be written again in

Akkadian, until the end of the **First Dynasty of Babylon**. It also includes the time of the **First Dynasty of Isin** and the dynasty of **Larsa**. It was dominated by the rise in the empire of **Hammurabi** and marked by a different cultural orientation than that of the **Neo-Sumerian** period.

There were changes in the royal ideology: Kings were now seen as arbiters of justice and "shepherds" of their people rather than remote and "divine." There was also a greater participation of private citizens in the economic exploitation of the country and a more intensive growth of rural settlements. Another development of this period was the shift of political power from the south to the north of **Babylonia** and the replacement of **Sumerian** as the official **language** of documentation by **Babylonian**.

OMENS (historical). The scrutiny of everyday occurrences (e.g., weather patterns) as well as geographical, astronomical, and even social behavior for the purposes of eliciting warnings about impending disasters was a veritable science in Mesopotamia. It was considered as a means of deciphering divine communications, which were encoded in a great variety of phenomena. The written records of earlier Mesopotamian kings were also studied as relevant case studies for ominous events. Especially the famous kings of the **Akkad** period were scrutinized; **Sargon of Akkad** was interpreted as a ruler blessed by the **gods**, but **Naram-Sin** evoked more negative associations. *See also* ASTROLOGY/ASTRONOMY.

– P –

PALACES. In archaeological terms, palaces are distinguished from large private residences and **temples**. They differ from the former by their greater size and number of rooms and by stricter measures of security reflected in the plan of buildings. The distinction between temples and palaces is less clear-cut in the prehistoric periods, but from the third millennium B.C. onward, certain architectonic features (e.g., niches and shallow buttresses) are typically found in temples rather than palaces.

Since the function of a palace in Mesopotamia was that of not simply a royal residence and a very large household but also an administrative center, such diverse functions were accommodated around separate courtyards surrounded by a suite of rooms.

There was also a division between the public and private sector. Reception areas, such as the throne room, were protected by a complex route of access and could be splendidly appointed with glazed tiles (as in **Nebuchadrezzar's** palaces in **Babylon**), wall reliefs (as in the **Neo-Assyrian** palaces), or wall paintings (as in **Dur-Kurigalzu**).

One of the best-known Mesopotamian palaces is the one built by **Zimri-Lim** at **Mari**. There is evidence of careful planning before construction began, as can be seen by the subterranean drainage channels. There was one very large and several smaller courtyards. The circulation system allowed for tight supervision. This palace, as various others in **Assyria**, had its own **archive**, which detailed the substantial economic activities of the palace, as well as the diplomatic correspondence and the **administration** of the kingdom. It is probable that most of the rooms as found in excavations were for storage purposes and that residential quarters and offices were located on upper floor levels. Evidence for the existence of such upper stories is generally indirect (stairwells, thickness of walls, lighting provisions, and the amount of rubble found within ground floor rooms).

Palaces in the first millennium B.C., especially in Assyria, also had pleasure gardens and parkland within their perimeter walls.

PARTHIAN PERIOD (c. 238 B.C.–A.D. 224). Parthia was the region in northern Iran where Indo-European **nomads** from Central Asia began to settle in the mid–first millennium B.C. This area was then controlled by the **Achaemenid Dynasty**. They began to form their own kingdom in the **Seleucid period**, when Arsaces, a leader of the Parni tribe, founded the Arsacid Dynasty around 238 B.C. He profited from the rebellions in Parthia and Bactria against the rule of **Seleucus II** and assumed control over most of central Iran, with a new capital at Dara.

His successors enlarged the Parthian territory eastward to the Indus and westward to the **Euphrates**. **Mithridates I** (reigned 171–c.139 B.C.) annexed Mesopotamia in 141, occupying **Babylon** and Seleucia. Having ousted the Seleucids, the Parthians remained in Mesopotamia while the region west of the Euphrates was under Roman control. They became wealthy due to the **trade** with luxury items along the Silk Road to China. This northern route contributed to the economic marginalization of southern Mesopotamia.

The Parthians established a new capital in Mesopotamia, Ctesiphon on the **Tigris**, which was destroyed by Trajan in A.D. 116. Thereafter, their power declined, and they were replaced by the **Sassanians** in A.D. 224.

PASTORALISTS. Nomadic or seminomadic herders of sheep and goats (in Mesopotamia). *See* NOMADS.

PERSIANS. Peoples speaking an Indo-European **language** who settled in Iran in the second millennium B.C. By the beginning of the first millennium, they spread westward to the Zagros, where they formed their first state, the **Median** kingdom (c. 720–550), with the capital at Ecbatana. After the elimination of **Elam**, they became a powerful force in western Iran, which was instrumental in bringing down the **Neo-Assyrian empire**. The Medes were in turn ousted by another Persian Dynasty, that of the **Achaemenids** (640–88). After the conquest of **Alexander the Great** and the subsequent rule of the **Seleucids** over Iran, new Persian polities formed, first the **Parthians** with the Arsacid Dynasty, and then the **Sassanians** (A.D. 224–642).

POTTERY. Deposits of pottery remains constitute the bulk of archaeological *tells* of Mesopotamia. The term *pottery* differentiates clay vessels and other household objects from figurines (called *terracotta*). The different shapes, decoration, burnishing, glazes, and sizes of pottery, the result of changes in taste and technology, furnish valuable and often vital clues to the relative dating of the object and its context. The technique of pottery sequences was pioneered by the archaeologist Flinders Petrie in the 1890s in Palestine. It is particularly useful for prehistoric periods, but pottery sequences are also relevant in later periods.

Pottery was invented in the **Neolithic period** about 7000 B.C. Such early pottery was made in a slab construction method and only lightly fired. The earliest known kiln comes form Yarim Tepe and dates from 6000. The most beautifully fashioned, thin-walled, and hand-painted pottery in the Near East dates from the **Chalcolithic period**. Decorated with often centrifugal designs and of elegant shapes, such tableware was in much demand throughout Mesopotamia and seems to have been used for banquets and other special occasions that called for the display of valuables. Coil-made pottery dominated until the invention of the slow wheel, a turntable rotated by hand, which first appeared in Mesopotamia around 4000 B.C. but mainly to fashion coarse, mass-produced jars.

Exquisite pottery became less important in the historical periods; **gold** and other **metals** replaced fired clay in prestige tableware. The fast wheel, used to "throw" pottery, was introduced in the late third millennium B.C., again for mass-produced ware.

Potters often worked together in separate quarters of Mesopotamian **cities**; they could work for a large organization in teams (as in the time of the **Third Dynasty of Ur**) or as private craftsmen.

PRIESTS. Mesopotamian **temples** commanded considerable manpower to work the agricultural estates, the various workshops, **administration**, and general maintenance of buildings and equipment. The service of the cult, the care for the divine statues residing in inner precincts of the temple, the daily offerings, and liturgies also demanded considerable personnel. There was no general distinction between those who worked in the "secular" sector and those who performed "priestly" functions. In fact, a number of sacerdotal functions could be carried out on a part-time basis (so-called prebends). Those who had any contact with the sacred precincts of the temple had to ensure that they were in a state of ritual purity, attained by ablutions as well as by the incantation of purificatory formulas.

Some categories of priests, especially those with intimate contact with divine statues, had to fulfill specific physical, ethical, and psychological requirements to qualify for the profession. Like **scribes**, certain high-status categories of priests belonged to families where the office passed from father to son. Literacy was mandatory for most cult specialists who had to be knowledgeable in liturgical procedures, chants, and prayers. Highly trained staff performed exorcistic and healing rituals, solicited and interpreted omens, and advised the king. Some classes of temple personnel wore distinguishing clothes, hats, and other accoutrements that are depicted on **cylinder seals** or in **Assyrian** reliefs. Ritual nudity, as shown on Early Dynastic plaques, was discontinued after the **Akkadian period**.

The daily services included musicians, singers, cult performers, and dancers, both male and female.

A great number and variety of professional titles for temple personnel has been preserved in the administrative records as well as in lexical lists, but it is not always clear which function was implied at any given period. The highest office in the administrative hierarchy during the **Uruk period** was that of the *EN*. In the Predynastic period, this was used as the title of the city ruler, especially at **Ur**; in later times, however, it denoted purely cultic responsibility. Great prestige was given to the office of the female *EN* (Akkadian *entu*) who served the moon god (*see* NANNAR) at Ur and who was often of royal blood. During the **Old Babylonian period**, the institution of the *naditu* women flourished, who lived in a cloisterlike enclosure. The exact function of many other female cult specialists who appear in administrative, omen, and literary texts remains obscure.

– R –

RIM-SIN I (reigned 1822–1763 B.C.). **Babylonian** king of **Larsa**. In the aftermath of the collapse of the **Third Dynasty of Ur**, it was at first the **city** of **Isin** that won supremacy in Mesopotamia. Rim-Sin fought long and hard to challenge Isin's position from his own power base at Larsa. He defeated a coalition of other cities led by the king of **Uruk**, and in his 13th year (1796), he captured Isin, which left him in control over the whole of southern Babylonia (the north was more fragmented into rival polities, such as the kingdom of **Babylon**).

Rim-Sin was thus one of the most powerful rulers in Mesopotamia at this time, and he also enjoyed an unusually long reign of 60 years that allowed him to implement important **administrative** and legal reforms concerning land ownership. His reluctance to join in a pan-Babylonian coalition against **Elam** resulted in **Hammurabi**'s anger and attack on Larsa in 1764. He took Rim-Sin prisoner to Babylon where he presumably died.

RIMUSH (reigned c. 2284–2276 B.C.). King of **Akkad**, son and successor of **Sargon of Akkad**. According to his own inscriptions he had to repress widespread revolts in the **Sumerian** cities at the beginning of his reign. He also campaigned against **Elam**, from where he returned with rich booty. He only stayed on the throne for nine years and was replaced (perhaps violently) by his brother **Manishtusu**.

ROYAL INSCRIPTIONS. Mesopotamian kings since the **Early Dynastic period** were keen to transmit records of their achievements for posterity. They furnish some of the most important sources for Mesopotamian history. The earliest examples of such texts consist only of a few lines to record the name and title of the king, perhaps with a mention of his most important conquest. They are generally couched in the first-person singular as personal testimony.

Since it was a royal responsibility to repair **city** walls and **temple** buildings, the kings commemorated such activities on **building inscriptions** that were deposited within the architectural structure of the edifice. The royal inscriptions of kings from the **Akkad Dynasty** were engraved on stone monuments and set up in the courtyard of the **Enlil** temple at **Nippur**. Some of them were written in both **Sumerian** and **Akkadian** and enumerate the campaigns of the kings, as well as their building activities, and they include lengthy references to the **gods** of **Sumer** and **Akkad**, who were said to have entrusted **kingship** to the rulers.

Such ideologically weighted passages were already formulated by some Early Dynastic rulers. The royal inscriptions of the Akkad kings were studied by later generations of **scribes**, and extant examples are mainly **Old Babylonian** copies of the originals. They were to serve as models and inspiration for future generations of scribes who had to compose royal inscriptions.

Not all such texts became part of the scribal tradition. The beautifully worded inscriptions of **Gudea**, the ruler of **Lagash**, for instance, were deposited in the temples of **Girsu** and left there. The kings of the **Third Dynasty of Ur** preferred a different style in which the king was addressed in the third person. Such texts are known as "royal hymns."

The **Assyrian** kings, too, gave a special form to the genre and developed **annals** that were royal inscriptions composed annually to record the mainly military achievements of the monarchs. Annals are also written in the first person. Other Assyrian royal inscriptions were engraved on **palace** wall reliefs to accompany the visual representations. They deal not only with conquest but also with civic projects, such as the building of aqueducts, or the royal hunt. The Assyrian inscriptions abound in detail and observations and can comprise hundreds of lines of texts.

The **Neo-Babylonian** examples concentrate on the kings' architectural projects, such as the works in **Babylon** under **Nebuchadrezzar II** or at **Harran** by **Nabonidus**.

– S –

SAMSU-ILUNA (reigned 1749–1712 B.C.). **Babylonian** king of the **First Dynasty of Babylon**, son and successor of **Hammurabi**. He managed to hold together the substantial kingdom created by his father despite mounting internal and external pressures. In his ninth year, he had to do battle against the **Kassites** and also faced a general revolt led by the king of **Larsa**, Rimush II, whom he defeated. Otherwise, the country enjoyed a measure of stability, as the many **administrative** and legal tablets from his 38-year reign document.

SARGON II (reigned 721–705 B.C.). **Assyrian** king who acceded to the throne in unclear circumstances after the death of Shalmaneser V. His succession was not uncontested, though he was backed by the citizens of **Assur**. There were also rebellions from **Assyria**'s vassals, and in 720 Sargon faced a coalition of Syrian contingents at Qarqar, which he defeated. He then marched south toward the Egyptian border where he stationed a garrison at Gaza. He was less successful in **Babylonia** where the Assyrian **army** was beaten by the **Elamite** allies.

Sargon's northern campaigns against **Urartu** and the Mushki (i.e., the Phrygians under their king Midas) took up several years. Midas, who had been accused of fomenting rebellions against Assyria, was forced to a peace treaty, and the Urartians were beaten in battle. Sargon also sacked the **city** of Musasir, as the wall reliefs in the **palace** of his new city, **Dur-Sharruken** (Sargon's Fort), illustrate.

Sargon could then concentrate on sorting out Babylonia; he chased **Merodach-baladan** into exile and assumed direct rule over the country. Sargon died on another campaign in Anatolia. His grandiose new foundation "Sargon's Fort" was abandoned by his successors.

SARGONIDS. The **Assyrian** Dynasty founded by **Sargon II** in 721 B.C., which also included his son **Sennacherib**, his grandson **Esarhaddon**, and **Ashurbanipal**.

SARGON OF AKKAD (reigned c. 2340–c. 2284 B.C.). King and founder of the **Akkadian Dynasty**. Sargon became the subject of a whole variety of **cuneiform** texts where he is generally portrayed as an exemplary ruler. He was described as destined by the **gods** (especially **Ishtar**) to conquer the "four corners of the universe" and presiding over peace and prosperity. Some of these accounts also credit him with a mysterious birth (by a priestess) and a miraculous Moses-like rescue from abandonment in a basket in the river. He was said to have journeyed very far and to have settled disputes in Anatolia. Much of this is fictional, but even the evidence of his **royal inscriptions**, which were copied in the **Old Babylonian period**, is confusing, and the chronology of events referred to in his royal inscriptions remains problematic.

It appears that Sargon began his career as a courtier of King Ur-Zababa of in **Kish**. His rise to power was triggered by his victory over **Lugalzagesi** of **Uruk**. He then gained control over all the other **Sumerian cities** but based himself at **Akkad**, presumably a new foundation. He always called himself "king of Akkad." During his long reign, he claims to have led various campaigns abroad: He subdued **Elam** to the east and moved westward, conquering **Mari** and other cities in Upper Mesopotamia and southern Anatolia. Sargon promoted the use of the Semitic **language Akkadian** in his inscriptions. His daughter **Enheduanna** was appointed **priestess** of the moon god at **Ur**.

SASSANIAN DYNASTY (A.D. 224–651). A **Persian** dynasty named after an ancestral figure called Sasan. King Ardashir I (reigned A.D. 224–241) founded a new, sometimes called Neo-Persian empire, after he had defeated Artabanus V, the **Parthian** king of the Arsacid Dynasty in 224. His territory stretched from the **Euphrates** to the Indus River. The Sassanians revitalized what they considered to have been the cultural traditions of the **Achaemenid Dynasty** to formulate a truly Persian national identity.

Zoroastrianism was the official religion, and the fire cult was vigorously promoted. Ardashir and later his son, Shapur I (reigned A.D. 241–272), also attacked Roman possessions in Armenia, Anatolia, and Syria, but following the counterattacks, they had to be content with the same western frontier as that of the Arsacid Empire, and their only non-Iranian province remained the district of the **Tigris** and Euphrates as far as the Mesopotamian desert, while the west and the north remained under Roman control. Under their rule, southern Mesopotamia became a peripheral outpost, marginalized because of border conflicts with Rome and later Byzantium, and with a dwindling population.

The Sassanian royal house was beset by internal rivalries resulting in intrigues and assassinations. The long struggle against Rome had exhausted the treasury and the vitality of the dynasty. The final blow came from the **Arabs**. The battle of Kadisiya in A.D. 637 brought victory to the Islamic Arabs and marked the end of the last Zoroastrian dynasty in Iran.

SCRIBES. Since the invention of **writing** in the late fourth millennium B.C., scribes were instrumental in the development of the **administrative** structures that made Mesopotamian **cities** economically competitive. Literate bureaucrats became a mainstay of Mesopotamian institutions, forming a kind of civil service sector that operated in large **temple** estates, the **palace**, and, to a lesser extent, for the private businesses. Centralized states, such as the **Third Dynasty of Ur** or the **Neo-Assyrian Empire**, were particularly reliant on their services.

One of their main responsibilities was accounting. Scribes had to keep track of daily expenditure (on rations for the laborers, equipment, materials, etc.), tally the income from diverse sources, and keep annual records that showed the balance of each account. In **Assyria**, scribes also accompanied the **army** on campaign; several reliefs show how they counted severed heads or hands for the battle statistics or itemized **tribute** payments. Scribes formed part of the personnel within a hierarchically structured labor organization. They underwent more or less lengthy training, and relatively few assumed positions of authority.

Apart from the bureaucratic function, scribes were concerned with the classification of knowledge. They composed lists of signs and lexical lists that constitute an attempt to provide reference works for scribal training and at the same time codify the material and intellectual repertoire of Mesopotamian civilization. They were also concerned to preserve important oral traditions, such as myths, proverbs, songs, and esoteric wisdom. As such, scribes became guardians of a literary tradition that was accorded the value of antiquity and the weight of authority. This gave the highly trained scribes considerable influence at court, for instance, since they were able to underpin ideological changes or, indeed, to resist them. A number of literary works are now thought to have been inspired by political motives of the time (*see* CREATION MYTHS; ROYAL INSCRIPTIONS).

As an intellectual elite Mesopotamian, a scribe had the most leverage in connection with esoteric knowledge, such as divination (*see* OMENS), **magic**, and **astrology/ astronomy**. This is particularly evident in the late **Neo-Assyrian** Empire.

In the late period, the prestige of scribes seems to have been higher than before. Although at the time of the Third Dynasty of Ur, King **Shulgi** had boasted of having a solid scribal education, as did **Ashurbanipal** much later, literacy was not a requirement for the exercise of **kingship**. While in previous centuries most scribes, except for the purposes of bureaucratic responsibility, remained anonymous, from the **Neo-Babylonian period** onward, scribes wrote their names and pedigree on the tablets they copied or composed. From such "colophons," it appears that many came from scribal families who had practiced the arts of writing for generations. One of the most famous of these scribal ancestors was **Sin-leqqe-unninni**, the reputed author of the **Gilgamesh epic**.

SEALAND (Babylonian *mar tamtim*). The name for the southern-most region of **Babylonia**, including the extensive marshlands of the gulf. The region was important for its access to the sea and seaborne **trade** and the marshes were a well-known refuge for political adversaries. In the first millennium B.C., the Sealand was controlled by the **Chaldean** tribes.

SEALAND DYNASTIES. There were two: (1) The first Dynasty of the Sealand was established during the lifetime of **Samsu-iluna** (reigned 1749–1712 B.C.) in the **Old Babylonian period** to the detriment of **Babylonia**'s sea **trade**; little is known about this dynasty, which was founded by Iluma-ilum. (2) The Second Sealand Dynasty lasted from

1026 to 1006 B.C. and was founded by Simbar-Shipak (reigned 1026–1010). He controlled much the same area as the **Second Dynasty of Isin** and was recognized as a legitimate king in **Babylon**. After his reign, rulers followed each other in quick succession due to **palace** intrigues.

SECOND DYNASTY OF ISIN (1155–1027 B.C.). After the **Elamite** attacks on **Babylonia**, which brought the **Kassite Dynasty** to an end, the center of power shifted southward again where a new dynasty was founded by Marduk-kabit-ahheshu in c.1155 at **Isin**. There were 11 kings altogether, though only some of them are known from contemporary sources. The most outstanding ruler was **Nebuchadrezzar I** (c. 1126–c. 1105), who defeated **Elam** and returned the abducted statues of **Marduk** and his consort Sarpanitum. Another successful and long-reigning king was **Marduk-nadin-ahhe** (reigned 1100–1083 B.C.), a contemporary of the **Assyrian** king **Tiglath-pileser I**, although the end of his reign was overshadowed by famine and unrest caused by intensified **tribal** immigration by the **Arameans**. This was to remain a source of instability until the demise of the Second Dynasty of Isin during the time of its last king, Nabu-shumu-libur (reigned 1034–1027).

SELEUCID DYNASTY (305–141 B.C.). Dynasty founded by **Seleucus I Nicator**, who was one of the generals in the **army** of **Alexander the Great**. In the struggles over the succession to Alexander's empire, Seleucus obtained most of the Asiatic territories, all of Persia, Bactria, and Mesopotamia, and he introduced a new dating system in **Babylonia** that began on 3 April 311. Greek became the **language** of **administration**. The capital was a new foundation, Seleucia-on-the-Tigris. He and all of his successors were engaged in constant, often violent, confrontations with the Ptolemies, another Macedonian dynasty who ruled from Egypt. The object of these fights were the fertile and wealthy regions in Syria and Palestine. The Seleucids lost Mesopotamia to the **Parthians** in 141 B.C.

SELEUCUS I NICATOR (reigned 305–281 B.C.). Macedonian general who accompanied **Alexander the Great** on his campaign to India. After Alexander's death in 321, he assumed the office of regent after the murder of Perdiccas. When the empire was partitioned, he became satrap of **Babylonia**. He was dislodged by **Antigonus**, fled to Egypt to Ptolemy I, and eventually returned to **Babylon** after 315. He then campaigned to gain control over the Iranian provinces. His coronation as king of Babylonia was hotly contested by Antigonus, who continued to raid and devastate the country, but he was finally defeated in 301 at Ipsus in Syria.

Seleucus now controlled the former satrapy of Syria and half of Anatolia and thus commanded an empire of almost the size of Alexander's (with the exception of Egypt). He founded several new cities, including the new capital Seleucia-on-the-Tigris, initiated a new dating system and the era of the **Seleucids**, made Greek the official **language**, and promoted Hellenistic culture in Mesopotamia.

SEMIRAMIS (Assyrian Sammu-ramat). **Assyrian** queen, wife of **Shamshi-Adad V** (reigned 823–811 B.C.), mother of **Adad-nirari III**. This **woman** achieved remarkable fame and power in her lifetime and beyond. According to contemporary records, she had considerable influence at the Assyrian court; she was able to erect her own inscribed monuments in the ceremonial center of **Assur**. She even accompanied her husband on a military campaign, a most unusual undertaking for an Assyrian queen. After the death of Shamshi-Adad, she assumed the office of regent for five years while Adad-nirari was a minor.

Semiramis became the subject of legendary tales, and **Herodotus** credits her with building the embankments in **Babylon**. According to Diodorus Siculus, she was semidivine, nourished as an infant by doves, of exceptional beauty, and became the wife of the Assyrian king Ninus. She then had the most extraordinary career, founding Babylon and a world empire that stretched from Egypt to India, to return eventually to **Nineveh**, where she changed into a dove, having handed her empire to her son Ninyas.

SENNACHERIB (Assyrian Sin-ahhe-eriba) (reigned 704–681 B.C.). Assyrian king. Despite the plentiful and varied sources for his reign, the sequence of events is still disputed. Sennacherib, whose name ("Sin has compensated [for dead] brothers") suggests that he was not a first-born, was groomed for royal succession by his father **Sargon II**, and was entrusted with **administrative** duties from an early age. Even so, his succession after Sargon's sudden death on campaign was not unproblematic and unleashed a series of revolts. The Egyptian pharaoh incited the kings of Sidon, Ascalon, and Judah to rebel against Assyrian rule, an uprising that was put down by Sennacherib's general.

Merodach-baladan had meanwhile returned to **Babylon** and assembled a large force of **Chaldean**, **Aramean**, **Arab**, and **Elamite** troops. Sennacherib marched to **Babylonia**, defeated the coalition, appointed a new ruler, Bel-ibni, and led a punitive campaign against the **Bit-Yakin** tribe in the marshes. He then replaced the unreliable Bel-ibni with his own son and continued to rout the southern tribes with the help of a fleet of Phoenician-built ships he had transported by land and river to the Persian Gulf.

While he was busily engaged in the south, the Elamites invaded northern Babylonia and kidnapped his son, the regent in Babylon. This led to another series of clashes between Elamite **Babylonian** coalitions and the Assyrians, while the son of his old foe Merodach-baladan had assumed the throne of Babylon. Sennacherib set siege to the **city**, which held out for 15 months, and vented his fury on the "holy city." This deed was not only abhorred as sacrilege by the Babylonians but also caused much consternation in Assyria where the **gods** of Babylon were held in high esteem.

Sennacherib is also remembered for his ambitious building program at **Nineveh**, which he made into his capital. He was very interested in engineering and personally supervised the construction of aqueducts and transport of the colossal human-headed bulls that guarded the **palace** gates. He was also very fond of plants and collected a great variety of species from all over the empire to grace the gardens of Nineveh. He died a violent death, perhaps at the hand of one of his own sons.

SHALMANESER III (reigned 858–824 B.C.). **Assyrian** king, son and successor of **Ashurnasirpal II**. Having inherited the vast empire his father had built, he was hard-pressed to maintain Assyrian hegemony in the face of widespread revolts. He relied on diplomacy coupled with the show of force when deemed necessary and thus managed to expand Assyrian influence even further.

The most persistent problems were in Syria. Here a coalition of local rulers was formed who assembled their troops for a violent confrontation with Assyrian forces. This alliance was commanded by the leader of the influential **tribe** Bit-Adini. Shalmaneser defeated them, and Bit-Adini became an Assyrian province.

Some time later, though, he faced a much more serious contingent of rebellious polities led by the kings of Hamath and Damascus. Here, too, he claimed victory in a great battle at Qarqar on the Orontes in 853, but the coalition was to continue its resistance activities for some years after that.

Shalmaneser was on friendly terms with **Babylonia** and supported its king Marduk-zakir-shumi when he faced a rebellion by his own brother. Shalmaneser used the opportunity to show his strength to the **Aramean** and **Chaldean** tribes and made a tour of the major **Babylonian temples**. He also campaigned in Anatolia, especially against **Urartu**. In his capital **Kalhu**, he built temples, a **ziggurat**, and a large fortress.

SHAMASH. Babylonian sun **god**. According to the personal names from the **Akkad** period, the sun deity, as in other Semitic cultures, may have originally been female. In Mesopotamia, Shamash became identified with the **Sumerian** sun god **Utu**, whose shrine was at **Larsa**.

In the **Old Babylonian period**, Shamash came to be seen as the supreme arbiter of justice—**Hammurabi** on the stele with his **law** code is seen to receive the symbols of **kingship** from the sun god. At this time, the main sanctuary of the sun god was at **Sippar**, where he resided in the Ebabbar, the "shining house," to the detriment of the temple at Larsa.

In the Babylonian hymns and prayers, Shamash is not only invoked to safeguard the rights of individuals but to guard all those on a journey, such as merchants and soldiers, and to combat evil in the many apotropaic and curative rituals and incantations.

The wife of Shamash was Aya, who was the patron of a special category of cloistered (*naditu*) **women** during the Old Babylonian period.

SHAMASH-SHUMA-UKIN (reigned 667–648 B.C.). **Assyrian** king of **Babylon**. He was the eldest son of King **Esarhaddon** of Assyria, who had appointed his younger son, **Ashurbanipal**, to be his successor while he destined Shamash-shuma-ukin to rule Babylon. If this arrangement was meant to secure brotherly unity between the two countries, it did not work out this way. Ashurbanipal's position was much stronger, and he treated his older brother like any other vassal ruler, making him swear an **oath** of allegiance and maintaining a policy of noninterference as long as there was no trouble.

Shamash-shuma-ukin was no doubt under pressure from the citizens of Babylon to push for a speedy return of the divine statues that his grandfather **Sennacherib** had removed from their sanctuaries, but Ashurbanipal prevaricated. Neither did he come to punish the raids by **nomadic tribes** that Babylonia suffered at this time.

Shamash-shuma-ukin decided to find support elsewhere and sought allies among **Arab** and **Chaldean** tribes and from **Elam**. Babylonia became split into a pro-Assyrian faction, which comprised the old **cities** in the south and the rebellious party led by the Chaldeans. Although Ashurbanipal seems to have been reluctant to intervene with arms, clashes between Assyrian and rebel forces went on for several years. The **Babylonian** side was weakened by mutiny among the Elamite troops and by the capture of the Chaldean leader Nabu-bel-shumati. Ashurbanipal then brought down his full force and set siege to Babylon, which was taken after two years, having caused terrible deprivation and suffering to the inhabitants. Shamash-shuma-ukin probably died in the final assault in his **palace**.

The conflict between the brothers and the renewed destruction of Babylon did much to incite hatred against Assyria.

SHAMSHI-ADAD I (reigned 1813–1781 B.C.). **Amorite** king of **Assyria**, who usurped the throne of **Assur**. Shamshi-Adad built up a powerful kingdom that stretched from the foothills of the Zagros to the valleys of the Habur and Balik in Syria and included much of northern **Babylonia**. He captured **Mari**, where he put one of his sons in charge; the **archives** in the Mari palace furnish much detail about Shamshi-Adad's maneuvers. Like his younger contemporary, **Hammurabi** at **Babylon**, he was one of those Amorite rulers who were very skillful in the use of diplomacy and the making of alliances, backed up by a shrewd and decisive deployment of force. Unlike Hammurabi, who inherited and built up a well-functioning **administrative** apparatus, Shamshi-Adad, despite employing Babylonian **scribes**, relied primarily on his personal connections and judgment. It was therefore not surprising that the large territory he had held together disintegrated rapidly after his death.

SHAMSHI-ADAD V (reigned 823–811 B.C.). **Assyrian** king. He fought for four years to sustain his succession after the death of his father **Shalmaneser III**. He was perhaps even helped in this by the king of **Babylon**, Marduk-zakir-shumi. When there were problems in Babylon after the death of his ally, Shamshi-Adad responded in a particularly brutal way: He invaded **Babylonia** and ravaged the countryside, having taken the new king Marduk-balassu-iqbi to **Nineveh**, where he was flayed.

SHAR-KALI-SHARRI (reigned c. 2223–2198 B.C.). **Akkadian** king, son of **Naram-Sin**. According to the surviving inscriptions from his reign, Shar-kali-sharri devoted much of his time to defending the Akkadian empire from external and internal threat. Soon after his accession, he had to drive back the **Elamites** who had invaded the region north of **Akkad** and besieged the town of Akshak. Elam, though repulsed from Akkad, continued to grow in strength and influence. The **Gutians** also conducted persistent raids into the valleys of the **Tigris**, which abated after Shar-kali-sharri managed to capture their king Asharlag. In the west, he campaigned against the **Amorites** and pushed them back behind Jebel Bisri. His most important building project was the reconstruction of the **temple** of **Enlil** at **Nippur**.

Shar-kali-sharri abandoned the use of the divine determinative that his father Naram-Sin had introduced. Despite his efforts and successful military campaigns, he was not able to protect his state from disintegration, and after his death, written sources dried up in a time of increased anarchy and confusion.

SHULGI (reigned c. 2094–c. 2047 B.C.). **Sumerian** king of the **Third Dynasty of Ur**. He was the second king of this dynasty founded by his father **Ur-Nammu** and concentrated on setting up a solid framework for the efficient and unified **administration** as well as defense of a centralized state that encompassed all of Mesopotamia. He created a standing **army** that was able to respond rapidly to any foreign threat and a host of bureaucrats to supervise the implementation of new **tax** regulations, as well as the state-owned and -managed production and distribution of **agricultural** and artisanal goods.

Scribal training had to be intensified to meet the demand for literate personnel. All records were written in Sumerian. Shulgi also introduced a new official calendar to replace the many different, local systems of reckoning time. There were also standardized **weights and measures**. **Temple** estates also came under the supervision of state-appointed officials.

To legitimize such radical reforms, which curtailed the economic independence of the Sumerian **cities** to an unprecedented degree, Shulgi elevated **kingship** to a divine office and, like in the times of **Naram-Sin** of **Akkad**, wrote his name with the divine determinative and ordered a cult of his statues. He was enthusiastically lauded by royal hymns, which describe his intimate relations with the great gods of **Sumer** (he was the "brother" of the sun god, and the "husband" of **Inanna**), as well as physical and intellectual qualities.

In his foreign policy, Shulgi used diplomacy (especially dynastic **marriages**) as well as military campaigns. His greatest success was the conquest of Anshan (in western Iran), which became part of his empire. Shulgi may have died a violent death in a **palace** revolt; he was succeeded by his son **Amar-Sin**.

SHURUPPAK (modern Fara). **Sumerian city** in southern Mesopotamia. It was inhabited from the **Jemdet-Nasr period** (c. 3000 B.C.) until the end of the **Third Dynasty of Ur** (c. 2000). The city knew its greatest extent (some 200 hectares) in the **Early Dynastic period**. From this time of Early Dynastic III (mid–third millennium) come a large quantity of **administrative** tablets with details about extensive land management involving thousands of workers, as well as literary works and lexical tables. There is also evidence of relationships and collaborative projects with other Sumerian cities, such as **Uruk**, Adab, **Nippur**, and **Lagash**. In the Sumerian tradition, Shuruppak was the home of the flood hero Utnapishtim.

SHUTRUK-NAHHUNTE I (reigned c. 1185–1155 B.C.). **Elamite** king, probably the founder of a dynasty known as the Shutrukides. Having consolidated his rule over **Elam**, he launched a carefully prepared attack against **Babylonia**. He took **Sippar**, **Kish**, and **Babylon**, deposed the last **Kassite** king Zababa-shum-iddina, and imposed heavy **tribute** on the population. He returned to Elam with enormous booty, which included several ancient monuments, such as the stele with **Hammurabi**'s **laws** and statues of **Akkadian** kings. In Babylon, he appointed his own son Kudur-Nahhunte as king.

SILVER. Since there were no metal deposits in Mesopotamia it had to be imported from outside. The most important sources were in Anatolia, in Cappadocia and the Taurus Mountains, referred to as the "silver mountains." In Mesopotamia, silver was used for luxury objects and jewelry since the **Uruk** period and became a standard of value and medium of exchange in the late third millennium B.C. It could be fashioned into rings, rods, or coils and had to be weighed for each transaction. Coins were only introduced in the late first millennium.

SIN. **Akkadian** name of the moon **god** whom the **Sumerians** called Suen or **Nannar**. In writing this was expressed by the number 30, the days of the lunar month. He was also addressed as the "fruit that renews itself" (after the waning of the moon) and the "horned bull." Like Nanna, he was closely associated with the fertility of cattle but also of **women**, as his epithet "midwife" suggests.

Apart from the ancient moon sanctuary at **Ur**, there was an important **temple** of Sin at **Harran**.

Although Sin was always popular throughout Mesopotamian history, as the many personal names composed with Sin prove, he never assumed the status of **Enlil** or **Marduk**, except for the time when the **Babylonian** king **Nabonidus** heavily promoted his cult in the sixth century B.C.

SIN-LEQQE-UNNINNI. **Babylonian** master **scribe** and incantation priest in the **Kassite period**. In the Mesopotamian scribal tradition, he is reputed as the author of the **Gilgamesh epic**.

SIPPAR (modern Abu Habbah and Tell ed-Der). **Babylonian city** on the river **Euphrates**. The site was occupied since the **Uruk** period in the fourth millennium B.C. and was not abandoned before the **Parthian period,** in the second century A.D. Most of the excavated monuments date from the **Old Babylonian** and **Neo-Babylonian periods**. Sippar was in fact composed of two towns that eventually grew together. One was dominated by the **temple** of a goddess called Anunnitum, the other by the larger sanctuary of the sun god **Shamash**.

Apart from a single reign of an antediluvian king (according to the **Sumerian King List**), Sippar was never the seat of a dynasty. Its main prestige derived from the cult of the sun god and the commercial activities, which were favored by the location of the city in central **Babylonia**, along the navigable Euphrates, and in close proximity also to the **Tigris**. Merchants of Sippar traveled north and westward to Anatolia and Syria, as well as east to Iran. Sippar, like **Nippur** and **Babylon**, was one of the privileged cities that enjoyed special **tax** status and whose citizens were exempt from conscription.

Most of the written documentation from the Old Babylonian period was found in the "cloister" of the so-called *naditu* **women,** who were placed there by their fathers in order to "pray continuously" but who were also free to invest their shares of paternal property. The tablets from the Neo-Babylonian period come mainly from the Shamash temple. An important library has recently been discovered by Iraqi archaeologists.

SLAVERY. In Mesopotamia, slaves were mainly used in a domestic context and not in large-scale public projects as in the Roman Empire. The **cuneiform** sign for slave denotes a person "from the mountains," which means a foreigner.

They could be prisoners of war, captured on campaigns against the peoples on the periphery of Mesopotamia, where skirmishes between the **nomadic** tribal populations and the sedentary people were often used as a pretext by Mesopotamian rulers to conduct military expeditions that were little more than slave raids. The men and **women** thus captured could be sold or distributed as personal gifts to individual retainers.

There was also commercial slavery, with slave markets in the major **cities,** although it is not clear how these slaves were procured in the first place.

Once acquired, slaves were marked with a special tonsure and skin mark, and they became the property of their owner, to be passed on to his heirs, hired out, or sold as a chattel (*see* INHERITANCE). Any children of slaves were also slaves.

Only wealthy households could afford to have slaves, and only very affluent families had more than one or two. Male slaves worked in all kinds of capacities, in the fields or workshops; they could also be trained as **scribes** and work as secretaries and clerks. Any profit they managed to make was theirs to invest, and there is evidence that some wealthy businessmen had started out as slaves.

The position of female slaves was slightly different; they worked in the house, fields, or textile workshops, but they were also used as concubines—proverbs warn against the disruptive influence of a pretty slave girl in the house. In the **Old Babylonian period**, a barren woman could select a slave girl to bear her husband children on her behalf who were then treated as her own offspring. Slaves could be officially freed or adopted into a family.

Not all slaves were foreigners or the descendants of captured persons. It was possible for Mesopotamian citizens to sell their children into slavery and to enslave themselves and/or their wives to their debtors. The duration of their bondage was in proportion to their debt and ended when the amount originally owing had been earned in labor. When the pressures of usurious loans were too high and debt slavery became too widespread (as in the late Old Babylonian period), kings could decree amnesties to release people from debt slavery.

SUMER. Modern name for the country in southern **Babylonia** (south of **Nippur**) that the Sumerians called *kengi*. The **Akkadian** inscriptions speak of Sumer (*šumerum*) and (the northern) **Akkad** as constituent of the "country." Although Sumer was never a coherent political unit, it was linked by cultural and economic practices and norms and the acceptance of urbanism. Already in the fourth millennium B.C. (**Uruk period**), such links can be surmised from the way the **city** seals appear in **administrative** texts and lists.

In the **Early Dynastic period**, there was great rivalry between individual cities and competition over water rights that led to armed clashes. On the other hand, there is also evidence of collective action, which could mobilize large numbers of people in common tasks.

SUMERIAN. Language spoken in southern Mesopotamia until the beginning of the second millennium B.C. It was expressed in writing since the

Early Dynastic period (earlier forms of **cuneiform** were not meant to reflect a particular idiom). Sumerian texts were written in the "main dialect" (*emegir*), and a secondary dialect was used for female speakers in the texts (*emesal*). It is not related to any other known languages. Its structure is agglutinative and ergative, and it differs greatly from the Semitic languages (e.g., **Akkadian**) that were current in Mesopotamia since the earliest written records.

Most Sumerian sources date from the late third millennium B.C., the time of the **Third Dynasty of Ur**, when Sumerian was the official language for all documents. From the Early Dynastic period, there are important text collections from Abu-Salabkih and **Shuruppak**. Most of the extant copies of Sumerian literary texts (myths, prayers, hymns, humorous dialogues, fables, proverbs, and **royal inscriptions**) date from the **Old Babylonian period**. Sumerian probably became extinct as a spoken language by the mid–second millennium, but it continued to be transmitted in writing as part of advanced **scribal** training until the very end of cuneiform literacy.

SUMERIAN KING LIST. A compilation of dynasties and the names of kings by a **Babylonian** scholar at the time of the **First Dynasty of Isin**. It begins in remote antiquity and the divine institution of **kingship** and ends with the reign of Sin-magir (1827–1817 B.C.). The Sumerian King List chronicles the transfer of hegemony ("kingship") from one **city** to another and thus obscures the reality that several dynasties existed at the same time.

SUPPILULIUMA I (reigned c. 1370–1330 B.C.). **Hittite** king. He was responsible for the expansion of the Hittite Empire into Upper Mesopotamia and Syria. Most important was his defeat of the kingdom of **Mitanni**, previously the most powerful state in this area. He sacked the Mitanni capital, Washshukanni, and appointed the Mitanni crown prince as his vassal ruler. He then asserted his authority over other Syrian states by attacking Aleppo, **Amurru**, and Alalakh, but he conducted a peace treaty with the **Babylonian** king (possibly **Kadashman-Enlil I**), whose daughter he married.

SYNCHRONISTIC HISTORY. This designates a chronicle work from the **Neo-Assyrian period**, written around 800 B.C. during the reign of **Adad-nirari III**. It concerns events after the destruction of **Babylon** by **Sennacherib** and lists **Assyrian** and **Babylonian** relations in two columns so that synchronicities become apparent.

– T –

TAXATION. Compulsory contributions toward public services are a feature of all complex societies. Mesopotamia had two kinds of levies that could be imposed by the main institutional bodies: the **temple**, the state (*see* PALACE), or the **city**. First there were the contributions in labor (corvée duty) or armed service (military duty). Both are well attested since the third millennium B.C. The former could be seen as a legacy of previous social systems where maintenance tasks were performed collectively. Corvée workers were essential for highly labor-intensive jobs such as the clearing and dredging of canals and other irrigation installations, as well as the construction of city walls and public buildings. This workforce was primarily constituted of young men. They also formed the main contingent of fighters in case of military campaigns and for defense (*see* WARFARE).

Taxes in kind levied by temples on their sharecroppers were generally a tenth of the yield ("tithe"). Temples were themselves subject to taxation to the state at times when there was a strong centralized government, as during the time of the **Third Dynasty of Ur**.

That the city ruler could demand payments in **silver** for all kinds of professional activities is made clear in **royal inscriptions** of **Uruinimgina** of **Lagash** from the 24th century B.C. He was at pains to reduce the exorbitant sums paid to officials for divorces, the brewing of **beer**, or the burial of the dead.

In the **Akkad** period, King **Naram-Sin** introduced a country-wide taxation scheme in which contributions were levied on provinces (city-states) and collected at the capital for distribution. Tax was payable on crops, livestock, **trade**, and craft production. Payments in kind and in silver had to be accounted for, stored, and distributed as required. The **administration** of the tax system made considerable demands on the bureaucratic structure of the state. The detailed workings of the system can best be studied in the documents from the time of the Third Dynasty of Ur.

During the **Old Assyrian period**, merchants doing business in Anatolia paid taxes to the city of **Assur** on leaving with their export goods (e.g., 10 percent on the textiles) and on arrival at **Kanesh**, the trade colony, where the tax payments were used for the maintenance of the colony.

In the **Neo-Assyrian Empire**, taxable services extended to any lucrative trade, and there were variable rates for different commodities. Tax collectors could be accompanied by soldiers to enforce people's contributions.

Just as individual kings could invent new taxes and new sources of revenue, they could also reduce the tax burden and exempt temples or cities from payments. Such pronouncements are known from a number of rulers and usually as a reaction to massive rises of insolvency and debt slavery.

TELL. Arabic word that denotes a mound-shaped hill composed of accumulated layers of debris of habitation, partially eroded by the elements.

TEMPLES. Mesopotamian temples combined several important functions. **Cities** were primarily identified by their tutelar deities, and the temples were the houses of the **gods** in a specific place. They provided continuity across time. Rising above the plains, they served as landmarks that could be seen above the low-rise skylines of Mesopotamian cities. In temples the gods were worshipped with sacrifice and rituals, and a large staff looked after the daily services (*see* PRIESTS).

Temples were also very large households and owned extensive tracts of **agricultural** land. They were therefore important economic entities. The yields of the fields and pastures, as well as the products of workshops attached to the temples, were primarily used to "feed the gods." In fact, they also sustained a large number of people attached to the temple as lifelong or temporary personnel.

Temples, much like monasteries in the Middle Ages in Europe, were also centers of learning and **scribal** training. A great number of **cuneiform** tablets were discovered in temple ruins. The forecourts also served to administer justice before the symbols of such deities as **Shamash**, **Marduk**, or **Enlil** (*see* LAWS).

Mesopotamian temples were thus complex institutions that played a vital role in Mesopotamian society since a substantial proportion of citizens either depended on the temples entirely for their livelihood or had regular involvement in their economic and/or cultic activities. Temples were able to give loans at lower rates than the private sector and took certain responsibilities toward the destitute.

The relationship between the state and the temples was marked by mutual dependence. The king derived much of his legitimacy from divine approval that was ratified by the consent of the leading temple authorities (e.g., those of **Assur** or **Babylon**). It was a royal duty to repair and maintain the architectural fabric of the country's major sanctuaries, and they also received a share of wartime booty. In turn, temple estates could be **taxed** and more or less heavily supervised. In some periods major appointments at the top end of temple hierarchies were made by the king.

Temples were sometimes a source of economic and social stability at times when there was political upheaval or during periods of foreign occupation (such as in the **Achaemenid** or **Seleucid** periods).

Architecturally temples can be distinguished from other monumental structures by the elaborately recessed facades and the furnishings in the cult rooms, which included one or several niches for the divine statues with an altar in front of it. The entrance to the cult room was placed in the long wall of the rectangular chamber, with the image placed against the short wall (the "bent axis approach") or, as often in **Assyria**, with the doorway in the short wall opposite the god's statue ("direct axis"). Like **palaces**, the temples were composed of one or several courtyards, subsidiary buildings grouped around them, and they had strong perimeter walls. Major temples could also boast a **ziggurat**. Because the building and restoration of the sacred "house" was a potentially dangerous undertaking due to the possible anger of the disturbed gods, temple architecture was inherently conservative. The solution most frequently adopted was to rebuild directly on the razed walls of the previous building while incorporating the rubble within a platform above which the renewed structure arose. Only when a sanctuary was severely dilapidated could any deviations from the original plan be considered.

All such undertakings, even minor restoration work, could only begin once positive and unanimous **omens** had been received through divination. Due to the practice of interring inscribed pegs or tablets within the brickwork or beneath the wall, we can ascribe successive restoration phases to particular kings who also mentioned their building activities in their **year names** or **annals**.

THIRD DYNASTY OF UR (c. 2112–2004 B.C.). A dynasty founded by **Ur-Nammu** who expelled the **Gutian** kings and united the country in a single state that reached from the Persian Gulf to the region of **Sippar**. His son **Shulgi** (reigned 2094–2047 B.C.) expanded the influence of Ur to include western Iran (the Susiana and Anshan), and his grandson **Amar-Sin** annexed **Assyria**. Shulgi also implemented strong centralization in terms of **administration** and **taxation** and standardized **weights and measures** across his whole domain. The workings of the Ur bureaucracy are well known due to many thousands of tablets that survive from this era.

The Ur empire was threatened by the intensified influx of **Amorite** tribes, and Shu-Sin, the successor and brother of Amar-Suen, built a huge wall in an attempt to stave them off. The Ur state disintegrated during the

reign of **Ibbi-Sin**; his governor **Ishbi-Erra**, installed at **Isin**, declared independence from Ur, and in 2007, the **Elamites** destroyed the capital and
deported the king.

TIGLATH-PILESER I (Assyrian Tukulti-apil-eshara) (reigned 1115–
1076 B.C.). **Assyrian** king of the **Middle Assyrian period**. He was one
of the most important Assyrian kings of this period, not only because of
his wide-ranging military campaigns—especially in Anatolia, where he
subjugated numerous peoples—but because of his building activities, especially at **Assur**, and his encouragement of the **scribal** arts. He established a library at Assur and collected numerous tablets on all kinds of
scholarly subjects. He also issued a legal decree, the so-called Middle
Assyrian **laws**, and laid out parks and gardens stocked with foreign and
native trees and plants.

A persistent problem of Tiglath-pileser's 39-year-long reign was the
Arameans, who caused disruption throughout the Syrian dependencies
of Assyria. There was also a serious conflict with **Babylonia** when **Neb-
uchadrezzar I** began to make incursions into Assyrian-held territory.
Tiglath-pileser retaliated by attacking Babylonian **cities**. He conquered
Babylon and destroyed the **palace** of King Marduk-nadin-ahhe.

TIGLATH-PILESER III (reigned 744–727 B.C.). **Assyrian** king who succeeded Ashur-nirari V, probably in the course of a palace coup at **Kalhu**.
He repressed all resistance to his rule and set about regaining Assyrian
influence in the Near East. He was a tireless campaigner, leading his
powerful **army** for every year but one of his 17-year-long reign. He began by subduing **Aramean** tribes in **Babylonia**, where he garnered general support on a grand tour of the major sanctuaries. He spent the next
few years campaigning in Anatolia, where he punished a disloyal vassal
of Arpad and strengthened his position in the Taurus region by building
fortresses. Most important was a direct attack on the powerful kingdom
of **Urartu**, which left Assyria without their interference.

After these successes in the north, he directed his attention to the west,
marching down the Syrian coast to capture Gaza. Most Syrian rulers
were made to pay **tribute**, but they formed a strong opposition to
Tiglath-pileser, under the leadership of Rakhianu of Damascus, which
took several years and many armed confrontations to subdue.

In the east, Tiglath-pileser stabilized his borders along the Zagros,
forcing the Mannaeans to pay tribute. When a rebellion broke out in
Babylonia, after the death of Nabonassar, he intervened directly by cap-

turing the Babylonia pretender to the throne and declared himself the rightful king of **Babylon**, and he took part in the ceremonies of the Babylonian New Year **festival**.

TIN. Tin was essential for the production of **bronze**, which is an alloy of **copper** and tin. It was always a very precious commodity and, like all metals, had to be imported to Mesopotamia. The first experiments in casing true tin bronze occurred in the late **Uruk period**, as isolated finds from Tepe Gawra document. A flagon discovered at **Kish** and dating from the **Jemdet-Nasr period** (beginning of the third millennium B.C.) is one the earliest tin bronze objects. Finds from the **Ur** cemetery suggest that tin bronze was preferred for metal vessels, while **silver** bronze was used for **weapons**. Actual tin artifacts are so far only known from finds in some early **Old Babylonian** tombs.

No **cuneiform** sources reveal the place of origin of tin, only its sites of distribution. It is likely that tin was mined in eastern Anatolia during the third millennium and exported from there to many distant places. In the early second millennium, however, **Assyrian** merchants brought tin to Anatolia, where it was traded for locally produced silver. It has been suggested that at that time tin came from much farther east, from Afghanistan, perhaps because Anatolian mines had become exhausted. **Mari** also was an important station of distribution in the early **Old Babylonian period**. In the later second and in the first millennium, eastern Anatolia once again supplied tin, as **Hittite** and Assyrian sources seem to indicate.

TRADE. Mesopotamia's primary source of wealth was surplus-producing **agriculture**. But the geophysical conditions of the land made it also singularly devoid of mineral or **metal** resources. Since mountainous regions to the north (Anatolia) and the east (Iran) were inversely endowed, this stimulated active exchanges of goods since the Paleolithic period, when worked and unworked flint and obsidian from Anatolia were distributed widely across the ancient Near East. Due to the considerable mobility of human groups, moving either from camp to camp in a form of transhumance or as **nomads**, raw materials and technologies were disseminated relatively quickly right through the **Chalcolithic** period. Such informal but effective networks of exchange and distribution became considerably more organized and centralized in the **Uruk period**.

The urbanization of Mesopotamia allowed for a concentration and specialization of crafts that relied on regular supplies of raw materials and a skilled workforce. The far-flung outposts of the Uruk culture in western and southwestern Iran and southern Anatolia, with their warehouses and literate personnel, were responsible for the smooth movements of goods in and out of southern Mesopotamia. **Gold, copper, silver**, and minerals such as hematite and lapis lazuli, as well as other hard stones, were worked into jewelry, artifacts used for ritual purposes, and the display of status.

With the emergence of wealthy Mesopotamian city-states in the **Early Dynastic period**, the demand for such commodities rose to new heights, as the fabulous equipment of the so-called Royal Graves at **Ur** show. Of particular importance was gold and lapis lazuli. Two literary texts written in **Sumerian** (from the time of the **Third Dynasty of Ur**) describes how the **city** of Uruk began its trade with the fabled city called Aratta, situated in the Iranian highlands, and the main center of the lapis lazuli import from its source in Badashkan (Afghanistan). The king of Uruk wishes to beautify the **temple** for the city-**goddess Inanna** and asks her, who is also worshipped at Aratta, to induce its ruler to send "gold, silver and lapis lazuli," as well as skilled artisans. In one text, he sends an army to force Aratta into submission; in the other, the two cities begin a form of contest that leads to regular contacts and the delivery of grain to the famished Arattians. Diplomacy and exchange between friendly polities as well as military aggression were employed by Mesopotamian rulers to ensure the supply of precious metals and stones.

In centralized states, such as the **Akkadian Dynasty** or the Third Dynasty of Ur, long-distance trade was supervised and regularized by the state. **Sargon of Akkad** boasts of having ships from **Magan and Meluhha** moor at his capital, and foreign merchants thronged the streets. The government invested in quays, warehouses, tow paths for the river traffic, as well as the maintenance of overland roads and rest houses, as **Shulgi**, the king of Ur, reports. Mercantile activities were duly **taxed** and became an important source of revenue.

As the countries around Mesopotamia also developed their own stratified states and affluent elites, demand grew for luxury items produced in Mesopotamia. These were textile goods (woolen cloth, finished garments, embroidered robes), leather ware, wooden and inlaid furniture, **bronze** weapons, highly crafted metal, and stone artifacts and jewelry. Such products were exported all over the Near East, including Egypt, during the second millennium and then again during the **Neo-Babylonian period**.

While the state could be instrumental in opening trade routes through **warfare** or diplomacy and by maintaining infrastructure, the actual business of import and export was left to merchants who had their own institutional body, the *karum* or "quay." The word derives from the mercantile quarter of Mesopotamian cities, which were usually just beyond the city walls, at a convenient landing place by the main waterway. Each karum had its own regulatory body who would liaise with a state official. There are at present very few texts from any *karum* within Mesopotamia, and the most important source of mercantile documents comes from an **Assyrian** trade colony in Anatolia (*see* KANESH), which flourished in the early second millennium B.C.

The business was run by Assyrians who raised capital at home to buy **tin** from an as yet unclear source outside Anatolia, which they transported to Cappadocia on donkeys, a journey lasting some three months. They also exported Assyrian textiles, which were much in demand. In return they imported silver. The **cuneiform** tablets detail the **administrative** organization of the *karum*, the initial investments, profits, and expenses incurred for transport, gifts, and taxes (which had to be paid at **Assur** and at the local **palace** in Anatolia).

The volume of trade and the trade routes at any given time depended on a variety of factors, such as internal and external political stability, economic prosperity, and competition over primary resource areas. It fell markedly during the difficult centuries of tribal unrest and political upheaval between the 12th and the 9th century B.C. but flourished in the early **Old Babylonian period**, the mid-**Kassite period**, and during the **Neo-Assyrian** and Neo-Babylonian imperial expansion.

Within Mesopotamia, the rivers and canals were the most important means of transporting bulk items as well as passengers. Cities on the **Euphrates**, such as **Sippar**, **Mari**, or **Babylon**, had access to Syria and the Mediterranean in the west, importing wine, aromatics, ivory, and copper from Cyprus. Those on the **Tigris** and its sidearms (**Nineveh**, Assur, Esnunna) were better placed for the eastern and northern highlands and their resources in silver and precious stones.

Seaborne shipping from the Persian Gulf went eastward to the mouth of the Indus and westward to the Arabian Peninsula and the Sudanese coast, bringing gold, precious stones, and pearls, known as "fish-eyes." The southern city of Ur was for a long time the most active trade city, due to its proximity to the gulf. Maritime trade only declined when the **Parthians** blocked access to the sea to encourage the northern east-west link, later known as the Silk Road.

The domestication of the **camel** in the late second millennium B.C. opened up trade traffic across the Arabian Desert, especially for the incense and aromatics export.

TRIBUTE. Tribute is the enforced delivery of goods, services, or people imposed on a country or region after a military defeat. In contrast to booty and plunder, which is amassed by soldiers during **warfare**, tribute payments are meant to be maintained over a period of time, usually as long as the victorious country is able to assert its power. They serve to acknowledge the superiority and hegemony of the victor.

The earliest evidence for this practice in Mesopotamia dates from the first emergence of a centralized state during the **Akkad** period. **Naram-Sin** (reigned c. 2260–2224 B.C.) claims to have received tribute from the rulers of Subartu (later **Assyria**) and other unspecified "highlands," but in Mesopotamia such practices were not very common until the imperial expansion of Assyria in the late second and first millennium.

The Assyrians had a system of provinces and vassal states. While provinces were **taxed** by Assyrian officials, vassal kings had to raise the equivalent contribution as rent for their thrones and raise it from their people. The Assyrian **administration** at the capital kept careful watch over the regularity and extent of these payments. Refusal or inability to deliver was punished by retributive military action.

TUKULTI-NINURTA I (reigned 1244–1208 B.C.). **Assyrian** king of the **Middle Assyrian period**. He was one of the most famous Assyrian soldier kings who campaigned incessantly to maintain Assyrian possessions and influence. He reacted with spectacular cruelty to any sign of revolt and crushed a coalition of kings in Anatolia, the so-called Nairi. He subdued the Zagros region to the east and spread terror in the Van region.

In **Babylonia**, he took the **Kassite** king Kashtiliash V and his family prisoners and declared himself king of **Babylon**, which began the first period of direct Assyrian rule over Babylonia. This produced a strong **Babylonian** influence over Assyria as Tukulti-Ninurta was keen to benefit from the learning and cultural sophistication of the subdued nation. He built a new **palace**, called Kar-Tukulti-Ninurta, but also invested in grand rebuilding programs of **temples** at **Assur** and **Nineveh**. According to an Assyrian chronicle, Tukulti-Ninurta was assassinated in his new palace.

TUKULTI-NINURTA II (reigned 744–727 B.C.). *See* NEO-ASSYRIAN PERIOD.

TUMMAL CHRONICLE. An **Old Babylonian** chronicle that lists kings who contributed to the rebuilding of the Tummal, the **temple** of Ninlil at **Nippur**. The account begins with the **Early Dynastic** king Mebaragesi of **Kish**.

– U –

UBAID PERIOD (c. 5500–4000 B.C.). Prehistoric period named after the site Tell el-Ubaid, near **Ur**. It was the time when the first settlements appeared in the alluvial plains of southern Mesopotamia, with houses built of rammed earth. The characteristic **pottery** was hand shaped and hand painted. The goods deposited in Ubaid cemeteries, as well as the architectural evidence, seem to point to social stratification. *See also* ERIDU.

UMMA (modern Djokha). **Sumerian city** in south Mesopotamia. It was situated along a network of canals, which linked the major rivers **Euphrates** and **Tigris**. **Umma** was a city-state of some importance in the **Early Dynastic period**. Its history is known primarily from tablets found at **Lagash** and **Girsu** that document a long conflict over border territories. Some kings of Umma have left inscribed votive objects but are otherwise unknown.

A certain Enakale attacked **Eannatum** of Lagash in the 25th century B.C. and thereafter concluded a treaty and erected a dike to delineate the border. This seems to have been respected for some time until the **war** flared up again under his successors, and it only came to an end with **Lugalzagesi** (reigned c. 234–c. 2316) who attacked and destroyed Girsu, before conquering other Sumerian cities.

When Lugalzagesi was in turn defeated by **Sargon of Akkad**, Umma became part of the **Akkad** state. The **city** continued to prosper until the end of the third millennium B.C. The main deity of Umma was the **god** Shara.

UR (modern Tell Muqayyar). Important Mesopotamian **city** in southern **Babylonia**. It was situated on the **Euphrates** and had access to the Persian Gulf.

Ur has a long and continuous history of occupation, which began in the **Ubaid** period (c. 4500 B.C.) and ended around 450 B.C. It was the seat of the moon **god Nanna(r)**, or **Sin**. The earliest levels were not substantially excavated and are mainly known from **pottery** and tools. During the **Uruk period**, a monumental building with cone mosaic decoration was erected.

Ur began to develop into a major city in the third millennium B.C., during the **Early Dynastic period**. The **Sumerian King List** records two dynasties at Ur. The First Dynasty was more or less contemporary with the period of the so-called Royal Graves of Ur, excavated by Sir Leonard Woolley. The elaborate burial gifts demonstrate the considerable wealth of the elite. Of the four kings mentioned by the King List, only Mesannepadda is known from brief inscriptions on objects found in the graves. The question whether the other personages buried in the graves, both male and female, were sacrificial victims or secondary interments is still debated. According to the Sumerian King List, the Second Dynasty of Ur had four kings whose names are not preserved.

During the **Akkad** period, Ur formed part of the empire founded by **Sargon of Akkad** whose daughter, **Enheduanna**, served the moon god as the highest-ranking priestess. It was one of the cities that rebelled against **Naram-Sin**.

The apogee of Ur's importance was the **Third Dynasty of Ur** (c. 2100–2000), when the city became the capital of a large and prosperous empire. Most of the extant architectural structures and **cuneiform** tablets found at Ur date from this period. **Ur-Nammu**, the founder of the dynasty, built a large **ziggurat** that has been partially restored. His successors continued his building works in the sacred precinct that included the **temples** of Nanna and Ningal, as well as the residence of the *entu* priestesses. Although the city was destroyed by the **Elamites** in 2007, the temples plundered and torched, and the inhabitants massacred, it was soon inhabited again.

In the **Old Babylonian period**, Ur was an important center of learning, and from this time a number of residential building have been excavated that give a good impression of the densely built urban fabric of a Mesopotamian town. The "heirs" of Ur, the kings of **Isin** and **Larsa**, were keen to show their respect to the gods of Ur by repairing the devastated temples. Despite the ecological problems experienced by the south toward the mid–second millennium, Ur continued to function, and the **Kassite** kings were also eager to contribute to the moon god's temples. So did subsequent rulers: **Nebuchadrezzar I** rebuilt the *giparu* and revitalized the office of the *entu* priestess.

Assyrian kings and governors also invested in the sacred precinct at Ur, and finally **Nabonidus**, with his well-publicized devotion to Sin, ordered the reconstruction of the ziggurat. The city began to decline during the **Achaemenid** period, and records cease after the end of the fourth century B.C.

URARTU. Kingdom in eastern Anatolia and western Iran, with a central area between Lake Van and Lake Sevan. Its history is known from rock inscriptions in Urartian, a late dialect of **Hurrian**, as well as **Assyrian annals** and letters.

Urartu began with a confederation of Hurrian tribes in the ninth century B.C. and reached its greatest territorial expansion around 800 B.C. under king Menua (reigned c. 810–c. 785 B.C.).

The Urartians were skilled at building massive **fortifications** and impressive hydraulic projects, such as aqueducts, dams, and canals, some of which are still in use to this day.

The Urartian expansion conflicted with **Neo-Assyrian** imperial aspirations. **Tiglath-pileser III** waged several campaigns against Urartu and laid (an ultimately unsuccessful) siege to Tushpa in 735, which resulted in the mutual recognition of their borders and areas of influence. Such agreements did not last very long at the time when political allegiances were rapidly changing. The Assyrians were keen to secure their access to the northern **trade** routes and their supply of **metal**, **horses**, and manpower.

Urartu was also under pressure from Caucasian **nomads**, such as the Cimmerians, who ravaged their countryside. It was **Sargon II** in 714 who mounted the biggest military expedition against Urartu, which is vividly described in his **annals** of the eighth campaign. He marched across the ragged mountain at the head of his troops and managed to take the Urartian camp by surprise. He went on to sack one of their sacred sites, the **temple** of Musasir. The Urartians were not broken by these attacks, however, and under Rusa II the kingdom regained much of its power and influence. He also moved the capital from Tushpa to Toprakkale near Van.

Rusa's son Sarduri III submitted to **Ashurbanipal** in c. 636 and was defeated by the Cimmerians and **Elamites**. It was the combined and repeated onslaughts of the Cimmerians and the **Medes** who brought the Urartian kingdom to an end, following the disappearance of the Assyrian empire after 610 B.C.

UR-NAMMU (reigned 2113–2096 B.C.). King of **Ur**, founder of the **Third Dynasty of Ur**. He was a governor of Ur during the reign of Utuhegal of **Uruk** but made himself independent after his successful expulsion of the **Gutians**. He asserted his authority over other **Sumerian cities**, such as **Lagash**, to form a strongly centralized state, with the capital at Ur. He initiated ambitious building programs, such as the **ziggurat** at Ur, as well as at Uruk. He also ordered the construction of new canals, rebuilt the city walls of Ur, planted date palm orchards, and did much to enhance the economic and military security of the country. For such efforts he was lauded in a **Sumerian** hymn that also extols his dedication to the god **Enlil** of **Nippur**. Ur-Nammu was also the subject of other literary works, such as a text in which he visits the Netherworld. He was portrayed on a stone stele that shows him making an offering to a **deity**.

URUINIMGINA (previously read Urukagina) (reigned c. 2351–c. 2342 B.C.). **Sumerian** ruler of **Lagash**. During his reign, Lagash experienced years of prosperity. Uruinimgina initiated a series of reforms that curtailed excessive **taxation** and exorbitant fees charged by officials to the population for their services. He also claims to have put an end to the custom of **women** having more than one husband. He was the last independent ruler of Lagash in the **Early Dynastic period**, having suffered a defeat by **Lugalzagesi** of **Uruk**.

URUK (modern Warka). Important Mesopotamian **city** in the southern plains, situated along the old course of the **Euphrates**. Uruk was occupied from the late fifth millennium B.C. until the Muslim conquests in the seventh century A.D. It has been excavated almost continuously by German teams of archaeologists since the late 19th century, but only about a fifth of the vast ruin field have been explored in depth.

During the fourth millennium B.C., Uruk encompassed two settlements, each with a distinct series of habitation. In the historical period, they were associated with **Inanna** (the site of the Eanna **temple**) and **Anu** (also known in antiquity as Kullab), respectively. Uruk experienced rapid growth in the mid–fourth millennium that lasted until c. 3000 B.C. Huge architectural monuments were put up in rapid succession and built in a variety of techniques. The wall surfaces were decorated with characteristic patterns, often made from clay cones embedded in plaster. These structures, which have been designated as "temples," show a concern for symmetry and monumentality.

During this period, known as the **Uruk period**, writing on clay tablets was invented to deal with a complex system of distribution and exchange that linked southern Mesopotamia to southern and western Iran, Upper Mesopotamia, and southeast Anatolia. Uruk was at this time the only large urban center, and it may have been the hub of the **administration** of the Uruk network, if not the actual capital of a "pristine" state, as has been suggested.

By c. 3100, this system disintegrated, and there was upheaval at Uruk, as various large buildings were demolished.

In the **Early Dynastic period** when the process of urbanization had spread right across southern Mesopotamia, Uruk became the seat of several dynasties. At that time it became surrounded by a huge wall of some 10 kilometers in length that was attributed to **Gilgamesh**, who is listed as a king of the first Uruk dynasty in the **Sumerian King List**.

By the mid–third millennium, **Lugalzagesi** had assumed the throne of Uruk and conquered all the **Sumerian** city-states. He was defeated by **Sargon of Akkad**. However, building at the sacred precincts of Inanna and Anu continued under the Akkad kings and during the **Third Dynasty of Ur**, whose rulers claimed a special affinity with the ancient city.

After the fall of the **Ur** state Uruk went into decline, although the **Kassites** initiated some rebuilding at the **Ishtar temple**. The city revived in the first millennium, when the newly refurbished and enlarged temples controlled vast **agricultural** areas of production.

The intense economic activities at Uruk continued well into the **Seleucid** and early **Parthian periods**. Important tablet collections, of administrative as well as scholarly content, date from this late period. The city fared better under the Parthians and **Sassanians** than other Mesopotamian cities, but it was finally abandoned at the time of the **Arab** invasion of A.D. 634.

URUK PERIOD (c. 4000–3200 B.C.). A prehistoric period in Mesopotamia named after its most important archaeological site, **Uruk**. It is in turn divided into several phases (Early, Middle, and Late), as suggested by the 18 successive layers of the Uruk site Eanna. The fully fledged Uruk culture sets in at level X (c. 3800) when mass-produced thick-walled clay bowls with "beveled rims" make their first appearance. **Cylinder seals** were introduced in the time of level VII (c. 3600), and monumental architecture dates from the Middle Uruk period 1 levels VI–IV (c. 3500–3300). The buildings of level VI, such as the so-called Stone Cone Temple, were erected on large platforms and were of impressive size (28 by 19 meters). Those of level V ("Lime Stone Temple") were even bigger (62.5 by 11.30 meters), and the walls had elaborately articulated facades.

At this stage, **writing** appeared, in pictographic form, to facilitate the increasingly complex economic activities at Uruk itself and in those centers farther afield that belonged to the Uruk sphere of influence. The text on these "archaic" tablets can be understood but not read; they do not appear to express any particular **language**. The tablets are tallies, receipts for goods and services, allocations of fields and labor, calculations of yield, and so forth. The earliest lexical lists were also composed at this time.

The Uruk phenomenon is still much debated, as to what extent Uruk exercised political control over the large area covered by the Uruk artifacts, whether this relied on the use of force, and which institutions were in charge. Too little of the site has been excavated to provide any firm answers to these questions. However, it is clear that at this time, the urbanization process was set in motion, concentrated at Uruk itself. Other **cities** in Mesopotamia were coming into existence, as the city seals on the archaic tablets demonstrate. There was an unprecedented amount of coordination and collaboration in respect to the organization of **agricultural** labor and the distribution of goods and services over a large area.

UTU. The **Sumerian** name of the sun **god** (*see* SHAMASH).

– W –

WARFARE. Violent confrontations between groups of people usually arise from disputes over access to resources such as water, game, and exploitable territories. While there is little evidence from the prehistoric period for organized military action, the presence of walls around settlements (as in Jericho), caches of slingshot, and human skeletal remains with marks of wounds indicate that warlike practices were not uncommon. Seals from the **Uruk period** show naked captives with their arms tied behind their backs being prodded along—they had been interpreted as prisoners of war.

During the first half of the third millennium B.C., Mesopotamia was divided into competing **city**-states, and there is documentary and visual evidence for intercity warfare. The best-known conflict is that between **Lagash** and **Umma**, which fought for generations over some fields at their mutual borders. The texts describe that hostile actions were perceived as an insult to the local **gods** who were said to lead the troops of their city to battle. The famous "Stele of Vultures" (now in the Louvre) depicts the god Ningirsu marching at the head of a tight formation of helmeted soldiers carrying spears and shields (*see* WEAPONS). They trample over the naked bodies of their dead enemies.

The victorious party could inflict punishment on the defeated, setting fire to buildings and looting **temples** and **palaces**. They could also impose a treaty that stipulated, as in the case of Umma, where the new boundaries are and what financial and material reparations were to be made. Spoils of war were deposited in the temple of the city god.

When the country became unified under the rule of the **Akkadian Dynasty**, this was first of all the result of superior military force against other Mesopotamian cities. The **royal inscriptions** of **Sargon of Akkad**, for instance, enumerate the number of battles he won and the cities he forced to submit to his hegemony. He also emphasizes that "5,400 men" daily ate at his table, which may indicate a sizeable bodyguard if not a corps of soldiers.

The **Akkadian** kings also initiated sorties and campaigns abroad, to **Elam** in the east, Syria in the northwest, and Upper Mesopotamia. Such raids were meant to inspire fear in the population, impressing upon them the superiority of the Akkadian power. It brought not only booty from sacked towns and villages but also more formal recognition of Akkadian rights over **trade** routes and **tribute** payments. Furthermore, conquered territories could be distributed to deserving individuals.

The increased use of warfare since the mid–third millennium helped to strengthen the role of kings as leaders of the armed forces, who had a special mandate from the gods (the Akkadian kings stressed the support of **Ishtar**) to defend their realm and to enrich it by aggressive sorties abroad. It appears, though, that most of the fighting was against other Mesopotamian cities keen to shake off the yoke of Akkad. In fact, the pacification of rebellious cities became a main theme in the royal inscriptions of **Naram-Sin**.

Another threat against the stability of a unified country was the uncontrollable influx of **tribal** groups in search of land. This was met with organized resistance and the punishment of tribal leaders although the evasive "guerilla tactics" employed by many tribal immigrants often proved undefeatable.

In the mid–second millennium B.C., "international" conflicts arose between "great powers" (e.g., Egypt, **Mitanni**, the **Hittites**, and **Assyria**) over the control of "colonial" territories, especially Syria and the Levant. Not only were these regions agriculturally productive and populous, but they gave access to the flow of commodities to and from the Mediterranean, Anatolia, and the east. These often intense rivalries were to lead to large armies marching across vast distances to do battle far away from their homeland. The local rulers became implicated as vassals, having to support garrisons of their occupying forces. Such wars continued to affect the Near East throughout the first millennium B.C., abated briefly during the **Achaemenid** period, and flared up again when the **Seleucids** clashed with the Ptolemies and the Romans with the Parthians.

The greatest military power in Mesopotamia was Assyria. The expansion of the **Middle Assyrian** and the **Neo-Assyrian** Empires demanded constant campaigning to secure Assyria's access to vital raw materials, especially **metals, horses**, and manpower. The Assyrian **army** was recruited from subdued territories as well as the mainland, well equipped, and trained by experienced military personnel. The king was the overall commander, and the most successful Assyrian kings (such **Tiglath-pileser III**, **Sargon II**, **Adad-nirari I** and **II**) were indefatigable campaigners who year after year led their troops to punish rebellious vassals, conquer new lands, and fight against troublesome tribal groups. They could also be represented by a chief commander, who was not infrequently a **eunuch**.

The technology of warfare underwent several important changes. In the third millennium B.C., the main body of the soldiers fought on foot, using spears and axes, although archery contingents also played a role. The king and other commanding officers rode in sturdy boxlike **chariots** driven by donkeys. In the second millennium, horses began to play an increasingly important part. Chariots became much lighter and easier to maneuver. Chariot teams driven into the serried ranks of foot soldiers provided a better view of the action and generally made an impressive and frightening impact. They were to become the elite troops of the mid–second millennium.

The foot soldiers armed with spears were augmented by mounted archers and spear men by the Assyrians in the first millennium. Their armies also included siege engines and battering rams to break down city walls. They used soldiers from subjugated areas for specialist tasks, such as fighting in mountainous terrain, the desert (on **camels**), the marshland, or on ships. There were also ritual specialists, diviners to be consulted about the right timing of attacks, priests, bureaucrats to count prisoners and casualties, cooks, baggage trains, musicians, and **women** camp followers.

Psychological warfare was not unknown, as the epic "Gilgamesh and Agga of Kish" as well as other **Sumerian** literary texts document. Exaggerated boasts about the strength of one's troops, terrible threats, and intimidation were meant to secure the submission of the other party. Severe punishments meted out to rebellious subjects was another favored technique, much employed by the **Assyrians**. The walls of royal palaces were covered with propagandistic depictions of the might and invincibility of the Assyrian forces and dreadful fate awaiting traitors. Impaling, flaying, and gouging out of eyes were some of the more gruesome Assyrian punishments meant to dissuade their subjects from insurrection.

WEAPONS. In the prehistorical periods, it is not possible to differentiate between tools and weapons, due to the multipurpose design of early equipment. Bows and arrows can be used to shoot at game animals but also at other human beings; hammers and axes, too, can be applied to all manners of materials, as well as other people's heads. The much increased specialization and Mesopotamia's organization into competing **city**-states in the third millennium B.C. contributed to the professionalization of soldiers.

Texts and visual depictions, as well as grave goods, show the military equipment of the period. Fighting men were protected by tight-fitting (leather?) caps, cloaks, and shields. They used stone-headed maces and **bronze** daggers for hand-to-hand combat. Projectile weapons, such as spears and arrows, were made of stone, bone, and wood. Kings and members of the elite were given ceremonial weapons made of **gold** when they were buried. They may have also played a role in courtly ritual and display and could be offered to **gods** as votive gifts.

In the second millennium B.C., improvements in molding techniques led to elaborately worked and decorated daggers and axes as well as mass-produced bronze arrowheads. Bows underwent several changes in design; it seems that composite bows, made from layers of different materials to improve strength and elasticity, were invented already in the third millennium.

Of great importance was the introduction of **chariot** troops in the mid–second millennium. Cavalry units were first used effectively by the **Assyrians**.

Assyrian reliefs give the best and most detailed evidence for weaponry of the first millennium. Soldiers wore pointed helmets, coats of mail, shin guards, and long as well as round, bronze-coated shields. The infantry had spears and daggers, while cavalry units were armed with spears or bows and arrows.

WEIGHTS AND MEASURES. While there is considerable evidence for weights from diverse historical periods in the form of weight stones of various shapes, other measuring standards have to be deducted from architectural remains and the written evidence. Most **cities** had their own standards, but centralized states since the **Akkadian Dynasty** began to impose unified weights and measures to be used throughout the country.

A similar system was adopted by the **Third Dynasty of Ur** and remained in use throughout all subsequent periods. Such measures were also used for teaching purposes in **scribal** education. Since the basic mathematical system was sexagesimal, basic units were divided or multiplied in a sexagesimal manner.

The measurements for length were based on the human body. The basic was the forearm or cubit (**Akkadian** *ammatu*)—about 50 centimeters. A "foot" was 2/3 of a cubit, a "palm" 1/2, and a "finger" 1/30 of a cubit. Larger units were the "rod" consisting of six cubits and the "cord" of 120 cubits. A mile (Akkadian *beru*) was 180 cords or 21,600 cubits (10,692 kilometers). Surfaces were measured by "garden plots" (Akkadian *musaru*) = c. 35 square meters; there were also multiples called *iku* = 100 *musaru* and *buru* = 18 *iku* = 6 hectare. The capacity measure was the SILA (Akkadian *qu*) = c. 1 liter.

Different names and proportions were used for solid and liquid matter, and the terminology changed in different epochs. The basic weight unit was the mina = c. 500 grams, subdivided in shekels (Akkadian *šiqlu*) =1/60 of a mina, and a "grain" (Akkadian *še*) = 1/180 of a mina. The multiples were the talent (Akkadian *biltu*) = 60 minas.

WOMEN. There is documentary, visual, and archaeological evidence for the role women played in Mesopotamian society through the ages. In many early textual sources, however, the gender of persons mentioned is not always clear. It appears that in the **Uruk period** there was, at least ritually, a complementarity between male and female; the highest male office (EN) had a female equivalent (NIN), and both are depicted as officiating side by side at important functions. During the **Early Dynastic period**, women could also occupy highly prestigious offices, as the grave goods in the "Royal Tombs" at **Ur** and inscribed votive gifts demonstrate. According to the **Sumerian King List**, there was even a female ruler of **Kish**.

It seems, though, that female status at high levels diminished progressively after the Early Dynastic period. There were some remnants of influential positions, such as that of the *entu* **priestess** of the moon god at Ur, which was often held by daughters of the ruling king. Princesses and queens owed their social rank to their relationship with the king and especially some queens could at times hold the balance of power after their husband's death (*see* SEMIRAMIS). Royal daughters, on the other hand, could be married off to secure political alliances and to provide an informal intelligence system.

Written documents also shed some light on the legal position of women in Mesopotamia. They could hold and acquire property, **slaves**, and other valuables; invest their dowries as appropriate; engage in business ventures of various kinds; and begin litigation. They were not, however, able to be witnesses in legal disputes. Of particular interest are the documents that belonged to the *naditu* women at **Sippar**, who lived in seclusion and engaged in business activities and performed various cultic duties at the temple.

Marriages were generally monogamous and arranged by parents; girls married earlier than men and, when widowed, could marry again. Since Mesopotamian society was patriarchal, women could instigate divorce only in cases of gross neglect and cruelty, and male adultery was not a justifiable reason. Women could be divorced on grounds of barrenness, refusal to perform marital duties, and when they became "hateful" to their husbands. This was less easy if they had borne children. Female adultery was punished with great severity, according to the Code of **Ur-Nammu**, with the death penalty (while the male lover was spared). In **Hammurabi's law** code, the accused adulterous couple was bound together and thrown in the river; if the river "accepted" them and they drowned, it was both proof of guilt and punishment.

Most legal documents referring to women (in marriage contracts, divorce settlements, **inheritance** suits, or business affairs) concern women of the affluent groups of society. Some high-status women, such as the privileged cloistered *naditu* women, even employed their own female secretaries. These texts make it clear that such women could dispose of considerable wealth, deriving from their dowries, their husband's gifts, or their own enterprise at their own discretion.

While the main contribution of all women was to bear and raise children, they also formed part of the workforce in Mesopotamia. The names of thousands of "ordinary" women are known from the **administrative** texts of large institutions, such as **temples** and **palaces** where they were employed in a great variety of occupations. They performed domestic work, such as the endless grinding of grain at millstones; backbreaking towing of barges along canals; reed cutting and other heavy **agricultural** work; domestic chores; and, importantly, in the textile workshops. They also performed services in the **temples**, ranging from administrative duties to praying, dancing, or singing. Altogether, working women (and their children) were an integral and important part of Mesopotamia's urban society. This is also documented by the numerous professional titles preserved in the lexical lists.

Women laborers were paid half the rations of men's, generally 30 liters per month (six days were deducted from her productivity to take account of menstruation).

Women could also engage in business. Most commonly they were tavern keepers, where they sold different varieties of **beer**, lent small sums of **silver**, and provided some form of entertainment. They were often partners in business with their husbands; in **Old Assyrian Assur**, they oversaw the **trade** activities at home while their men folk were abroad, and sometimes they produced some of the merchandise themselves (e.g., textiles) for a share of the profits. Similar practices are also known from the **Old-** and **Neo-Babylonian periods**.

Women's movements and opportunities appear to have been more restricted in Assyria, where they were also under the obligation to wear a veil in public.

In Mesopotamian literature, women were active both as authors (*see* ENHEDUANNA), composing hymns, prayers, and love songs (as during the time of the **Third Dynasty of Ur**), and as performers in cultic or courtly settings. The most prominent female personage in literary texts is the **goddess Inanna-Ishtar** whose ambition, vitality, and independence is matched by charm, sex appeal, and ingenuity. In **Sumerian** love songs, she embodies the much admired libidinous powers of female sexuality, while some later **Babylonian** texts place more emphasis on the destructive aspects of her personality.

Fear of seductive women is also much in evidence in the **omen** literature, especially in antiwitchcraft incantations.

WRITING. Writing was first invented to provide a durable record for economic transactions that transcended simple barter. In the **Neolithic period**, small tokens of different shapes, or with marks on them, were used for a simple form of accounting.

In the fourth millennium B.C., when **Uruk** became a major center for distribution and exchange, the greater complexity of **administration** demanded more sophisticated recording systems, and small clay tablets were used, imprinted with abstracted pictorial representations and signs for numbers. They could be used, for example, to compute projected yields, as proof for delivered goods, expenditure of labor and rations. This form of writing was in use throughout the considerably large sphere of influence of the **Uruk** culture. It provided a medium for information that could be understood by bureaucrats with some basic training, but it did not attempt to record sentences in a particular idiom.

This step happened after the breakup of the Uruk period, and the original pictographs were also used to refer to the phonetic value of the depicted subject; thus the picture of a bee could be used to represent the notion of "to be" in English.

The language of the earliest readable texts was **Sumerian**, and the Sumerian syllabary became the primary referent when the same signs were used to express other **languages**, such as **Elamite** or **Akkadian**. This extended use complicated the writing system considerably and required an extended period of **scribal** education. This was facilitated by the lists of syllables and signs, with columns for pronunciation. There were also lexical lists, divided into subject categories such as "wood, trees, and wooden objects," "metal and metallic objects," living beings, professional, geographical terms, divine names, and so forth. Such syllabaries and lexical lists were not only transmitted throughout Mesopotamian history but also used as basic reference texts in such foreign cultures when **cuneiform** was adopted to express local languages.

By the end of the second millennium B.C., west Semitic peoples invented new systems of writing that were more suitable for the linguistic peculiarities of their languages and quicker to learn. One such experiment was the cuneiform syllabary of Ugarit, a wealthy trading kingdom in northwest Syria. Farther south, under the influence of Egyptian hieroglyphics, another form of writing was invented that singled out those hieroglyphs with consonantal values. Few records exist, except for some rock-cut inscriptions, but the idea of representing the main constituents of Semitic languages, the consonantal roots, were developed in different forms.

Since the **Arameans** were a populous people who spread across the whole of the Near East, Aramean writing became the most widespread. Aramean, written on parchment or some similar flat surface with ink, was used by **Assyrian** officials alongside cuneiform since the eighth century. It was adopted as the main official script by the **Achaemenids** and remained in use well into the Roman era.

– Y –

YEAR NAMES. During the **Akkad Dynasty**, a system of dating was introduced in which years were named in hindsight after a significant event, such as the appointment of a senior official or priest, a military campaign, or the inauguration of an important building. The current year,

as well as those in which nothing special occurred, was called "year after such and such happened." Lists of year names were collected and collated with the regnal years of kings. This system was used throughout
southern Mesopotamia for centuries but not in **Assyria**, where they used
the **eponym** dating. The lists of year names, as well as year names
recorded in administrative records, are an important source of historical
information, especially for those periods in which written documentation
is sparse.

– Z –

ZIGGURAT. This loan word, derived from the **Akkadian** *ziqqurratu,* designates architectural structures that resemble stepped pyramids in outline. They were built solidly, with no internal chambers, from mud brick,
with sometimes an outer mantle of baked brick. Ziggurats had religious
significance; they were usually part of a **temple** complex and had a
chapel at the top-most platform. This was reached by a series of ramps
and steps. No ziggurat is preserved well enough to allow a valid reconstruction. **Assyrian** ziggurats were usually directly attached to a "low
temple," while **Babylonian** ziggurats were free-standing. In general, all
these structures provided a lofty stage, a kind of ladder for the **gods** to
come closer to Earth and for the priests to draw nearer to the heavens.
They also formed landmarks that were visible from afar.

ZIMRI-LIM (reigned c. 1775–1761 B.C.). King of **Mari** in the **Old Babylonian period**. When **Shamshi-Adad I** conquered Mari, Zimri-Lim,
then a child, went into exile to the kingdom of Yamhad, whose daughter he married. After the death of Shamshi-Adad, he returned to claim
the throne. He was skillful at using his contacts with Yamhad and other
Syrian polities to extend his influence in **Middle Babylonia** and formed
alliances with other rulers, such as **Hammurabi** of **Babylon**. He maintained good relations with the **nomadic** tribes around Mari and established a profitable network of **trade** along the **Euphrates** and beyond.
The wealth thus generated he invested in building a vast and sumptu-
ously appointed **palace**. The reign of Zimri-Lim is unusually well documented thanks to a surviving **archive** in the palace that details his
diplomatic and military activities. He was defeated by Hammurabi
when the latter attacked and sacked the palace in c. 1761 B.C.

Appendix I: Mesopotamian Rulers

Appendix II: Museums

Select Bibliography

Appendix I
Rulers of Mesopotamia

The numbers indicate regnal year. Dates for all of the third and much of the second millennium are provisional. Several dynasties or individual reigns were contemporary with others.

EARLY DYNASTIC PERIOD

Kish

Mebaragesi	c. 2650 ?
Agga	c. 2600 ?
Mesalim	c. 2550 ?

Ur

Meskalamdug	c. 2620 ?
Akalamdug	c. 2600 ?

Lagash

Enhegal	c. 2570
Lugal-saengur	c. 2550
Ur-Nanshe	c. 2494–2465
Akurgal	c. 2464–2455
Eannatum	c. 2454–2425
Enannatum I	c. 2424–2404
Enmetena	c. 2403–c. 2375
Enannatum II	c. 2374–c. 2365
Enentarzi	c. 2364–c. 2359
Lugalanda	c. 2358–2352
Uruinimgina	c. 2351–2342

Uruk

Lugalzagesi	c. 2341–2316

AKKADIAN EMPIRE

Akkad

Sargon	c. 2340–2284?
Rimush	c. 2284–2276
Manishtusu	c. 2275–2261
Naram-Sin	c. 2260–c. 2224
Shar-kali-sharri	c. 2223–c. 2198
[Gutian rule]	

NEO-SUMERIAN PERIOD

Uruk (2nd Dynasty)

Utuhegal	c. 2119–2112

Lagash

Gudea	c. 2141–c. 2122

Third Dynasty of Ur

Ur-Nammu	c. 2113–c. 2096
Shulgi	c. 2094–2047
Amar-Sin	c. 2046–c. 2038
Shu-Sin	c. 2037–c. 2027
Ibbi-Sin	c. 2026–2004?

OLD BABYLONIAN PERIOD

First Dynasty of Isin

Ishbi-Erra	c. 2017–c. 1985
Shu-ilishu	c. 1984–c. 1975

Iddin-Dagan	c. 1974–1954
Ishme-Dagan	c. 1953–c. 1935
Lipit-Ishtar	c. 1934–c. 1923
Ur-Ninurta	c. 1923–c. 1896
Bur-Sin	c. 1895–c. 1874
Lipit-Enlil	c. 1873–c. 1869
Erra-imitti	c. 1688–c. 1861
Enlil-bani	c. 1860–c. 1837
Zambiya	c. 1836–c. 1834
Iter-pisha	c. 1833–c. 1831
Ur-dukuga	c. 1830–1828
Sin-magir	c. 1827–c. 1817
Damiq-ilishu	c. 1816–c. 1794

Dynasty of Larsa

Naplanum	c. 2025–c. 2005
Emisum	c. 2004–c. 1977
Samium	c. 1976–c. 1942
Zabaya	c. 1941–c. 1933
Gungunum	c. 1932–c. 1906
Abisare	c. 1905–c. 1895
Sumuel	c. 1894–1866
Nur-Adad	c. 1865–1850
Sin-iddinam	c. 1849–c. 1843
Sin-eribam	c. 1842–c. 1841
Sin-iqisham	c. 1840–1836
Silli-Adad	c. 1835
Warad-Sin	c. 1834–c. 1823
Rim-Sin I	c. 1822–1763
Rim-Sin II	c. 1741–?

First Dynasty of Babylon

Sumu-abum	c. 1894–c. 1881
Sumula'el	c. 1880–c. 1845
Sabium	c. 1844–1831
Apil-Sin	c. 1830–c. 1813
Sin-muballit	c. 1812–c. 1793
Hammurabi	c. 1792–c. 1750

Samsuiluna	c. 1749–c. 1712
Abi-esuh	c. 1711–c. 1684
Ammiditana	c. 1683–c. 1647
Ammisaduqa	c. 1646–c. 1626
Samsu-ditana	c. 1625–c. 1595

OLD ASSYRIAN PERIOD

Puzur-Ashur I?	Early 20th century
Shalim-Ahhe	c. 1970?
Ilu-shuma	c. 1960–c. 1939
Erishum I	c. 1939–c. 1900
Ikunum?	(Early 19th century)
Sargon I(?)	(Early 19th century)
Puzur-Ashur II(?)	(Mid–19th century)
Naram-Sin	(Late 19th century)
Shamshi-Adad I	c. 1813–c. 1781
Ishme-Dagan	c. 1780–c. 1741

Mari

Yaggid-Lim	c. 1820–c. 1811
Yahdun-Lim	c. 1810–c. 1795
Sumuyaman	c. 1794–?
(Shamshi-Adad)	
(Yasmah-Adad)	
Zimri-Lim	c. 1775–1761

MIDDLE BABYLONIAN PERIOD

Kassite Dynasty

Gandash	c. 1729–?
Agum I	(Early 18th century)
Kashtiliash I	c. 1660–?
Burnaburiash I	c. 1530–1500?
Karaindash	c. 1413–?

Kadashman-Harbe?	(Late 15th century?)
Kurigalzu I	(Early 14th century?)
Kadashman-Enlil I	c. 1374–c. 1360
Burnaburiash II	c. 1359–c. 1334
Karahardash	c. 1333
Nazi-bugash	c. 1333
Kurigalzu II	c. 1332–c. 1308
Nazi-Maruttash	c. 1307–c. 1282
Kadashman-Turgu	c. 1281–c. 1264
Kudur-Enlil	c. 1263–c. 1255
Kudur-Enlil	c. 1254-1225
(Tukulti-Ninurta	c. 1225)
Enlil-nadin-shumi	c. 1224
Kadashman-Harbe II	c. 1223
Adad-shum-iddina	c. 1222–1217
Adad-shum-usur	c. 1216–1187
Marduk-apla-iddina I	c. 1171–c. 1159
Zababa-shum-iddina	c. 1158
Enlil-nadin-ahi	c. 1157–1155

Second Dynasty of Isin

Marduk-kabit-ahheshu	c. 1154–c. 1141
Itti-Marduk-balatu	c. 1140–c. 1133
Ninurta-nadin-shumi	c. 1132–c. 1127
Nebuchadnezzar I	c. 1126–c. 1105
Enlil-nadin-apli	c. 1104–c. 1111
Marduk-nadin-ahhe	c. 1110–c. 1083
Adad-apla-iddina	c. 1082–c. 1070
Marduk-ahhe-eriba	c. 1069–c. 1048
Marduk-zer-x(?)	c. 1046–c. 1035
Nabu-shum-libur	c. 1034–1027

Second Sealand Dynasty

Simbar-Shipak	c. 1026–c. 1010
Ea-mukin-zeri	c. 1009
Kashshu-nadin-ahi	c. 1008–1006

Bazi-Dynasty

Eulmash-shakin-shumi	c. 1005–c. 989
Ninurta-kudurri-usur I	c. 988–c. 987
Shirikti-Shuqamuna	c. 986
[Elamite ruler]	
Mar-biti-apla-usur	c. 985–c. 980

MIDDLE ASSYRIAN PERIOD

Ashur-rabi I (?)	(Early 15th century)
Ashur-nadin-ahhe I	(Mid–15th century)
Enlil-nasir II	c. 1432–c. 1427
Ashur-nirari II	c. 1426–c. 1420
Ashur-bel-nisheshu	c. 1419–c. 1411
Ashur-rem-nisheshu	c. 1410–c. 1403
Ashur-nadin-ahhe	c. 1402–c. 1393
Eriba-Adad I	c. 1392–c. 1366
Ashur-uballit I	c. 1365–c. 1330
Enlil-nirari	c. 1329–c. 1320
Arik-den-ili	c. 1319–c. 1308
Adad-nirari I	c. 1307–c. 1275
Shalmaneser I	c. 1274–c. 1245
Tukulti-Ninurta I	c. 1244–c. 1208
Ashur-nadin-apli	c. 1207–c. 1204
Ashur-nirari III	c. 1203–c. 1198
Enlil-kudurri-usur	c. 1197–c. 1193
Ninurta-apil-Ekur	c. 1192–c. 1180
Ashur-dan I	c. 1179–c. 1134
Ninurta-tukulti-Assur	c. 1133?
Mutakkil-Nusku	c. 1133?
Ashur-resh-ishi	c. 1133–c. 1116
Tiglath-pileser I	c. 1115–c. 1076
Ashared-apil-Ekur	c. 1076–c. 1075
Ashur-bel-kala	c. 1074–1057
Eriba-Adad II	c. 1056–c. 1055
Shamshi-Adad II	c. 1054–c. 1051
Ashurnasirpal I	c. 1050–c. 1032
Shalmaneser II	c. 1031–c. 1020
Ashur-nirari IV	c. 1019–c. 1014

Ashur-rabi II	c. 1013–c. 973
Ashur-resh-ishi	c. 972–c. 968
Tiglath-pileser II	c. 967–c. 934

NEO-BABYLONIAN PERIOD

Dynasty of E

Nabu-mukin-apli	c. 979–c. 945
Ninurta-kudurri-usur	c. 944
Mar-bit-ahhe-iddina	c. 943–c. 906
Shamash-mudammiq	c. 905–c. 896
Nabu-shuma-ukin	c. 895–c. 871
Nabu-apla-iddina	c. 870–c. 855
Marduk-zakir-shumi	c. 854–c. 819
Marduk-balassu-iqbi	c. 818–c. 813
Baba-aha-iddina	c. 812–?
[six unknown kings]	
Marduk-bel-zeri?	
Marduk-apla-usur?	
Eriba-Marduk	c. 770–c. 761
Nabu-shuma-ishkun	c. 760–c. 748
Nabu-nasir	747–734
Nabu-nadin-zeri	733
Nabu-shuma-ukin II	732
Nabu-mukin-zeri	731–729
(Tiglath-pileser	728–727)
(Shalmaneser	726–722)
Marduk-apla-iddina	721–710
(Sargon	709)
[Succession unclear for several rulers]	
(Esarhaddon)	
Shamash-shum-ukin	667–648
Kandalanu	647–627?

NEO-ASSYRIAN PERIOD

Ashur-resh-ishi II	c. 972–c. 968
Tiglath-pileser II	c. 967–c. 935

Ashur-dan II	c. 934–912
Adad-nirari II	911–891
Tukulti-Ninurta II	890–884
Ashurnasirpal II	883–859
Shalmaneser III	858–824
Shamshi-Adad V	823–811
Adad-nirari III	810–783
Shalmaneser IV	782–773
Ashur-dan III	772–755
Ashur-nirari V	754–745
Tiglath-pileser III	744–727
Shalmaneser V	726–722
Sargon II	721–705
Sennacherib	704–681
Esarhaddon	680–669
Ashurbanipal	668–?
Ashur-etil-ilani	630?/626?
Sin-shar-ishkun	622?–610
Ashur-uballit III	609

NEO-BABYLONIAN PERIOD

Chaldean Dynasty

Nabopolassar	626–605
Nebuchadnezzar II	604–562
Amel-Marduk	561–560
Neriglissar	559–557
Labashi-Marduk	556
Nabonidus	555–539

ACHAEMENID PERIOD

Cyrus II	c. 559–530
Cambyses II	530–522
Darius I	522–486
Xerxes	486–465
Artaxerxes I	465–244/3

Darius II	423–405
Artaxerxes II	405–359
Artaxerxes III	359–338
Artaxerxes IV	338–336
Darius III	336–330

HELLENISTIC PERIOD

Alexander the Great	(reigned in Babylon since 331–321)
Antigonous Monophthalmos	321–301
Seleucus I Nicator	(reigned in Babylon since 301)–281
Antiochus I Soter	281–261
Antiochus II	261–246
Seleucus II	246–226
Antiochus III the Great	223–187
Seleucus III Philopator	187–176
Antiochus IV Epiphanes	176–164
Antiochus V Eupator	164–162
Demetrios I Soter	162–150
Antiochus VI Sidetes	164–129

PARTHIAN PERIOD

Phraates I ruled Babylonia	since 129–127
Artabanus	c. 127–123
Mithridates II the Great	c. 123–88
(Romans occupy Mesopotamia)	
Phraates III	70–58 B.C.

Appendix II

Museums with Mesopotamian Collections

An asterisk indicates large or important collections.

A Worldwide Directory of Museums with Near Eastern Collections, can be found on the website of Akkadica <www.akkadica.org> under "Museum Links," Brussels 2002.

Belgium
Musées Royaux d'Art et d'Histoire
Parc du Cinquantaine, 10
B-1000 Bruxelles

Canada
Montreal Museum of Fine Arts
1379 Sherbrooke Street West
Montreal, Quebec H3G 2T9

Royal Ontario Museum
100 Queen's Park
Toronto, Ontario M5S 2C6

Denmark
The National Museum of Denmark
Department of Classical and Near Eastern Antiquities
Ny Vestergarde, 10
Dk-1220 Copenhagen

France
Ecole pratique des hautes études
45-47, rue des Ecoles
F-75005 Paris

Musée du Louvre*
34, Quai du Louvre
F-75058 Paris

Germany
Staatliche Museen, Vorderasiatisches Museum*
Pargamonmuseum
Berlin-Mitte

Uruk-Warka Sammlung
Ruprechts-Karl Universität
Hauptstrasse 126
Heidelberg

Hilprecht Sammlung
Friedrich-Schiller Universität
Kalaische Straße 1
07745 Jena

Archäologische Staatssammlungen, München
Museum für Vor- und Frühgeschichte
Archäologische Museen
Karmeliterstrasse 1
60311 Frankfurt am Main

Iraq
The Iraq Museum*
The General Directorate of Antiquities
Baghdad

Israel
Bible Lands Museum
Granot, 25
Jerusalem 93706

The Israel Museum
Hakiriya
Jerusalem 91710

Italy
Museo Archeologico
Via della Colonna, 38
I -50121 Florence

Vatican Museum
00120 Vatican City

Netherlands
National Museum of Antiquities
Rapenburg 28
NL-2301 Leiden

Russia
State Pushkin Museum of Fine Arts
Oriental Department
Volchonka, 12
121019 Moscow

State Hermitage Museum
Oriental Department
Dvortsovaya Naberezhnaya, 34
191186 St. Petersburg

Syrian Arab Republic
Aleppo National Museum*
The Directorate of Aleppo Antiquities
Aleppo

The National Museum of Damascus*
The General Directorate of Museums and Antiquities
Damascus

Turkey
Museum of Anatolian Civilisations
Hisar cad.
Ulus
Ankara

United Kingdom
City Museums and Art Gallery
Department of Antiquities
Chamberlain Square
Birmingham B3 3DH

Royal Museum of Scotland
Chambers Street
Edinburgh EH1 1JH

Liverpool Museum
William Brown Street
Liverpool L3 8EN

British Museum*
Department of Western Asiatics
Great Russell Street
London WC1 3DG

The Manchester Museum
University of Manchester
Oxford Road
Manchester M13 9PL

The Ashmolean Museum
Department of Antiquities
University of Oxford
Beaumont Street
Oxford OX1 2PH

United States
Kelsey Museum of Ancient and Medieval Archaeology
University of Michigan
434 South State Street
Ann Arbor, Michigan 48104

The Walters Art Gallery
600 North Charles Street
Baltimore, Maryland 21201-5185

The Semitic Museum
Harvard University
Cambridge, Massachusetts 02138

Oriental Institute Museum*
University of Chicago
1155 East 58th Street
Chicago, Illinois 60637-1569

Peabody Museum
Yale University
New Haven, Connecticut 06520

Metropolitan Museum of Art*
1000 Fifth Street
New York, New York 10028-0198

University Museum of the University of Pennsylvania*
33d and Spruce Street
Philadelphia, Pennsylvania 19104

National Museum of Natural History
Smithsonian Institution
Washington, D.C. 20560

Select Bibliography

The history, archaeology, societies, and material cultures of ancient Mesopotamia are discussed in a great number of academic specialist journals, books, monographs, and edited volumes. Such publications go back to the late 19th century when the cuneiform tablets discovered in Mesopotamian archaeological sites began to be copied, transcribed, and translated. Now the main centers of assyriological scholarship are in Germany, Britain, France, and the United States. The Netherlands, Belgium, Austria, Italy, the Scandinavian countries (notably Finland), Russia, and the Czech Republic also have specialist departments at their universities, and more recently Japan has also begun to make contributions, especially in Sumerian studies. Equally important is the work done by archaeologists and assyriologists in the Middle East, in Iraq, Syria, Turkey, and Israel. The majority of scholarly publications are written in German, English, or French.

The sources in this bibliography are a selection of works on various topics, meant as a starting point for references, as well as giving examples of recent contributions and debates, primarily using sources in English. More comprehensive bibliographies can be found in most of the works quoted here, as well as in specialist library databases of universities. Some departments also have websites giving information of archaeological excavation, and, increasingly, cuneiform sources are also available online. Databases can be accessed through keywords such as *Mesopotamian archaeology, Babylon, Assyria, Sumer, Assyriology, Ancient Near East,* and so on.

A number of reference works and general source books summarize current knowledge on the topics covered in the book. The most exhaustive and scholarly encyclopedia is the *Reallexikon der Assyriologie and Archäologie* (with articles in German, French, and English). The first volume was published in Berlin in 1928. It is a work in progress (up to letter *N*) and now published by Walter de Gruyter (Berlin and New York). Less comprehensive and more accessible is the five-volume collection of essays *Civilizations of the Ancient Near East* (1995). For Mesopotamian history, the *Cambridge Ancient History* (Vols. I, II, III/1, III/2, IV, VI [rev. ed.] [1972–1994]) provides authoritative accounts, although some earlier editions are now outdated. Concise historical overviews are provided by *The Ancient Near East: c. 3000–300 B.C.* (1995) and *The Ancient Near East: A History* (2d ed., 1998). Also very useful is the *Cultural Atlas of Mesopotamia and the Ancient Near East* (1990). Historical reference works are *Who's Who in the Ancient Near East* (1999) and a recent edition by the British Museum *Dictionary of the Ancient Near East* (2000).

For peoples of ancient Mesopotamia, there is *The Sumerians* (1963), *The Babylonians* (1995), *The Babylonians: An Introduction* (2002), and *Peoples of Old Testament Times* (1973).

Other subjects are covered here in alphabetical order.

Agriculture

Breckwoldt, T. "Management of Grain Storage in Old Babylonian Larsa." *Archiv für Orientforschung* 42/43 (1995–1996): 64–88.

Charles, M. "Irrigation in Lowland Mesopotamia." In "Irrigation and Cultivation in Mesopotamia, part 1." *Bulletin on Sumerian Agriculture* 4 (1988): 1–39.

Civil, Miguel. *The Farmer's Instructions: A Sumerian Agricultural Manual*. Aula Orientalis Supplements 5. Barcelona: Ausa, 1994.

Ellis, Maria de J. "Agriculture and the State in Ancient Mesopotamia." In *Introduction to the Problems of Land Tenure*. Philadelphia: Babylonian Fund, University Museum, 1976.

Englund, Robert K. "Regulating Dairy Production in the Ur III Period." *Orientalia* 64, no. 4 (1995): 377–429.

Hesse, B. "Animal Husbandry and Human Diet in the Ancient Near East." In *Civilizations of the Ancient Near East,* ed. Jack M. Sasson. New York: Scribner, 1995, 203–22.

Jacobsen, Thorkild. *Salinity and Irrigation Agriculture in Antiquity*. Bibliotheca Mesopotamica 14. Malibu, Calif.: Undena, 1982.

Jas, R. M., ed. *Rainfall and Agriculture in Northern Mesopotamia (MOS Studies): Proceedings of the Third MOS Symposium, Leiden 1999*. Istanbul: Nederlands Historisch-Archaeologisch Instituut te Istanbul, 2000.

Klengel, Horst, and Johannes Renger, eds. *Landwirtschaft im alten Orient: Ausgewählte Vorträge der XLI Rencontre Assyriologique Internationale Berlin 4.–8. 1994*. Berlin: Reimer, 1999.

Liverani, Mario, and Wolfgang Heimpel. "Observations on Livestock Management in Babylonia." *Acta Sumerologica* 17 (1995): 127–44.

Powell, Michael A. "Salt, Seeds and Yields in Sumerian Agriculture: A Critique of the Theory of Progressive Salination." *Zeitschrift für Assyriologie* 75 (1985): 7–38.

Redman, Charles. *The Rise of Civilization: From Early Farmers to Urban Society in the Ancient Near East.* San Francisco: Freeman, 1978.

Walters, Stanley D. *Waters for Larsa: An Old Babylonian Archive Dealing with Irrigation. Yale Near Eastern Researches.* New Haven, Conn.: Yale University Press, 1970.

Zeder, Melinda A. *Feeding Cities: Specialized Animal Economy in the Ancient Near East.* Washington, D.C.: Smithsonian Institution Press, 1991.

Archaeology

Burney, Charles. *From Village to Empire: An Introduction to Near Eastern Archaeology.* Oxford: Phaidon, 1977.

Curtis, John, ed. *British School of Archaeology in Iraq: Fifty Years of Mesopotamian Discovery: The Work of the British School of Archaeology in Iraq 1932–1982.* London: British School of Archaeology in Iraq, 1982.

Henrickson, Elizabeth, and Ingolf Thuesen, eds. *Upon This Foundation: The "Ubaid" Reconsidered.* Carsten Niebhur Institute publications 10. Copenhagen: Museum Tusculanum, 1989.

Larsen, Mogens T. *The Conquest of Assyria: Excavations in an Antique Land 1840–1860.* London: Routledge, 1994.

Lloyd, Seton. *Foundations in the Dust: A Story of Mesopotamian Exploration.* Rev. ed. London: Oxford University Press, 1980.

——. *The Archaeology of Mesopotamia: From the Old Stone Age to the Persian Conquest,* rev. ed. London: Thames & Hudson, 1985.

Millard, Allan. "The Bevel-Rimmed Bowls: Their Purpose and Significance." *Iraq* 50 (1988): 49–57.

Moorey, Peter R. S. *Ur "of the Chaldees": A Revised and Updated Edition of Sir Leonard Woolley's Excavations at Ur.* Ithaca, N.Y.: Cornell University Press, 1982.

——. *Ancient Mesopotamian Materials and Industries: The Archaeological Evidence.* Oxford: Clarendon, 1994.

Oates, Joan. *Babylon,* rev. ed. London: Thames & Hudson, 1986.

Russell, John M. *The Final Sack of Nineveh: The Discovery, Documentation, and Destruction of King Sennacherib's Throne Room at Nineveh, Baghdad.* New Haven, Conn.: Yale University Press, 1998.

Woolley, Charles Leonard. *Ur Excavations: Vol. 2. The Royal Cemetery.* London: British Museum, 1934.

——. *Ur Excavations: Vol. 4. The Early Periods.* London: British Museum, 1955.

Wright, Rita P., ed. *Gender and Archaeology.* Philadelphia: University of Pennsylvania Press, 1996.

Young, Gordon D. *Mari in Retrospect: Fifty Years of Mari and Mari Studies.* Winona Lake, Ind.: Eisenbrauns, 1992.

Young, T. Cuyler, and Louis D. Levine, eds. *Mountains and Lowlands: Essays in the Archaeology of Greater Mesopotamia.* Bibliotheca Mesopotamica 7. Malibu, Calif.: Undena, 1977.

Young, T. Cuyler, P. E. L. Smith, and P. Mortensen, eds. *The Hilly Flanks and Beyond: Essays on the Prehistory of Southwestern Asia Presented to Robert J. Braidwood November 15, 1982.* Studies in Ancient Oriental Civilization No. 36. Chicago: Oriental Institute of Chicago, 1983.

Art and Architecture

Amiet, Pierre. *Art in the Ancient World: A Handbook of Style and Forms.* London: Faber & Faber, 1981.

Barnett, Richard D., and W. Forman. *Assyrian Palace Reliefs and Their Influence on the Sculptures of Babylonia and Persia.* London: British Museum Publications, 1960.

Collon, Dominique. *First Impressions: Cylinder Seals in the Ancient Near East.* London: British Museum Publications, 1995.

Crawford, Harriet E. W. *The Architecture of Iraq in the Third Millennium B.C.* Mesopotamia 5. Copenhagen: Akademisk Forlag, 1977.

Curtis, John E., and Julian E. Reade. *Art and Empire: Treasures from Assyria in the British Museum.* London: British Museum Publications, 1995.

Frankfort, Henri. *The Art and Architecture of the Ancient Near East.* 4th ed. Harmondsworth: Penguin, 1970.

Gates, M. H. "The Palace of Zimri-Lim at Mari." *Biblical Archaeology* 47 (1984): 70–87.

Gunter, Ann C., ed. *Investigating Artistic Environments in the Ancient Near East.* Washington, D.C.: Arthur M. Sackler Gallery, Smithsonian Institution, 1990.

Hallo, William W., and Irene Winter, eds. *Seals and Seal Impressions: Proceedings of the XLV Rencontre Assyriologique Internationale.* Bethesda, Md.: CDL, 2001.

Johansen, Flemming. *Statues of Gudea, Ancient and Modern.* Mesopotamia 6. Copenhagen: Akademisk Forlag, 1978.

Porada, Edith. *Ancient Art in Seals.* Princeton, N.J.: Princeton University Press, 1980.

Strommenger, Eva, and Manfried Hirmer. *The Art of Ancient Mesopotamia.* London: Thames & Hudson, 1965.

Veenhof, Klaas R., ed. *Houses and Households in Ancient Mesopotamia: Papers Read at the 40e Rencontre Assyriologique Internationale, Leiden, July 5–8, 1993.* Istanbul: Nederlands Historisch-Archaeologisch Instituut te Istanbul, 1996.

Westenholz, Joan E. "The King, the Emperor, and the Empire. Continuity and Discontinuity of Royal Representation in Texts and Language." In *The Heirs of Assyria: Proceedings of the Opening Symposium of the Assyrian and Babylonian Intellectual Heritage Project Held in Tuärminne, Finland, October 8–11, 1998,* ed. Sanno Aro and R. M. Whiting. Helsinki: Neo-Assyrian Text Corpus Project, 2000, 99–126.

Zettler, Richard, and Lee Horne, eds. *Treasures from the Royal Tombs at Ur.* Philadelphia: University of Pennsylvania, Museum of Archaeology and Anthropology, 1998.

Astrology/Astronomy

Brown, David. *Mesopotamian Planetary Astronomy-Astrology.* Groningen: Styx, 2000.

Galter, Hannes D., ed. *Die Rolle der Astronomie in den Kulturen Mesopotamiens. Beiträge zum 3. Grazer Morgenländischen Symposium 23.–27. September 1991.* Graz: Kult, 1993.

Hunger, Hermann, ed. *Astrological Reports to Assyrian Kings.* Helsinki: Helsinki University Press, 1992.

Koch-Westenholz, Ulla. *Mesopotamian Astrology: An Introduction to Babylonian and Assyrian Celestial Divination.* Copenhagen: Carsten Niebuhr Institute of Near Eastern Studies, Museum Tusculanum Press, 1995.

Rochberg, Francesca. *Babylonian Horoscopes: Transactions of the American Philosophical Society 88,* Part 1. Philadelphia: American Philosophical Society, 1998.

Rochberg-Halton, Francesca. *Aspects of Babylonian Celestial Divination: The Lunar Eclipse Tablets of Enuma Anu Enlil.* Horn, Austria: Berger, 1988.

Chronology

Aström, Paul, ed. *High, Middle or Low? Acts of an International Colloquium on Absolute Chronology.* 3 vols. Gothenburg: Aströms, 1987–1989.

Bickerman, Elias. *Chronology of the Ancient World.* London: Thames & Hudson, 1980.

Gasche, H., J. Amstrong, and S. W. Cole. *Dating the Fall of Babylon: A Reappraisal of Second-Millennium Chronology.* Chicago: University of Ghent and the Oriental Institute of the University of Chicago, 1998.

Grayson, Albert K. "The Chronology of the Reign of Ashurbanipal." *Zeitschrift für Assyriologie* 70 (1980): 227–45.

Jacobsen, Thorkild. *The Sumerian King List.* Chicago: Chicago University Press, 1939.

Michalowski, Piotr. "History as Charter: Some Observations on the Sumerian King List." *Journal of the American Oriental Society* 103 (1983): 237–48.

Na'aman, N. "Statements of Time-Spans by Babylonian and Assyrian Kings and Mesopotamian Chronology." *Iraq* 46 (1984): 115–24.

———. "Chronology and History of the Late Assyrian Empire." *Zeitschrift für Assyriologie* 81 (1991): 242–67.

Parker, Richard A., and Waldo Dubberstein. *Babylonian Chronology, 626 B.C.–A.D. 45.* 3d. ed. Chicago: University of Chicago Press, 1956.

Sollberger, Edmond. "The Tummal Inscription." *Journal of Cuneiform Studies* 16 (1962): 4–47.

Collections of Essays in Honor of Individual Scholars and on Symposia

Archi, Alfonso, ed. *Circulation of Goods in Non Palatial Contexts in the Ancient Near East*. Rome: Ateneo, 1984.

Cameron, Averil, and Amélie Kuhrt, eds. *Images of Women in Antiquity*. Rev. ed. London: Routledge, 1993.

Cogan, Mordechai, and Yisrael Epha'al, eds. *Ah, Assyria . . . Studies in Assyrian History and Ancient Near Eastern Historiography Presented to Hayim Tadmor*. Jerusalem: Magnes, 1991.

Cohen, Mark E., Daniel C. Snell, and D. B.Weisberg, eds. *The Tablet and the Scroll: Near Eastern Studies in Honor of William W. W. Hallo*. Bethesda, Md.: CDL, 1993.

Dandamayev, Mohammed, et al., eds. *Societies and Languages of the Ancient Near East: Studies in Honor of I. M. Diakonoff*. Warminster: Aries & Phillips, 1982.

Dietrich, Manfried A. and Ostwald Loretz, eds. *Mesopotamica-Ugaritica-Biblica: Festschrift für Kurt Bergerhof zur Vollendung seines 70. Lebensjahres am 7. Mai 1992*. Neukirchen-Vluyn: Neukirchner, 1993.

———. *Dubsar anta-men: Festschrift für Willem H. Ph. Römer zur Vollendung seines 70. Lebensjahres*. Muenster: Ugarit, 1998.

Ellis, Maria de J., ed. *Essays on the Ancient Near East in Memory of J. J. Finkelstein*. Hamden, Conn.: Archon, 1977.

George, Andrew, and I. L. Finkel, eds. *Wisdom, Gods and Literature: Studies in Assyriology in Honour of W. G. Lambert*. Winona Lake, Ind: Eisenbrauns, 2000.

Goedicke, Hans, and J. J. M. Roberts, eds. *Unity and Diversity: Essays in the History, Literature and Religion of the Ancient Near East*. Johns Hopkins Near Eastern Studies. Baltimore, Md.: Johns Hopkins University Press, 1975.

Güterbock, Hans G., and Thorkild Jacobsen, eds. *Studies in Honor of Benno Landsberger*. Assyriological Studies 16. Chicago: Oriental Institute, 1967.

Haex, O. M. C., H. H. Curvers, and P. M. M. G. Akkerman, eds. *To the Euphrates and Beyond: Archaeological Studies in Honour of Maurits N. van Loon*. Brookfield, Va.: Balkma, 1989.

Leichty, Erle, Marie de J. Ellis, and Pamela Gerardi, eds. *A Scientific Humanist: Studies in Memory of Abraham Sachs*. Philadelphia: University Museum, 1988.

Lieberman, Stephen J., ed. *Sumerological Studies in Honor of Thorkild Jacobsen on His Seventieth Birthday, June 7th 1974*. Chicago: University of Chicago Press, 1976.

Marks, John H., and Robert M. Good, eds. *Love and Death in the Ancient Near East: Essays in Honor of Marvin H. Pope*. Guildford, Conn.: Four Quarters, 1987.

Mauer, Gerlinde, and Ursula Magen, eds. *Ad bene et fideliter seminandum: Festgabe für Karlheins Deller zum 21. Februar 1987*. Kevelaar: Butzon & Becker, 1988,

Postgate, J. Nicholas, ed. *Societies and Languages of the Ancient Near East: Studies in Honour of I. M. Diakonoff*. Warminster: Aris & Phillips, 1982.

Rochberg-Halton, Francesca, ed. *Language, Literature and History: Philological and Historical Studies Presented to Erica Reiner*. New Haven, Conn.: American Oriental Society, 1987.

Sasson, Jack M., ed. *Studies in the Literature of the Ancient Near East Dedicated to S. N. Kramer*. New Haven, Conn.: American Oriental Society, 1984.

Soldt, W. H., ed. *Veenhof Anniversary Volume: Studies Presented to Klaas R. Veenhof on the Occasion of His Sixty-fifth Birthday*. Istanbul: Nederlands Historisch-Archaeologisch Instituut te Istanbul, 2001.

van Driel, G., et al., eds. *Zikir Šumim: Assyriological Studies Presented to F. R. Kraus on the Occasion of His Seventieth Birthday*. Leiden: Brill, 1982.

Wunsch, Cornelia, ed. *Mining the Archives: Festschrift for Christopher Walker on the Occasion of His 60th Birthday, 4 October 2002*. Dresden: ISLET, 2002.

Crafts and Material Culture

Barber, E. J. W. *Prehistoric Textiles: The Development of Cloth in the Neolithic and Bronze Ages with Special Reference to the Aegean*. Princeton, N.J.: Princeton University Press, 1991.

Forbes, Robert J. *Metallurgy in Antiquity*. Leiden: Brill, 1950.

———. *Studies in Ancient Technology*. 8 vols. Leiden: Brill, 1955–1964.

Hartman, L., and A. Leo Oppenheim. *On Beer and Brewing Techniques in Ancient Mesopotamia According to the XXIIIrd Tablet of the Series HAR.ra.hubullu*. Supplement, *Journal of the American Oriental Society*. Baltimore, Md.: American Oriental Society, 1950.

Herrmann, Georgina, ed. *The Furniture of Western Asia: Ancient and Traditional. Papers presented at the Institute of Archaeology, University College London, 28–30 June 1993*. Mainz: Zabern, 1996.

Hodges, H. *Technology in the Ancient World*. Harmondsworth: Penguin, 1970.

Levey, Martin. *Chemistry and Chemical Technology in Ancient Mesopotamia*. Amsterdam: Elsevier, 1959.

Liebowitz, H. A., B. A. Nakahi, and E. Stern. "Furniture and Furnishings." In *The Oxford Encyclopedia of Archaeology in the Near East 2*, ed. Eric M. Meyers. Oxford: Oxford University Press, 1997, 352–58.

Moorey, Peter R. S. *Materials and Manufacture in Ancient Mesopotamia: The Evidence of Art and Archaeology: Metals and Metalwork, Glazed Materials and Glass*. Oxford: B.A.R., 1985.

———. *Ancient Mesopotamian Materials and Industries: The Archaeological Evidence*. Oxford: Clarendon, 1994.

Muhly, James D. *Copper and Tin*. New Haven. Conn.: Connecticut Academy of Arts and Sciences, 1973.

Oppenheim, A. Leo, et al. *Glass and Glassmaking in Ancient Mesopotamia: An Edition of Cuneiform Texts Which Contain Instructions for Glassmakers with a Catalogue of Surviving Objects*. Corning, N.Y.: Corning Museum of Glass, 1970.

Peregrine, Peter. "Some Political Aspects of Craft Specialization." *World Archaeology* 23 (1991): 1–11.

Postgate, J. Nicholas, and Marvin A. Powell, eds. *Trees and Timber in Mesopotamia*. *Bulletin of Sumerian Agriculture*. Cambridge: Cambridge University Press, 1992.

Potts, Daniel T. *Mesopotamian Civilization: The Material Foundations*. New York: Athlone, 1997.

Simpson, E. "Furniture in Ancient Western Asia." *In Civilizations of the Ancient Near East,* ed. Jack M. Sasson, New York: Scribner, 1995, 167–71.

Szarzynska, Krystyna. *Sheep Husbandry and Production of Wool, Garments and Cloths in Archaic Sumer*. Warsaw: Agade, 2002.

van de Mieroop, Marc. *Crafts in the Early Isin Period: A Study of the Isin Craft Archive from the Reign of Isbi-Erra and Su-Ilisu*. Leuven: Departement Oriëntalistik, 1987.

Waetzoldt, Hartmut. *Untersuchnungen zur neusumerischen Textilindustrie*. Rome: Centro per le Antichità e la Storia dell'Arte del Vicino Oriente, 1972.

Daily Life

Averbeck, Richard E., Mark W. Chavalas, and David B. Weisberg, eds. *Life and Culture in the Ancient Near East*. Bethesda, Md.: CDL, 2003.

Bottéro, Jean. "The Cuisine of Ancient Mesopotamia." *Biblical Archaeology* 481 (1985): 30–47.

———. *Textes Culinaires Mésopotamiens*. Winona Lake, Ind.: Eisenbrauns, 1995.

———. *Everyday Life in Ancient Mesopotamia*. Edinburgh: Edinburgh University Press, 2001.

Collon, Dominique. "Clothing and Grooming in Western Asia." In *Civilizations of the Ancient Near East,* ed. Jack M. Sasson. New York: Scribner, 1995, 503–15.

Dayagi-Mendels, Michael. *Perfumes and Cosmetics in the Ancient World*. Jerusalem: Israel Museum, 1989.

Ellison, R. "Diet in Mesopotamia: The Evidence of the Barley Ration Texts (c. 3000–1400 B.C.)." *Iraq* 43 (1981): 35–45.

Greengus, Alan. "Old Babylonian Marriage Ceremonies and Rites." *Journal of Cuneiform Studies* 20 (1966): 55–72.

Milano, Lucio, ed. *Drinking in Ancient Societies: History and Culture of Drinking in the Ancient Near East. Papers of a Symposium held in Rome, 17–19 May 1990*. Padua: Sargon, 1994.

Nemet-Nejat, Karen R. *Daily Life in Ancient Mesopotamia*. Westport, Conn.: Greenwood, 1999.

Powell, Marvin A., ed. *Labor in the Ancient Near East*. New Haven, Conn.: American Oriental Society, 1987.

Snell, Daniel D. C. *Life in the Ancient Near East*. New Haven, Conn.: Yale University Press, 1999.

Stol, Martin. "Private Life in Mesopotamia." In *Civilizations of the Ancient Near East,* ed. Jack M. Sasson. New York: Scribner, 1995, 485–501.

Geography

Adams, Robert McC. *Heartland of Cities*. Chicago: University of Chicago Press, 1981.

———. *Land behind Baghdad*. Chicago: University of Chicago Press, 1965.

Adams, Robert McC., and Hans J. Nissen. *The Uruk Countryside: The Natural Setting of Urban Societies*. Chicago: Chicago University Press, 1972.

Butzer, K. W. "Environmental Change in the Near East and Human Impact on the Land." In *Civilizations of the Ancient Near East,* ed. Jack M. Sasson. New York: Scribner, 1995, 123–51.

Horowitz, Wayne. *Mesopotamian Cosmic Geography*. Winona Lake, Ind.: Eisenbrauns, 1987.

Jacobsen, Thorkild. *Salinity and Irrigation Agriculture in Antiquity*. Bibliotheca Mesopotamica 14. Malibu, Calif.: Undena, 1982.

Lees, G. M., and N. L. Falcon. "The Geographical History of the Mesopotamian Plain." *Geographical Journal* 118 (1952): 24–39.

Levine, Louis D. *Geographical Studies in the Neo-Assyrian Zagros*. Toronto: Royal Ontario Museum, 1974.

Liverani, Mario, ed. *Neo-Assyrian Geography*. Rome: Università di Roma, Istituto di studi del vicino oriente, 1995.

Milano, Lucio, S. de Martino, F. M. Fales, and G. B. Lanfranchi, eds. *Landscapes, Territories, Frontiers and Horizons in the Ancient Near East. Papers presented to the XLIV Rencontre Assyriologique Internationale, Venice, 7–11 July 1997.* 3 vols. Padua: Sargon, 1999.

Nützel, W. "The Climate Changes of Mesopotamia and Bordering Areas." *Sumer* 32 (1976): 11–24.

Wagstaff, John M. *The Evolution of Middle Eastern Landscapes: An Outline to A.D. 1840*. London: Croom Helm, 1985.

Weiss, Harvey P. *The Origins of Cities in Dry-Farming Syria and Mesopotamia in the Third Millennium B.C.* Guildford, Conn.: Four Quarters, 1986.

General Introductions

Jacobsen, Thorkild. *Towards the Image of Tammuz and Other Essays on Mesopotamian History and Culture*. Cambridge, Mass.: Harvard University Press, 1970.

Oppenheim, A. Leo. *Ancient Mesopotamia. Portrait of a Dead Civilization*. 2d. ed. Chicago: Chicago University Press, 1977.

Postgate, John Nicholas. *The First Empires*. Oxford: Elsevier-Phaidon, 1977.

Roaf, Michael. *Cultural Atlas of Mesopotamia and the Ancient Near East*. Oxford: Facts on File, 1990.

Sasson, Jack M., et al., eds. *Civilizations of the Ancient Near East*. New York: Scribner, 1995.

Soden, Wolfram von. *The Ancient Orient: An Introduction to the Study of the Ancient Near East*. Grand Rapids, Mich.: Eerdmans, 1994.

Historiography

Abusch, Tzvi, P. A. Beaulieu, H. Huehnergard, P. Machinist, and P. Steinkeller, eds. *Historiography in the Cuneiform World: Proceedings of the XLV Rencontre Assyriologique Internationale*. Bethesda, Md.: CDL, 2001.

Dentan, Robert C., ed. *The Idea of History in the Ancient Near East*. New Haven, Conn.: Yale University Press, 1954 (reprint: 1983).

Finkelstein, Josef J. "Mesopotamian Historiography." *Proceedings of the American Philosophical Society* 107 (1963): 461–71.

Grayson, Albert Kirk. *Assyrian and Babylonian Chronicles*. 2 vols. Locust Valley, N.Y.: Augustin, 1970.

———. *Babylonian Historical-Literary Texts*. Toronto Semitic Texts and Studies 3. Toronto: University of Toronto Press, 1975.

Tadmor, Hayim, and M. Weinfeld, eds. *History, Historiography and Interpretation Studies in Biblical and Cuneiform Literatures*. Jerusalem: Magnes, 1983.

van de Mieroop, Marc. *Cuneiform Texts and the Writing of History*. London: Routledge, 1999.

HISTORY

General

Bottéro, Jean, Elena Cassin, and Jean Vercoutter, eds. *The Near East: The Early Civilizations*. 3 vols. London: Weidenfeld & Nicolson, 1965–1967.

Diakonoff, I. M. *Early Antiquity*. Chicago: University of Chicago Press, 1991.

Hallo, William W., and William K. Simpson. *The Ancient Near East: A History*. 2d. ed. New York, London: Harcourt Brace, 1998.

Kuhrt, Amélie. *The Ancient Near East, c. 3000–330 B.C.* London: Routledge, 1995.

Leick, Gwendolyn. *Who's Who in the Ancient Near East*. London: Routledge, 1999.

———. *Mesopotamia: The Invention of the City*. London: Penguin, 2001.

Nissen, Hans. *The Early History of the Ancient Near East 9000–2000 B.C.* Chicago: University of Chicago Press, 1988.

Postgate, John Nicholas. *Early Mesopotamia: Society and Economy at the Dawn of History*. London: Routledge, 1992.

Roux, Georges. *Ancient Iraq*. Harmondsworth: Penguin, 1966.

Prehistory

Adams, Robert McC. *Heartland of Cities*. Chicago: University of Chicago Press, 1981.

Adams, Robert McC., and Hans Nissen. *The Uruk Countryside*. Chicago: University of Chicago Press, 1972.

Algaze, Guillermo. *The Uruk World System: The Dynamics of Expansion of Early Mesopotamian Civilization*. Chicago: University of Chicago Press, 1993.

Bartl, Karin, Reinhard Bernbeck, and Marlies Heinz, eds. *Zwischen Euphrat und Indus: Aktuelle Forschungsprobleme in der Vorderasiatischen Archäologie*. Hildesheim: Olms, 1995.

Charvát, Petr. *On Peoples, Signs and States: Spotlights on Sumerian Society, c. 3500– 2500 B.C. Prague:* Oriental Institute, 1997.

———. *Mesopotamia: Before History*. London: Routledge, 2002.

Henrickson, Elizabeth, and Ingolf Thuessen, eds. *Upon This Foundation: The "Ubaid" Reconsidered*. Carsten Niebuhr Institute Publications 10. Copenhagen: Museum Tusculanum, 1989.

Huot, Jean-Louis, ed. *Préhistoire de la Mésopotamie*. Paris: Centre National de la Recherche Scientifique, 1987.

Johnson, Gregory. "Late Uruk in Greater Mesopotamia: Expansion or Collapse?" *Origini* (1988–1989) 14: 595–613.

Maisels, Charles Keith. *The Emergence of Civilization: From Hunting and Gathering to Agriculture, Cities, and the State in the Near East*. London: Routledge, 1990.

Matthews, Roger. "Defining the Style of the Period: Jemdet Nasr 1926–28." *Iraq* 54 (1992): 1–34.

———. *Cities, Seals, and Writing: Archaic Seal Impressions from Jemdet Nasr and Ur. Materialien zu den frühen Schriftzeugnissen des Vorderen Orients 2*. Berlin: Gebrüder Mann, 1993.

Pollock, Susan. "Bureaucrats and Managers, Peasants and Pastoralists, Imperialists and Traders: Research on the Uruk and Jemdet-Nasr Periods in Mesopotamia." *Journal of World Prehistory* 6 (1992): 297–336.

———. *Ancient Mesopotamia: The Eden That Never Was*. Cambridge: Cambridge University Press.

Stein, Gil. "On the Uruk Expansion." *Current Anthropology* (1990) 31: 66–69.

Strommenger, Eva. *Habuba-Kabira: Eine Stadt vor 5000 Jahren*. Mainz: Philip von Zabern, 1980.

Early Dynastic Period

Charvát, Petr. *On Peoples, Signs and States: Spotlights on Sumerian Society, c. 3500– 2500 B.C.* Prague: Oriental Institute, 1997.

Cooper, Jerrold J. *Reconstructing History from Ancient Inscriptions: The Lagash-Umma Border Conflict*. Sources from the Ancient Near East 2/1. Malibu, Calif.: Undena, 1983.

———. *Sumerian and Akkadian Royal Inscriptions: Vol. I. Pre-Sargonic Inscriptions.* Winona Lake, Ind.: Eisenbrauns, 1986.

Hansen, D. P. "Royal Building Activity at Sumerian Lagash in the Early Dynastic Period." *Biblical Archaeology* 55 (1992): 206–11.

Jacobsen, Thorkild. "Primitive Democracy in Ancient Mesopotamia." *Journal of Near Eastern Studies* 2 (1943): 159–72.

———. "Early Political Development in Mesopotamia." *Zeitschrift für Assyriologie* 52 (1957): 91–140.

Katz, Dina. "Gilgamesh and Akka: Was Uruk Ruled by Two Assemblies?" *Révue d'Assyriologie* 81 (1987): 105–14.

Maekawa, Kazuya. "The Development of the é-mí in Lagash during Early Dynastic III." *Mesopotamia* 8–9 (1973–1974): 77–144.

———. "Female Weavers and Their Children in Lagash: Pre-Sargonic and Ur III." *Acta Sumerologica* 2 (1980): 81–125.

Martin, Harrriet P. *Fara. A Reconstruction of the Ancient Mesopotamian City of Shuruppak.* Birmingham: Martin and Associates, 1988.

Matthews, Roger. "Fragments of Officialdom from Fara." *Iraq* 54 (1991): 1–15.

Pollock, Susan. "Of Priestesses, Princes and Poor Relations: The Dead in the Royal Cemetery of Ur." *Cambridge Archaeological Journal* 1/2 (1991): 171–89.

Akkadian Period

Cooper, Jerrold S. *Sumerian and Akkadian Royal Inscriptions: Vol. I. Pre-Sargonic Inscriptions.* American Oriental Society Translation Series I. Winona Lake, Ind.: Eisenbrauns, 1986.

Foster, Benjamin. *Umma in the Sargonic Period.* Hamden, Conn.: Archon, 1986.

Frayne, Douglas. *Sargonic and Gutian Periods (2334–2113 B.C.): Royal Inscriptions of Mesopotamia. Early Periods. Vol. 2.* Toronto: University of Toronto Press, 1993.

Gelb, Igance J., and Burkhart Kienast. *Die altakkadischen Königsinschriften des dritten Jahrtausends v. Chr.* Stuttgart: Steiner, 1990.

Glassner, Jean-Jacques. *La chute d'Akkade: l'évenement et sa mémoire.* Beiträge zum Vorderen Orient. Berlin: Reimer, 1986.

Liverani, Mario, ed. *Akkad: The First World Empire: Structure, Ideology, Traditions.* Padua: Sargon, 1993.

Michalowski, Piotr. "New Sources Concerning the Reign of Naram-Sin." *Journal of Cuneiform Studies* 32 (1980): 233–46.

Tinney, Stephen. "A New Look at Naram-Sin and the 'Great Rebellion.'" *Journal of Cuneiform Studies* 47 (1995): 1–14.

Sumerian History

Civil, Miguel. "Šu-Sin's Historical Inscriptions: Collection B." *Journal of Cuneiform Studies* 21 (1967): 24–38.

Crawford, Harriet E. W. *Sumer and the Sumerians.* Cambridge: Cambridge University Press, 1991.

Edzard, Dietz Otto. *Gudea and His Dynasty: Royal Inscriptions of Mesopotamia. Early Periods 3/1*. Toronto: University of Toronto Press, 1997.

Falkenstein, Adam. *The Sumerian Temple City*. Monographs of the Ancient Near East I/1. Malibu, Calif.: Undena, 1954.

Foster, Benjamin. "A New Look at the Sumerian Temple State." *Journal of the Economic and Social History of the Orient* 24 (1981): 225–34.

———. *Administration and Use of Institutional Land in Sargonic Sumer*. Mesopotamia 9. Copenhagen: Akademisk Forlag, 1982.

Hallo, William W. "A Sumerian Amphyctyony." *Journal of Cuneiform Studies* 17 (1960): 112–41.

———. "Women of Sumer." In *The Legacy of Sumer*, ed. Denise Schmandt-Besserat. Malibu, Calif.: Undena, 1960, 23–40.

Katz, D. "Gilgamesh and Akka: Was Uruk Ruled by Two Assemblies?" *Révue d'Assyriologie* 81 (1987): 105–14.

Kramer, Samuel Noah. *History Begins at Sumer*. 3d ed. Philadelphia: University of Pennsylvania Press, 1981.

Pollock, Susan. "Of Priests, Princes, and Poor Relations: The Dead in the Royal Graves of Ur." *Cambridge Archaeological Journal* 1 (1991): 171–89.

———. "Women in a Men's World: Images of Sumerian Women." In *Engendering Archaeology: On Women and Prehistory*, ed. Joan Gero and Margaret Conkey. Oxford: Blackwell, 1991, 366–87.

Schmandt-Besserat, Denise, ed. *The Legacy of Sumer*. Bibliotheca Mesopotamica 4. Malibu, Calif.: Undena, 1976.

Steinkeller, Peter. "The Date of Gudea and His Dynasty." *Journal of Cuneiform Studies* 40 (1988): 47–53.

Third Dynasty of Ur

Buccellati, Giorgio. *Amorites of the Ur III Period*. Naples: Istituto Orientale di Napoli, 1966.

Flückiger-Hawker, Esther. *Urnammu of Ur in Sumerian Literary Tradition*. Freiburg: Université de Fribourg, Vandenhoeck and Ruprecht, 1999.

Frayne, Douglas R. *Ur III Period (2212–2004 B.C.): The Royal Inscriptions of Mesopotamia. Early Periods 3/2*. Toronto: University of Toronto Press, 1997.

Kärki, Ilmari. *Königsinschriften der dritten Dynastie von Ur*. Helsinki: Societas Orientalis Fennica, 1986.

Klein, Jacob. *The Royal Hymns of Shulgi, King of Ur*. Philadelphia: American Philosophical Society, 1981.

———. "Shulgi King of Ur: King of Neo-Sumerian Empire." In *Civilizations of the Ancient Near East*, ed. Jack M. Sasson, New York: Scribner, 1995, 843–58.

Kramer, Samuel Noah. "The Ur-Nammu Code: Who Was Its Author?" *Orientalia* 52 (1983): 453–56.

Michalowski, Piotr. "The Death of Shulgi." *Orientalia* 46 (1977): 220–25.

Moorey, P. R. S. "Where Did They Bury the Kings of the Third Dynasty of Ur?" *Iraq* 46 (1984): 1–18.

Steible, Horst. *Die neusumerischen Bau-und Weihinschriften. Teil 2,* Freiburger Altorientalische Studien 9/2. Wiesbaden: Steiner, 1991.

Steinkeller, Peter. "The Administrative and Economic Organization of the Ur III State: The Core and the Periphery." In *The Organization of Power: Aspects of Bureaucracy in the Ancient Near East,* eds. McGuire Gibson and Robert D. Biggs. Chicago: Oriental Institute of the University of Chicago, 1987, 19–42.

Old Babylonian Period

Batto, Bernard F. *Studies on Women at Mari.* Baltimore, Md.: Johns Hopkins University Press, 1974.

Frayne, Douglas R. *Old Babylonian Period (2003–1595 B.C.): The Royal Inscriptions of Mesopotamia. Early Period.* Vol. 4. Toronto: Toronto University Press, 1990.

Dalley, Stephanie. *Mari and Karana: Two Old Babylonian Cities.* London: Longman, 1984.

Gadd, Cyril J. "Hammurabi and the End of His Dynasty." In *Cambridge Ancient History 2.* 2d ed. Cambridge: Cambridge University Press, 1973, 176–227.

Gasche, Hermann, J. A. Armstrong, and S. W. Cole. *Dating the Fall of Babylon.* Chicago: University of Ghent and the Oriental Institute of the University of Chicago, 1998.

Harris, Rivkah. "The Process of Secularization under Hammurapi." *Journal of Cuneiform Studies* 15 (1961): 17–24.

———. *Ancient Sippar: A Demographic Study of an Old Babylonian City (1994–1595 B.C.).* Istanbul: Nederlands Historisch-Archaeologisch Intituut te Istanbul, 1975.

Horsnell, Malcolm J. A. *The Year Names of the First Dynasty of Babylon.* Vol. II. Hamilton, Canada: Mcmaster University Press, 1999.

Jacobsen, Thorkild. "The Reign of Ibbi-Suen." *Journal of Cuneiform Studies* 7 (1953): 36–47.

Stol, Marten. *Studies in Old Babylonian History.* Leiden: Nederlands Historisch-Archaeologisch Instituut, 1976.

Stone, Elizabeth. "Economic Crisis and Social Upheaval in Old Babylonian Nippur." *In Mountains and Lowlands: Essays in the Archaeology of Greater Mesopotamia,* ed. T. Cuyler Young and Louis D. Levine. Bibliotheca Mesopotamica 7, Malibu, Calif.: Undena, 1977, 267–89.

———. "The Social Role of the Naditu Women in the Old Babylonian Nippur." *Journal of the Economic and Social History of the Orient* 25 (1982): 50–70.

———. *Nippur Neighborhoods.* Chicago: University of Chicago Press, 1987.

van de Mieroop, Marc. "The Reign of Rim-Sin." *Révue d'Assyriologie* 87 (1993): 47–69.

Young, G. D., ed. *Mari in Retrospect.* Winona Lake, Ind.: Eisenbrauns, 1992.

Yuhong, W. *A Political History of Eshnunna: Mari and Assyria during the Early Old Babylonian Period*. Changchun: Institute of History of Ancient Civilizations, Northeast Normal University, 1994.

Middle Babylonian Period

Brinkman, John A. *A Political History of Post-Kassite Babylonia*. Rome: Biblical Institute, 1968.

———. "'The Monarchy of the Kassite Dynasty' in *Le Palais et la royauté*." In *XIX Rencontre Assyriologique Internationale, Paris 1971*, ed. Pierre Garelli. Paris: Geuthner, 1974, 409–15.

———. *Materials and Studies for Kassite History: Vol. I. A Catalogue of Cuneiform Sources Pertaining to Specific Monarchs of the Kassite Dynasty*. Chicago: Oriental Institute of the University of Chicago, 1976.

———. "Kassiten." *Reallexikon der Assyriologie und Archäologie* 5 (1980): 464–73.

Frame, Grant. *Rulers of Babylonia: From the Second Dynasty of Isin to the End of the Assyrian Domination (1157–612 B.C.): Royal Inscriptions of Mesopotamia. Early Period*, vol. 2. Toronto: University of Toronto Press, 1995.

Lambert, Wilfred G. "The Reign of Nebuchadnezzar I: A Turning Point in the History of Mesopotamian Religion." In *The Seed of Wisdom. Essays in Honor of T. J. Meek*, ed. W. S. MacCullogh. Toronto: University of Toronto Press, 1963, 3–13.

Sassmannhausen, L. "The Adaptation of the Kassites to the Babylonian Civilization." In *Languages and Cultures in Contact: At the Crossroads of Civilization in the Syro-Mesopotamian Realm: Proceedings of the 42 Rencontre Assyriologique Internationale*, ed. Karel van Lerberghe and Gabrielle Voet. Leuven: Peeters, 1999, 409–24.

Sommerfeld, Walter. "The Kassites of Ancient Mesopotamia: Origins, Politics, and Culture." In *Civilizations of the Ancient Near East*, ed. Jack M. Sasson. New York: Scribner, 1995, 917–30.

Stein, Peter. *Die mittel-und neubabylonischen Königsinschriften bis zum Ende der Assyrerherrschaft*. Jenaer Beiträge zum Vorderen Orient 3. Wiesbaden: Harrassowitz, 2000.

Ward, William A., and Martha Sharp Jonkowsky, eds. *The Crisis Years: The 12th Century B.C.* Dubuque, Iowa: Kendall/Hunt, 1992.

Amarna Period

Cohen, Raymond, and Raymond Westbrook, eds. *Amarna Diplomacy: The Beginnings of International Relations*. Baltimore, Md.: Johns Hopkins University Press, 2000.

Moran, William L. *The Amarna Letters*. Baltimore, Md.: Johns Hopkins University Press, 1992.

Neo-Babylonian Period

Beaulieu, Pierre-Alain. *The Reign of Nabonidus King of Babylon 556–539 B.C.* New Haven, Conn.: Yale University Press, 1989.

——. "King Nabonidus and the Neo-Babylonian Empire." In *Civilizations of the Ancient Near East,* ed. Jack M. Sasson. New York: Scribner, 1995, 969–80.

Borger, Rykele. "Der Aufstieg des neubabylonischen Reiches." *Journal of Cuneiform Studies* 19 (1965): 59–78.

Brinkman, John A. "Babylonia under the Assyrian Empire 745–c. 627." In *Power and Propaganda: A Symposium on Ancient Empires,* ed. Mogens T. Larsen. Copenhagen: Akademisk Forlag, 1979, 223–50.

——. *Prelude to Empire: Babylonian Society and Politics, 747–626 B.C.* Philadelphia: University Museum, 1984.

Dandamayev, Mohammed. "The Neo-Babylonian Society and Economy." In *Cambridge Ancient History,* 3.2. Cambridge: Cambridge University Press, 1988, 252–75.

Frame, Grant. *Babylonia 689–627 B.C.: A Political History.* Istanbul: Nederlands Historisch-Archaeologisch Instituut te Istanbul, 1992.

——. "The 'First Families' of Borsippa during the Early Neo-Babylonian period." *Journal of Cuneiform Studies* 36 (1984): 67–80.

Funk, Bernhard. "Babylonien im 7. und 6. Jahrhundert." In *Gesellschaft und Kultur im alten Vorderasien,* ed. Horst Klengel. Berlin: Akademie Verlag, 1982.

Gadd, Cyril J. "The Harran inscriptions of Nabonidus." *Anatolian Studies 8* (1958): 35–92.

Sack, Ronald H. "Nebuchadnezzar and Nabonidus in Folklore and History." *Mesopotamia* 17 (1982): 67–131.

——. "The Nabonidus Legend." *Révue d'Assyriologie* 77 (1983): 67–131.

——. *Neriglissar—King of Babylon.* Neukirchen-Vluyn: Neukirchner, 1994.

Saggs, Henry W. F. *The Greatness that was Babylon.* London: Sidgwick & Jackson, 1962.

Stein, Peter. *Die mittel-und neubabylonischen Königsinschriften bis zum Ende der Assyrerherrschaft.* Jenaer Beiträge zum Vorderen Orient 3. Wiesbaden: Harrasowitz, 2000.

Wiseman, Donald J. *Nebuchadrezzar and Babylon: The Schweich Lectures of the British Academy.* London: Oxford University Press, 1985.

Old Assyrian Period

Dercksen, Jan G. *The Old Assyrian Copper Trade in Anatolia.* Istanbul: Nederlands Historish-Archaeologisch Instituut te Istanbul, 1996.

Grayson, Albert K. "The Early Development of the Assyrian Monarchy." *Ugarit Forschungen* 3 (1971): 311–19.

——. *Assyrian Royal Inscriptions.* Vol. I. Wiesbaden: Harrasowitz, 1972.

——. *Assyrian Rulers of the Third and Second Millennia B.C. (to 1115 B.C.)*. Toronto: University of Toronto Press, 1987.

Larsen, Mogens T. *Old Assyrian Caravan Procedures*. Istanbul: Nederlands Historisch-Archaeologisch Instituut te Istanbul, 1967.

——. *The Old Assyrian City State and Its Colonies*. Mesopotamia 4. Copenhagen: Akademisk Forlag, 1976.

Orlin, Louis L. *Assyrian Colonies in Cappadocia*. The Hague: Mouton, 1970.

Özgüç, Tahsin. *Kültepe-Kaniš II: New Researches at the Trading Center of the Ancient Near East*. Ankara: Türk Tarih Kurumu Basimevi, 1986.

Middle Assyrian Period

Grayson, Albert K. "Assyria: Ashur-Dan II to Ashur-nirari V (934–745 B.C.)." In *Cambridge Ancient History*, 3.1, 2d ed. Cambridge: Cambridge University Press, 1982, 253–59.

——. *Assyrian Royal Inscriptions 1*. Wiesbaden: Harrasowitz, 1972.

——. *Assyrian Royal Inscriptions 2*. Wiesbaden: Harrasowitz, 1976.

Munn-Rankin, M. "Assyrian Military Power 1300–1200 B.C." In *Cambridge Ancient History*, 2.2, 2d ed. Cambridge: Cambridge University Press, 1975, 274–79.

Saporetti, Claudio. *The Status of Women in the Middle Assyrian Period*. Sources and Monographs of the Ancient Near East 2/1. Malibu, Calif.: Undena, 1979.

Schaudig, Hanspeter. *Die Inschriften Nabonids von Babylon und Kyros' des Grossen samt den in ihrem Umfeld entstandenen Tendenzschriften: Textausgabe und Grammatik*. Münster: Ugarit, 2001.

Weidner, Ernst F. *Die Inschriften Tukulti-Ninurtas I und seiner Nachfolger*. Archiv für Orientforschung Beiheft 12. Graz: im Selbstverlag des Herausgebers, 1959.

Wiseman, Donald J. "Assyria and Babylonia c. 1200–1000 B.C." In *Cambridge Ancient History*, 2.2, 2d ed. Cambridge: Cambridge University Press, 1975, 469–70.

——. "Babylonia 605–539 B.C." *Cambridge Ancient History*, 3.2, 2d ed. Cambridge: Cambridge University Press, 1991, 229–51.

——. *Nebuchadnezzar and Babylon*. Oxford: Oxford University Press, 1985.

Neo-Assyrian Period

Fales, F. M., ed. A*ssyrian Royal Inscriptions: New Horizons in Literary, Ideological, and Historical Analysis: Papers of a Symposium Held in Cetona (Siena), 26–28 June 1980*. Rome: Isitituto per l'Oriente, Centro per le antichità e la storia dell'arte del vicino Oriente, 1981.

Grayson, Albert K. "Assyria 668–635 B.C.: The Reign of Ashurbanipal." In *Cambridge Ancient History*, 3.2, 2d ed. Cambridge: Cambridge University Press, 1991, 142–61.

Landsberger, Benno, Simo Parpola, and Hayim Tadmor. "The Sin of Sargon and Sennacherib's Last Will." *State Archives of Assyria Bulletin* 3 (1989): 1–51.

Lanfranchi, Giovanni, and Simo Parpola. *The Correspondence of Sargon: Part II. Letters from the Northern and North-Eastern Provinces.* State Archives of Assyria 5. Helsinki: Helsinki University Press, 1990.

Levine, Louis D. "Sargon's Eighth Campaign." In *Mountains and Lowlands.* Bibliotheca Mesopotamica 7, ed. Louis D. Levine and T. Cuyler Young. Malibu, Calif.: Undena, 1977, 135–51.

Liverani, Mario. "The Growth of the Assyrian Empire." *State Archives of Assyria Bulletin* II, no. 2 (1988): 81–98.

———. "The Ideology of the Assyrian Empire." In *Power and Propaganda: A Symposium on Ancient Empires. Studies in Assyriology, vol. 7,* ed. Mogens T. Larsen. Copenhagen: Akademisk Forlag, 1979, 297–317.

Luckenbill, Daniel D. *The Annals of Sennacherib.* Chicago: University of Chicago Press, 1924.

———. *Ancient Records of Assyria and Babylonia.* 2 vols. New York: Greenwood, 1968.

Luukko, Mikko, and Greta van Buylaere, eds. *The Political Correspondence of Esarhaddon.* State Archives of Assyria, vol. 16. Helsinki: Helsinki University Press, 2002.

Malbran-Labat, Florence. *L'Armée et l'Organisation Militaire de l'Assyrie.* Paris: Droz, 1982.

Melville, Sarah C. *The Role of Naqia/Zakutu in Sargonid Politics.* State Archives of Assyria 9. Helsinki: Neo-Assyrian Text Corpus Project, 1999.

Millard, Alan Ralph. *Eponyms of the Assyrian Empire 910–612 B.C.* State Archives of Assyria 2. Helsinki: Neo-Assyrian Text Corpus Project, 1994.

Na'aman, N. "Chronology and History in the Late Assyrian Empire (613–619 B.C.)." *Zeitschrift für Assyriologie* 81 (1991): 243–67.

Oates, Joan. "Assyrian Chronology 613–612 B.C." *Iraq* 27 (1965): 135–59.

Oded, Bustang. *Mass Deportations and Deportees in the Neo-Assyrian Empire.* Wiesbaden: Reichert, 1979.

Paley, Samuel M. *King of the World: Ashur-nasirpal II of Assyria 883–859 B.C.* New York: Brooklyn Museum, 1976.

Parpola, Simo. "A Letter from Šamaš-šumu-ukin to King Esarhaddon." *Iraq* 34 (1972): 21–34.

———. "The Murder of Sennacherib." In *Death in Mesopotamia: 26th Rencontre Assyriologique Internationale,* ed. Bendt Alster. Copenhagen: Akademisk Forlag, 1980, 171–82.

———. *The Correspondence of Sargon II: Part 1, Letters from Assyria and the West.* State Archives of Assyria 1. Helsinki: Helsinki University Press, 1987.

Parpola, Simo, and Kazuko Watanabe. *Neo-Assyrian Treaties and Loyalty Oaths.* State Archives of Assyria 2. Helsinki: Helsinki University Press, 1988.

Pongratz-Leisten, Beate. *Herrschaftswissen in Mesopotamien: Formen der Kommunikation zwischen Gott und König in 2. und 1. Jahrtausend v. Chr.* Helsinki: The Neo-Assyrian Text Corpus Project, 1999.

Porter, Barbara N. *Images, Power, and Politics: Figurative Aspects of Esarhaddon's Babylonian Policy.* Philadelphia: American Philosophical Society, 1993.

Postgate, John Nicholas. "The Land of Assur and the Yoke of Assur." *World Archaeology* 23 (1992): 247–63.

———. *Neo-Assyrian Royal Grants and Decrees.* Studia Pohl, Series Maior 1. Rome: Pontifical Biblical Institute, 1969.

———. *Taxation and Conscription in the Assyrian Empire.* Studia Pohl, Series Maior 3. Rome: Biblical Institute Press, 1974.

Reade, Julian. "The Neo-Assyrian Court and Army: Evidence from the Sculptures." *Iraq* 34 (1972): 87–112.

Saggs, Henry W. F. *The Might That Was Assyria.* London: Sidgwick & Jackson, 1984.

Starr, Ivan. *Queries to the Sungod: Divination and Politics in Sargonid Assyria.* State Archives of Assyria 4. Helsinki: Helsinki University Press, 1990.

Tadmor, Hayim. "The Campaigns of Sargon II of Assyria." *Journal of Cuneiform Studies* 12 (1958): 22–40, 77–100.

Thomas, F. "Sargon II, der Sohn Tiglath-pilesers III." In *Mesopotamica-Ugaritica-Biblica: Festschrift für Kurt Bergerhof zur Vollendung seines 70. Lebensjahres am 7. Mai 1992,* ed. Manfried Dietrich and Oswald Loretz. Neukirchen-Vluyn: Neukirchner Verlag,1993, 465–70.

Waetzold, Hartmut, and Harald Hauptmann, eds. *Assyrien im Wandel der Zeiten: 39 e Rencontre Assyriologique Internationale, Heidelberg 6–10, Juli 1992.* Heidelberg: Heidelberger Orientverlag, 1997.

Yamada, Shigeo. *The Construction of the Assyrian Empire: A Historical Study of the Inscriptions of Shalmaneser III (859–824 B.C.) Relating to his Campaigns in the West.* Boston: Brill, 2001.

Zawadzki, Stefan. *The Fall of Assyria and Median-Babylonian Relations in the Light of the Nabopolassar Chronicle.* Pozna'n: Adam Mickiewitz University Press, 1988.

Elam

Carter, Elizabeth, and Matthew W. Stolper. *Elam: Surveys of Political History and Archaeology.* Berkeley: University of California Press, 1984.

Hinz, Walther. *The Lost World of Elam.* London: Sidgwick & Jackson, 1972.

Waters, Matthew W. *A Survey of Neo-Elamite History.* State Archives of Assyria Studies, vol. 12. Helsinki: Neo-Assyrian Text Corpus Project, 2000.

Achaemenid Period

Briant, Pierre. *Histoire de l'empire perse: De Cyrus à Alexandre.* Paris: Fayard, 1996.

Cook, John M. *The Persian Empire.* London: Dent, 1983.

Curtis, John. *Ancient Persia.* London: British Museum Publications, 1989.

Dandamayev, Mohammed A. *A Political History of the Achaemenid Empire*. Leiden: Brill, 1989.

Herzfeld, Ernst. *The Persian Empire: Studies in Geography and Ethnography of the Ancient Near East*. Wiesbaden: Steiner, 1968.

Klengel, Horst. "Babylon zur Zeit der Perser, Griechen und Parther." *Forschungen und Berichte, Staatliche Museen zu Berlin* 5 (1962): 40–53.

Kuhrt, Amélie. "The Cyrus Cylinder and Achaemenid Imperial Policy." *Journal for the Study of the Old Testament* 25 (1983): 83–97.

Sancisi-Weerdenburg, Heleen, ed. *Achaemenid History Workshop*. Vols. 1–8. Leiden: Nederlands Instituut voor het Nabije Oosten, 1987–1994.

Wiesehöfer, Josef. *Ancient Persia from 550 B.C. to 650 A.D.* London: Tauris, 1996.

Young, T. Cuyler. "The Early History of the Medes and the Persians and the Achaemenid Empire to the Death of Cambyses." In *Cambridge Ancient History*. Vol. 4, 2d ed. Cambridge: University of Cambridge Press, 1988, 24–46.

Seleucid Period

Cohen, Getzel M. *The Seleucid Colonies: Studies in Founding, Administration and Organization*. Wiesbaden: Steiner, 1978.

Sherwin-White, Susan, and Amélie Kuhrt, eds. *Hellenism in the East: The Interaction of Greek and Non-Greek Civilizations from Syria to Central Asia after Alexander*. London: Duckworth, 1987.

———. *From Samarkhand to Sardis: A New Approach to the Seleucid Empire*. London: Duckworth, 1993.

Tarn, William W. *Seleucid-Parthian Studies*. London: Milford, 1930.

Wagner, Jörg. *Seleukia am Euphrat/Zeugma*. Wiesbaden: Reichert, 1976.

Laws and Legal Systems

Driver, G. R., and John C. Miles. *The Assyrian Laws*. 2 vols. Oxford: Clarendon, 1935.

———. *The Babylonian Laws*. 2 vols. Oxford: Clarendon, 1968.

Greengus, Samuel. "Legal and Social Institutions of Ancient Mesopotamia." In *Civilizations of the Ancient Near East,* ed. Jack M. Sasson. New York: Scribner, 1995, 469–84.

Jas, Remko. *Neo-Assyrian Judicial Procedures*. State Archives of Assyria V. Helsinki: Neo-Assyrian Text Corpus Project, 1996.

Joannès, Francis. *Rendre la Justice en Mésopotamie. Les Archives judiciaires du Proche-Orient ancien IIIe-Ier Millénaires avant J.-C.* Saint-Denis: Presses univérsitaires de Vincennes, 2000.

Kwasman, Theodore and Simo Parpola, eds. *Legal transactions of the royal court of Nineveh*. Helsinki: Helsinki University Press, 1991–2002.

Malul, Meir. *Studies in Mesopotamian Legal Systems*. Neukirchen-Vluyn: Neukirchner, 1988.

Roth, Martha. *Law Collections from Mesopotamia and Asia Minor*. Atlanta: Scholars Press, 1995.

VerSteeg, Russ. *Early Mesopotamian Law*. Durham, N.C.: Academic Press, 2000.

Westbrook, Raymond. "Cuneiform Law-Codes and the Origin of Legislation." *Zeitschrift für Assyriologie* 79 (1989): 201–22.

Yaron, Reuven. *The Laws of Eshnunna*. Leiden: Brill, 1969.

LITERATURE

Akkadian Literature

Cagni, Luigi. *The Poem of Erra. Sources from the Ancient Near East*. Vol. I. Malibu, Calif.: Undena, 1977.

Cooper, Jerrold S. *The Curse of Agade*. Baltimore, Md.: Johns Hopkins University Press, 1983.

Dalley, Stephanie. *Myths from Mesopotamia*. Oxford: Oxford University Press, 1989.

Foster, Benjamin. *Before the Muses: An Anthology of Akkadian Literature*. 2 vols. Bethesda, Md.: CDL, 1996.

——. *The Epic of Gilgamesh*. New York: Norton, 2001.

——. *From Distant Days: Myths, Tales and Poetry of Ancient Mesopotamia*. Bethesda, Md.: CDL, 1995.

George, Andrew. *The Epic of Gilgamesh: The Babylonian Epic Poem and Other Texts in Akkadian and Sumerian*. London: Allen Lane, 2001.

Goodnick-Westenholz, Joan. *Legends of the Kings of Akkade*. Winona Lake, Ind.: Eisenbrauns, 1997.

Harris, Rivkah. *Gender and Aging in Mesopotamia: The Gilgamesh Epic and Other Ancient Literature*. Norman: University of Oklahoma Press, 2000.

Heidel, Alexander. *A Babylonian Genesis*. Chicago: University of Chicago Press, 1951.

Lambert, Wilfred G. *Babylonian Wisdom Literature*. Oxford: Clarendon, 1960.

Lambert, Wilfred G., and Allan R. Millard. *Atra-hasis: The Babylonian Story of the Flood*. Oxford: Clarendon, 1969.

Leick, Gwendolyn. *Sex and Eroticism in Mesopotamian Literature*. London: Routledge, 1994.

Mindlin, M., M. J. Geller, and J. E. Wansbrough, eds. *Figurative Language in the Ancient Near East*. London: School of Oriental and African Studies, University of London, 1987.

Westenholz, Joan G. *Legends of the Kings of Akkade: The Texts*. Winona Lake, Ind.: Eisenbrauns, 1997.

Reiner, Erica. *"Your Thwarts in Pieces, Your Mooring Rope Cut": Poetry from Babylonia and Assyria*. Ann Arbor: Horace H. Rackham School of Michigan Graduate Studies at the University of Michigan, 1985.

Vanstiphout, Herman L. J., ed. *Genre in Mesopotamian Literature*. Leiden: Brill, 2001.

Vanstiphout, Herman L. J., and M. E. Vogelzang. *Mesopotamian Poetic Language: Sumerian and Akkadian*. Groningen: Styx, 2001.

Wassermann, N. *Wool from the Loom: The Development of Literary Genres in Ancient Literature*. Jerusalem: N.p., 2001.

Sumerian Literature

Alster, Bendt. "The Instructions of Shuruppak." *Orientalia* 60, no. 3 (1991): 141–57.

———. *Proverbs of Ancient Sumer: The World's Oldest Proverb Collections*. 2 vols. Bethesda, Md.: CDL, 1997.

Behrens, Hermann. *Enlil and Ninlil*. Studia Pohl: Series Maior 8. Rome: Biblical Institute Press, 1978.

Benito, Carlos A. *"Enki and Ninmah" and "Enki and the World Order."* Ann Arbor: University Microfilms, 1969.

Berlin, Adele. *Enmerkar and Enšuhkešdanna: A Sumerian Narrative Poem*. Philadelphia: University Museum, 1979.

Cohen, Mark. *Balag-Compositions: Sumerian Lamentation Liturgies of the Second and First Millennium B.C.* Sources from the Ancient Near East. Malibu, Calif.: Undena, 1974–1978.

Cooper, Jerrold S. *The Return of Ninurta to Nippur*. Analecta Orientalia 52. Rome: Pontificum Institutum Biblicum, 1978.

Jacobsen, Thorkild. *Harps That Once . . .: Sumerian Poetry in Translation*. New Haven, Conn.: Yale University Press, 1978.

Klein, Jacob. *The Royal Hymns of Shulgi, King of Ur*. Philadelphia: American Philosophical Society, 1981.

Kramer, Samuel Noah. *From the Tablets of Sumer*. Indian Hills, Colo.: Falcon Wings, 1956.

Michalowski, Piotr. *The Lamentation over the Destruction of Sumer and Ur*. Winona Lake, Ind.: Eisenbrauns, 1989.

Sjöberg, Ake, and E. Bergman. *The Collection of Sumerian Temple Hymns and the Kes Temple Hymn*. Locust Valley, N.Y.: Augustin, 1969.

Wasserman, Nathan. *Style and Form in Old-Babylonian Literary Texts*. Cuneiform Monographs, 27. Leiden: Brill, 2002.

Mathematics and Metrology

de Odorico, Mario. *The Use of Numbers and Quantifications in the Assyrian Royal Inscriptions*. State Archives of Assyria III. Helsinki: Neo-Assyrian Text Corpus Project, 1995.

Nemet-Najat, Karen. *Cuneiform Mathematical Texts as a Reflection of Everyday Life in Mesopotamia*. New Haven, Conn.: American Oriental Society, 1993.

Neugebauer, Otto, and A. Sachs, eds. *Mathematical Cuneiform Texts*. New Haven, Conn.: American Oriental Society, 1954.

Powell, Marvin A. "Ancient Mesopotamian Metrology." *Alter Orient und Altes Testament* 203 (1979): 90–105.

———. "Metrology and Mathematics in Ancient Mesopotamia." In *Civilizations of the Ancient Near East*, ed. Jack M. Sasson. New York: Scribner, 1941–1957, 1979.

Omen Collections

Friedman, Sally M. *If a City Is Set on a Height. Akkadian series Šumma alu ina melê sakin*. Philadelphia: Pennsylvania Museum, 1998.

Guinan, Ann. "Auguries of Hegemony: The Sex Omens of Mesopotamia." *Gender and History* 9, no. 3 (1997): 423–61.

Koch-Westenholz, Ulla. *Old Babylonian Extispicy: Omen Texts in the British Museum*. Istanbul: Nederlands Historisch-Archaeologisch Instituut te Istanbul, 1989.

———. *Babylonian Liver Omens: The Chapter Manzazu, Padanu and Pan takalti of the Babylonian Extispicy Series Mainly from Ashurbanipal's Library*. Carsten Niebuhr Institute Publications 25. Copenhagen: University of Copenhagen, 2000.

Leichty, Erle. *The Omen Series Summa Izbu: Texts from Cuneiform Sources*. Locust Valley, N.Y.: Augustin, 1970.

Reiner, Erica, and Donald Pingree. *Babylonian Planetary Omens*. Groningen: Styx, 1975–1998.

Peoples of the Ancient Near East

Hinz, Walther. *The Lost World of Elam: Re-creation of a Vanished Civilization*. London: Sidgwick & Jackson, 1972.

Kramer, Samuel Noah. *The Sumerians: Their History, Culture, and Character*. Chicago: University of Chicago Press, 1963.

Leick, Gwendolyn. *The Babylonians: An Introduction*. London: Routledge, 2002.

McQueen, James G. *The Hittites and Their Contemporaries in Asia Minor*. Rev. ed. London: Thames & Hudson, 1986.

Saggs, Henry W. F. *Babylonians*. London: British Museum Press, 1995.

———. *The Might That Was Assyria*. London: Sidgwick & Jackson, 1984.

Wilhelm, Gernot. *The Hurrians*. Warminster: Aris & Phillips, 1989.

Wiseman, Donald J., ed. *Peoples of Old Testament Times*. Oxford: Oxford University Press, 1973.

Political Structure

Finet, André. *La voix de l'opposition en Mésopotamie*. Brussels: Institut des Hautes Études Belgique, 1973.

Jacobsen, Thorkild. "Early Political Development in Mesopotamia." *Zeitschrift für Assyriologie* 52 (1957): 91–140.

Larsen, Mogens Trolle. *The Old Assyrian City-State and its Colonies.* Mesopotamia 4. Copenhagen: Akademisk Forlag, 1976.

Stein, Gil, and Martha Rothman, eds. *Chiefdoms and Early States in the Near East: The Organizational Dynamics of Complexity.* Madison: Prehistory Press, 1994.

Weisberg, David. *Guild Structure and Political Allegiance in Early Achaemenid Mesopotamia.* New Haven, Conn.: Yale University Press, 1967.

Yoffee, Norman. "Political Economy in Early Mesopotamian States." *Annual Review of Anthropology* 24 (1995): 415–30.

Religion

Abusch, Tzvi. *Mesopotamian Witchcraft: Towards a History and Understanding of Babylonian Witchcraft Beliefs and Literature.* Leiden: Brill, 2001.

Black, Jeremy A., and Anthony R. Green. *Gods, Demons and Symbols of Ancient Mesopotamia: An Illustrated Dictionary.* 2d. ed London: British Museum Press, 1992.

Bottéro, Jean. *Religion in Ancient Mesopotamia.* Chicago: University of Chicago Press, 2001.

Chamaza, G. W. V. *Die Omnipotenz Assurs: Entwicklungen in der Assur Theologie unter den Sargoniden, Sargon II, Sanherib, und Asarhaddon.* Alter Orient und Altes Testament 295. Muenster: Ugarit Verlag, 2002.

Ciraolo, L., and J. Seidel (eds.). *Magic and Dvination.* Leiden: Brill, 2002.

Cohen, Mark E. *The Canonical Lamentations of Ancient Mesopotamia.* 2 vols. Potomac, Md.: Capital Decsions, 1988.

Collins, P. "The Sumerian Goddess Inanna." *Papers from the Institute of Archaeology (University of London)* 5 (1994): 103–18.

Cunningham, Graham. *"Deliver Me from Evil": Mesopotamian Incantations 2500–1500 B.C.* Studia Pohl, Series Maior 17. Rome: Pontificio istituto biblico, 1997.

Dick, Michael B., ed. *Born in Heaven, Made on Earth: The Making of the Cult Image in the Near East.* Winona Lake, Ind.: Eisenbrauns, 1999.

Finet, André, ed. *La divination en Mésopotamie ancienne et dans les régions voisins: XIVe Rencontre Assyriologique Internationale, Strasbourg, 2–6 Juillet 1965.* Paris: Presses universitaires, 1966.

Finkel, Irvin L., and Markholm J. Geller. *Sumerian Gods and Their Representations.* Groningen: Styx, 1997.

Holloway, S. W. *Assur Is King! Assur Is King! Religion in the Exercise of Power in the Neo-Assyrian Empire.* Leiden: Brill, 2001.

Jacobsen, Thorkild. *The Treasures of Darkness: A History of Mesopotamian Religion.* New York, Conn.: Yale University Press, 1976.

Kingsbury, E. C. "A Seven Day Ritual in Old Babylonian Cult at Larsa." *Hebrew Union College Annual* 34 (1963): 1–34.

Krebernik, M. and Juergen van Oorschot (eds.). *Polytheismus und Monotheismus in den Religionen des Vorderen Orients.* Alter Orient und Altes Testament 298. Muenster: Ugarit Verlag, 2002.

Laessøe, Jørgen. *Studies on the Assyrian Ritual and Series Bît Rimki.* Copenhagen: Munsgaard, 1955.

Leick, Gwendolyn. *A Dictionary of Ancient Near Eastern Mythology.* 2d. ed. London: Routledge, 1998.

Matsushima, Eiko, ed. *Official Cult and Popular Religion in the Ancient Near East: Papers of the First Colloquium on the Ancient Near East—The City and Its Life: Held at the Middle Eastern Cultural Center in Japan (Mitaka, Tokyo).* Heidelberg: Winter, 1993.

McEwan, Gilbert J. P. *Priest and Temple in Hellenistic Babylonia.* Wiesbaden: Steiner, 1981.

Meyer, J. W. *Untersuchungen zu den Tonlebermodellen aus dem Alten Orient.* Neukirchen-Vluyn: Neukirchner, 1987.

Meyer, M., and Paul Mirecki. *Ancient Magic and Ritual Power.* Leiden: Brill, 2001.

Ringgren, Helmer. *Religions of the Ancient Near East.* London: S.P.C.K., 1973.

Oppenheim, Adolf Leo. *The Interpretation of Dreams in the Ancient Near East: With a Translation of the Assyrian Dream Book.* Philadelphia: American Philosophical Society, 1956.

Quaegebeur, J. *Ritual and Sacrifice in the Ancient Near East: Proceedings of the International Conference Organized by the Katholieke Universiteit Leuven from the 17th to the 20th of April 1991.* Leuven: Peeters, 1994.

Schwerner, D. *Die Wettergottgestalten Mesopotamiens und Nordsyriens in Zeitalter der Keilschrift.* Wiesbaden: Harrasowitz, 2001.

Scurlock, Joann. *Magico-Medical Means of Treating Ghost-Induced Illness in Ancient Mesopotamia.* Studies in Ancient Magic and Divination, 3. Leiden: Brill, 2002.

Walker, Christopher, and Michael Dick. *The Induction of the Cult Image in Ancient Mesopotamia: The Mesopotamian Mis Pî Ritual / Transliteration, Translation, and Commentary.* State Archives of Assyria Literary Texts V 1. Helsinki: Neo-Assyrian Text Corpus Project, 2001.

Watanabe, Kazko, ed. *Priests and Officials in the Ancient Near East: Papers of the Second Colloquium on the Ancient Near East—The City and Its Life—Held at the Middle Eastern Culture Center in Japan (Mitaka, Tokyo), March 22–24, 1991.* Heidelberg: Winter, 1999.

Wiggermann, F. A. M. *Mesopotamian Protective Spirits: The Ritual Texts.* Groningen: Styx, 1992.

Wilson, E. Jan. *"Holiness" and "Purity" in Mesopotamia.* Neukirchen-Vlyun: Neukirchner Verlag, 1994.

Society and Economy

Adams, Robert McC. *The Evolution of Urban Society: Early Mesopotamia and Prehispanic Mexico*. London: Weidenfeld & Nicolson, 1966.

Bongenaar, A. C. V. M., ed. *Interdependency of Institutions and Private Entrepreneurs: Proceedings of the Second MOS Symposium*. Leiden: Nederlands Instituut voor het Nabije Oosten, 2000.

Dandamaev, Mohammed. *Slavery in Babylonia from Nabopolassar to Alexander the Great 626–331 B.C.* De Kalb: Northern Illinois University Press, 1984.

Dercksen, Jan G. "'When We Met at Hattus': Trade According to Old Assyrian Texts from Alishar and Bogazköy." In *Veenhof Anniversary Volume: Studies Presented to Klaas R. Veenhof on the Occasion of his Sixty-Fifth Birthday*, ed. W. H. Soldt Leiden: Nederlands Instituut voor het Nabije Oosten, 2001, 39–65.

Diakonoff, I. M. "Slaves, Helots and Serfs in Early Antiquity." *Acta Antiqua Academiae Scientiarium Hungaricae* 22 (1974): 45–78.

——. "Socio-Economic Classes in Babylonia and the Babylonian Concept of Social Stratification." In *Gesellschaftsklassen im alten Zweistromland*, ed. Dietz O. Edzard. Munich: Verlag der bayerischen Akademie der Wissenschaften, 1972, 41–52.

——. "The Structure of Near Eastern Society before the Middle of the 2nd Millennium B.C." *Oikumene* (Budapest) 3 (1982): 7–100.

——. *Structure of Society and State in Early Dynastic Sumer*. Monographs on the Ancient Near East, Vol. I. Malibu, Calif.: Undena, 1974–1979.

Durand, Jean-Marie, ed. *La Femme dans le Proche-Orient Antique: XXXIIIe Rencontre Assyriologique Internationale, Paris, 7–10 Juillet 1986*. Paris: Éditions recherche sur les Civilisations, 1987.

Edzard, Dietz Otto, ed. *Gesellschaftsklassen im alten Zweistromland, 18 Rencontre Assyriologique Internationale, München, 29. Juni–3. Juli 1970*. Munich: Verlag der bayerischen Alademie der Wissenschaften, 1972.

Gelb, Ignace J. "Household and Family in Early Mesopotamia." In *State and Temple Economy in the Ancient Near East*. Vol. I, ed. E. Lipinski. Leuven: Department Oriëntalistiek, 1979.

Gelb, Ignace J., Piotr Steinkeller, and Robert Whiting. *Earliest Land Tenure Systems in the Near East: Ancient Kudurrus*. Oriental Institute Publications 104. Chicago: Oriental Institute of the University of Chicago, 1991.

Gibson, McGuire, and Robert D. Biggs, eds. *The Organization of Power: Aspects of Bureaucracy in the Ancient Near East*. Chicago: Oriental Institute of the University of Chicago, 1987.

Hawkins, J. D., ed. *Trade in the Ancient Near East: Papers Presented to the XXIII Recontre Assyriologique Internationale, University of Birmingham, 5–9 July, 1976*. London: British School of Archaeology in Iraq, 1977.

Jakob, S. *Untersuchungen zur mittelassyrischen Verwaltung und Sozialstruktur*. Leiden: Brill, 2001.

Klengel, Horst. *Gesellschaft und Kultur im alten Vorderasien*. Berlin: Akademie Verlag, 1982.

Mattila, Raija. *The king's magnates: a study of the highest officials of the Neo-Assyrian Empire*. Helsinki: The Neo-Assyrian Text Corpus Project, 2000.

Miller, N., ed. *Economy and Settlement in the Near East: Analyses of Ancient Sites and Materials*. MASCA Research Papers in Science and Archaeology, suppl. to vol. 7. N.p.: 1990.

Powell, Marvin. "Elusive Eden: Private Property at the Dawn of History." *Journal of Cuneiform Studies* 46 (1994): 99–104.

Renger, Johannes. "On Economic Structures in Ancient Mesopotamia." *Orientalia* 63, no. 3 (1994): 157–208.

Silver, Morris. *Economic Structures of the Ancient Near East*. London: Croom Helm, 1985.

Snell, Daniel C. *Flight and Freedom in the Ancient Near East*. Leiden: Brill, 2001.

van de Mieroop, Marc. "Women in the Economy of Sumer." In *Women's Earliest Records from Ancient Egypt and Western Asia: Proceedings of the Conference on Women in the Ancient Near East, Brown University, Providence, Rhode Island, November 5–7, 1987*, ed. Barbara Lesko. Atlanta: Scholars, 1987, 53–66.

———. *Society and Enterprise in Old Babylonian Ur*. Berlin: Reimer, 1992.

———. *The Ancient Mesopotamian City*. Oxford: Clarendon, 1997.

Veenhof, Klaas R., ed. *Houses and Households in Ancient Mesopotamia: Papers Read at the 40e Rencontre Assyriologique Internationale, Leiden, July 5–8, 1993*. Istanbul: Nederlands Historisch-Archaeologisch Intituut te Istanbul, 1996.

Yoffee, N. *The Economic Role of the Crown in the Old Babylonian Period*. Malibu, Calif.: Undena, 1977.

Zagarell, A. "Trade, Women, Class and Society in Ancient Western Asia." *Current Anthropology* 27 (1986): 415–30.

Zeder, M. A. *Feeding Cities: Specialized Animal Economy in the Ancient Near East*. Smithsonian Series in Archaeological Inquiry. Washington, D.C.: Smithsonian Institute, 1991.

Trade and Commerce

Archi, Alfonso, ed. *Circulation of Goods in Non-Palatial Context in the Ancient Near East*. Rome: Ateneo, 1984.

Bongenaar, A. C. V. M., ed. *Interdependency of Institutions and Private Entrepreneurs: Proceedings of the Second MOS Symposium, Leiden 1988*. Leiden: Nederlands Instituut voor het Nabije Oosten, 2000.

Dercksen, Jan G. *The Old Assyrian Copper Trade in Anatolia*. Istanbul: Nederlands Historisch-Archaeologisch Instituut te Istanbul, 1996.

———. *Trade and Finance in Ancient Mesopotamia*. Leiden: Nederlands Historisch-Archaeologisch Instituut voor het Nabije Oosten, 1999.

Edens, C. "Dynamics of Trade in the Ancient Mesopotamian 'World System.'" *American Anthropologist* 94 (1992): 118–39.

Larsen, Mogens T. *Old Assyrian Caravan Procedures*. Istanbul: Nederlands Historisch-Archaeologisch Instituut te Istanbul, 1967.

Leemans, Wilhelmus F. *The Old Babylonian Merchant: His Business and Social Position*. Studia et documenta ad iura Orientis Antiqui pertinentia III. Leiden: Brill, 1950.

———. *Foreign Trade in the Old Babylonian Period as Revealed by Texts from Southern Mesopotamia*. Studia et documenta ad iura Orientis Antiqui pertinentia VI. Leiden: Brill, 1960.

Lipinski, Edward, ed. *State and Temple Economy in the Ancient Near East*. Leuven: Department Oriëntalisiek, 1982.

Oates, Joan. "Mesopotamian Social Organisation: Archaeological and Philological Evidence." In *The Evolution of Social Systems,* ed. J. Friedman and M. J. Rowlands. London: Duckworth, 1977, 457–85.

———. "Ancient Trade: New Perspectives." *World Archaeology* 24, no. 3 (1993).

Oppenheim, A. Leo. "The Seafaring Merchants of Ur." *Journal of the American Oriental Society* 74 (1954): 6–17.

Powell, Marvin A. "Sumerian Merchants and the Problem of Profit." *Iraq* 39 (1954): 23–29.

Shiff, L. B. "The Nur-Sin Archive: Private Entrepreneurship in Babylon (603–507 B.C.)." Ph.D. diss., University of Pennsylvania, 1987.

Snell, Daniel. *Ledgers and Prices: Early Mesopotamian Merchant Accounts*. New Haven, Conn.: Yale University Press, 1982.

Stech, T., and V. C. Pigot. "The Metals Trade in Southwest Asia in the Third Millennium B.C." *Iraq* 48 (1986): 39–64.

Stolper, Matthew W. *Entrepreneurs and Empire: The Murašu Archive, the Murasu Firm, and the Persian Rule in Babylonia*. Istanbul: Nederlands Historisch-Archaeologisch Instituut te Istanbul, 1985.

Veenhof, Klaas R. *Aspects of Old Assyrian Trade and Its Terminology*. Leiden: Brill, 1972.

Wunsch, Cornelia. *Das Egibi Archiv 1: Die Felder und Gärten*. Groningen: Styx, 2000.

Yoffee, Norman. *The Economic Role of the Crown in the Old Babylonian Period*. Malibau, Calif.: Undena, 1977.

———. *Explaining Trade in Ancient Western Asia*. Malibu, Calif.: Undena, 1981.

Tribal Peoples

Buccellati, Giorgio G. *The Amorites of the Ur III Period*. Naples: Istituto Universitario Orientale, 1966.

Curtis, John, ed. *Later Mesopotamia and Iran: Tribes and Empires 1600–539 B.C.: Proceedings of a Seminar in Memory of Vladimir C. Lukoniv*. London: British Museum Publications, 1995.

Dietrich, Manfried. *Die Aramäer Südbabyloniens in der Sargonidenzeit (700–648)*. Neukirchen-Vlyun: Neukirchner, 1970.

Dion, Paul E. *Les Araméens à l'age du fer: Histoire politique et structures sociales*. Paris: Lecoffre, 1997.

Eph'al, Yisrael. *The Ancient Arabs: Nomads on the Borders of the Fertile Crescent 9th–5th Centuries B.C.* Leiden: Brill, 1982.

Heltzer, Michael. *The Suteans*. Naples: Istituto Universitario Orientale, 1981.

Luke, John T. *Pastoralism and Politics in the Mari Period*. Ann Arbor. Mich.: University Microfilms, 1965.

Matthews, Victor H. *Pastoral Nomadism in the Mari Kingdom*. Ann Arbor. Mich.: University Microfilm International, 1978.

Millard, Allan R. "Arameans." In *The Anchor Bible Dictionary,* ed. D. N. Freedman. New York: Doubleday, 1992, 345–50.

Schwartz, G. "Pastoral Nomadism in Ancient Western Asia." In *Civilizations of the Ancient Near East,* ed. Jack M.Sasson. New York: Scribner, 1995, 249–58.

Sommerfeld, Walter. "The Kassites of Ancient Mesopotamia: Origins, Politics and Culture." In *Civilizations of the Ancient Near East,* ed. Jack M. Sasson. New York: Scribner, 1995, 917–30.

Whiting, R. M. "Amorite Tribes and Nations." In *Civilizations of the Ancient Near East,* ed. Jack M. Sasson. New York: Scribner, 1995, 1231–42.

Warfare and Military Organization

Dalley, Stephanie. "Ancient Mesopotamian Military Organisation." In *Civilizations of the Ancient Near East,* ed. Jack M. Sasson. New York: Scribner, 1995, 413–22.

———. "Foreign Chariotry and Cavalry in the Armies of Tiglath-Pileser III." *Iraq 47* (1985): 31–38.

Epha'al, Yisrael. "Ways and Means to Conquer a City, Based on Assyrian Queries to the Sun God." In *Assyria 1995: Proceedings of the 10th Anniversary Symposium of the Neo-Assyrian Text Corpus Project, Helsinki, September 7–11, 1995,* ed. Simo Parpola and Robert M. Whiting. Helsinki: Neo-Assyrian Text Corpus Project, 1997, 49–53.

Gabriel, Richard A., and Kren S. Metz. *From Sumer to Rome: The Military Capabilities of Ancient Armies*. New York: Greenwood, 1991.

Gelb, Ignace J. "Prisoners of War in Early Mesopotamia." *Journal of Near Eastern Studies* 32 (1973): 70–98.

Klengel, Horst. "Krieg, Kriegsgefangene." *Reallexikon der Assyriologie* 6. Berlin: de Gruyter, 1980–1983, 241–46.

Malbran-Labat, Florence. *L'armée et l'organisation militaire de l'Assyrie d'après les lettres des Sargonides*. Paris: Droz, 1982.

Munn-Rankin, J. M. "Diplomacy in Western Asia in the Early Second Millennium B.C." *Iraq* 18 (1956): 68–100.

Postgate, John Nicholas. *Taxation and Conscription in the Assyrian Empire*. Rome: Biblical Institute Press, 1974.

Sasson, Jack M. *The Military Establishments at Mari*. Rome: Pontifical Institute, 1969.

Yadin, Yigael. *The Art of Warfare in Biblical Lands in the Light of Archaeological Evidence*. London: McGraw-Hill, 1963.

Women

Asher-Greve, Julia. "Stepping into the Maelstrom: Women, Gender and Ancient Near Eastern scholarship." *NIN—Journal of Gender Studies in Antiquity* 1 (2000): 1–22.

Bahrani, Zainab. *Women of Babylon: Gender and Representation in Mesopotamia*. London: Routledge, 2001.

Batto, Bernard F. *Studies on Women at Mari*. Baltimore, Md.: Johns Hopkins University Press, 1974.

Cameron, Averil, and Amélie Kuhrt, eds. *Images of Women in Antiquity*. London: Routledge, 1993.

Durand, Jean-Marie, ed. *La femme dans le Proche-Orient antique*. Paris: N.p., 1987.

Lesko, Barbara. *Women's Earliest Records from Ancient Egypt and Western Asia: Proceedings of the Conference on Women in the Ancient Near East, Brown University, Providence, Rhode Island, November 5–7, 1987*. Atlanta: Scholars Press, 1987.

Stol, Marten. "Women in Mesopotamia." *Journal of the Economic and Social History of the Orient* 38 (1995): 123–44.

Westenholz, Joan G. "Towards a New Conceptualization of the Female Role in Mesopotamian Society." *Journal of the American Oriental Society* 110 (1990): 510–21.

Wyke, Maria. *Gender and the Body in the Ancient Mediterranean*. Oxford: Oxford University Press, 1998.

Wyke, Maria, Léonie J.Archer, and Susan Fischler, eds. *Women in Ancient Societies: An illusion of the Night*. Basingstoke: Macmillan, 1994.

Writing

Driver, George R. *Semitic Writing from Pictograph to Alphabet*. 3d. rev. ed. Oxford: Oxford University Press, 1976.

Gelb, Ignace J. *A Study of Writing*. Rev. ed. Chicago: University of Chicago Press, 1963.

Gesche, Petra. *Schulunterricht in Babylonien im ersten Jahrtausend v. Chr*. Muenster: Ugarit, 1963 (reprint: 2000).

Healey, John F. *The Early Alphabet*. London: British Museum Publications, 1990.

Hooker, J. T., ed. *Reading the Past: Ancient Writings from Cuneiform to the Alphabet*. London: British Museum Publications, 1991.

Krispijn, Th. J. H. "The Early Mesopotamian Lexical Lists and the Dawn of Linguistics." *Jaarbericht Ex Oriente Lux* 32 (1991–1992): 12–22.

Liebermann, Stephen. "Of Clay Pebbles, Hollow Clay Balls, and Writing: A Sumerian View." *American Journal of Archaeology* 84 (1980): 339–58.

Michalowski, Piotr. "Early Mesopotamian Communicative Systems: Art, Literature, and Writing." In *Investigating Artistic Environments in the Ancient Near East,* ed. A. Gunter. Washington, D.C.: Arthur M. Sackler Gallery, Smithsonian Institute, 1990, 53–69.

———. *Letters from Early Mesopotamia.* Atlanta: Scholars Press, 1990.

———. "Writing and Literacy in Early States: A Mesopotamianist Perspective." In *Literacy: Interdisciplinary Conversations,* ed. Deborah Keller Cohen. Creskill, N.J.: Hampton, 1994, 49–70.

Millard, Allan R. "The Infancy of the Alphabet." *World Archaeology* 17 (1986): 390–98.

Nissen, Hans, Peter Damerow, and Robert K. Englund. *Archaic Bookkeeping: Early Writing and Techniques of Economic Administration in the Ancient Near East.* Chicago: University of Chicago Press, 1993.

Parpola, Simo. *Letters from Assyrian and Babylonian Scholars.* State Archives of Assyria 10. Helsinki: Helsinki University Press, 1993.

———. *Letters from Assyrian Scholars to the Kings Esarhaddon and Assurbanipal.* Helsinki: Helsinki University Press, 1970–1983.

Pedersén, Olof. *Archives and Libraries in the Ancient Near East, 1500–1300 B.C.* Bethesda, Md.: CDL, 1998.

Powell, Marvin A., ed. "Aspects of Cuneiform Writing." *Visible Language* 15, no. 4 (1981).

Schmandt-Besserat, Denise. *Before Writing: From Counting to Cuneiform.* 2 vols. Austin: University of Texas Press, 1992.

Veenhof, Klaas R., ed. *Cuneiform Archives and Libraries: Papers Read at the 30e Rencontre Assyriologique Internationale, Leiden, 4–8 July, 1983.* Leiden: Nederlands Historisch-Archaeologisch Instituut te Istanbul, 1986.

Walker, Christopher B. F. *Reading the Past: Cuneiform.* London: British Museum, 1987.

Periodicals

Acta Sumerologica
Akkadica
Analecta Orientalia
Archiv Orientalni
Archiv für Orientforschung
Baghdader Mitteilungen
Bibliotheca Orientalis
Bulletin of the American Schools of Oriental Research

Bulletin of Sumerian Agriculture
Journal of the American Oriental Society
Journal of the Ancient Near East Society
Journal of Cuneiform Studies
Journal of the Economic and Social History of the Orient
Journal of Near Eastern Studies
Mesopotamia
Mitteilungen der Altorientalischen Gesellschaft
Mitteilungen des Instituts für Orientforschung
NIN—Journal of Gender Studies in Antiquity
Orientalistische Literaturzeitschrift
Revue d'Assyriologie
State Archives of Assyria Bulletin
Studia Orientalia
Sumer
Welt des Orients
Zeitschrift für Assyriologie und verwandte Gebiete

About the Author

Gwendolyn Leick studied assyriology at the Karl-Franzens University of Graz (Austria) (Dr.phil) and at the School of Oriental and African Studies, London. She has taught since 1980 at various universities in Britain and is at present senior lecturer at the Chelsea College of Art and Design in London. She is the author of *A Dictionary of Ancient Near Eastern Architecture* (1988), *A Dictionary of Ancient Near Eastern Mythology* (1991), *Sex and Eroticism in Mesopotamian Literature* (1994), *Who's Who in the Ancient Near East* (1999) (all published by Routledge), as well as *Mesopotamia: The Invention of the City* (2002, Penguin). *The Babylonians: An Introduction* was published by Routledge in 2002.